INTERLINGUICITY, INTERNATIONALITY, AND SHAKESPEARE

Interlinguicity, Internationality, and Shakespeare

Edited by

MICHAEL SAENGER

McGill-Queen's University Press
Montreal & Kingston • London • Ithaca

ISBN 978-0-7735-4473-4 (cloth)
ISBN 978-0-7735-4474-1 (paper)
ISBN 978-0-7735-9689-4 (ePDF)
ISBN 978-0-7735-9690-0 (ePUB)

Legal deposit fourth quarter 2014
Bibliothèque nationale du Québec

Printed in Canada on acid-free paper that is 100% ancient forest free (100% post-consumer recycled), processed chlorine free

McGill-Queen's University Press acknowledges the support of the Canada Council for the Arts for our publishing program. We also acknowledge the financial support of the Government of Canada through the Canada Book Fund for our publishing activities.

Library and Archives Canada Cataloguing in Publication

Interlinguicity, internationality, and Shakespeare/edited by Michael Saenger.

Includes bibliographical references and index.
Issued in print and electronic formats.
ISBN 978-0-7735-4473-4 (bound). – ISBN 978-0-7735-4474-1 (pbk.). – ISBN 978-0-7735-9689-4 (ePDF). – ISBN 978-0-7735-9690-0 (ePUB)

1. Shakespeare, William, 1564–1616 – Criticism and interpretation. 2. Shakespeare, William, 1564–1616 – Knowledge – Language and languages. 3. Shakespeare, William, 1564–1616 – Language. 4. Shakespeare, William, 1564–1616 – Influence. 5. English language – Early modern, 1500–1700 – Foreign elements. 6. Language and history. I. Saenger, Michael, editor II. Title.

PR3069.L3167 2014 822.3'3 C2014-905028-3
C2014-905029-1

This book was typeset by Interscript in 10.5/13 Sabon.

Contents

Acknowledgments

The best thing an editor can do is ask a good question and then get out of the way, and it is my hope that I have not missed this goal by much. The pages that follow reflect vibrant exciting conversations, carried out over several years. I have been fortunate enough to join these distinguished scholars in the development of these ideas – in some cases for more than ten years. An acquisitions editor is normally an important job, but in this case Mark Abley has played a shaping and inspirational role. From my first conversations with him, his assistance and support have been erudite, skillful, poetic, deeply optimistic – in a word, indispensible. Essential support for this project was provided by Southwestern University. Finally, I must thank my students at Southwestern and my two assistants, Devin and Noah, who teach me new languages on a daily basis.

Patricia Parker's essay, "Shakespeare's Sound Government: Sound Defects, Polyglot Sounds, and Sounding Out," appeared first in *Oral Tradition* 24 (2009): 359–72, and appears with adjusted spelling by gracious permission of that journal. Robert N. Watson's essay draws from material published in "Shakespeare's New Words," *Shakespeare Survey* 65 (2013): 358–77, and appears by kind permission of Cambridge University Press. Parts of Paula Blank's essay, "Introducing 'Intrelinguistics': Shakespeare and Early/Modern English," appear here by kind permission of Stanford University Press.

Contributors

PAULA BLANK is professor of English at the College of William and Mary, where she teaches courses on Shakespeare, Early Modern English language and literature, and premodern sexualities. She is the author of two books, *Broken English: Dialects and the Politics of Language in Renaissance Writings* (Routledge, 1996) and *Shakespeare and the Mismeasure of Renaissance Man* (Cornell, 2006). Her current projects include a collection of original essays titled *The Proverbial "Lesbian" and Other Essays in Early Modern Language and Sexuality*; and *Shakespeare and Modern English*, a book about the ways we experience Shakespeare's language in relation to our own.

LAUREN COKER is a doctoral candidate in English at Saint Louis University. Her research focuses on Early Modern English literature with a particular emphasis on representations of the body and disability in Renaissance drama. Her publications include book reviews in *Comitatus* and, most recently, an essay on feigned disability on *Volpone*, featured in the 2013 collection *Recovering Disability in Early Modern England* from Ohio State University Press. She is currently completing her dissertation, "Metatheatricality and 'Disability Drag': Performing Bodily Difference on the Renaissance Stage." She teaches courses related to the novel, drama, Shakespeare, disability, first-year composition, and ESL at Saint Louis University.

BRIAN GINGRICH has an MA in German Studies from Stanford University and is a doctoral candidate in English at Princeton University. He studies narrative developments in America and Europe from the mid-nineteenth century onward, in the novel as well as in cinema. His particular interests include Freud, Barthes, critical theory, the visual arts, literary style, theories of desire, and the crossing of realism and modernism. His dissertation currently focuses on the role of pace in narratives of the late nineteenth and early twentieth centuries.

ALEXA HUANG is a general editor of *The Shakespearean International Yearbook*, director of the Dean's Scholars in Shakespeare program, and professor of English, Theatre, East Asian Languages and Literatures, and International Affairs at George Washington University, where she has co-founded and co-directs the Digital Humanities Institute. As Research Affiliate in Literature at MIT, she cofounded http://globalshakespeares.org. Her *Chinese Shakespeares: Two Centuries of Cultural Exchange* (Columbia University Press) received the Aldo and Jeanne Scaglione Prize of the MLA, an honourable mention by the Joe A. Callaway Prize of NYU, and the International Convention of Asian Scholars Colleagues' Choice Award. Her new book, *Weltliteratur und Welttheater: Ästhetischer Humanismus in der kulturellen Globalisierung* (2012), explores the role of aesthetic humanism in the recent historical record of globalization and examines the works of intercultural directors, translators, writers, and Nobel laureates Gao Xingjian and Mo Yan. She currently chairs the MLA committee on the New Variorum Edition of Shakespeare.

JAMES LOEHLIN is Shakespeare at Winedale Regents Professor of English and University Distinguished Teaching Professor at the University of Texas at Austin. His books include studies of *Henry IV, Parts I and II*, *Henry V*, and Chekhov's *The Cherry Orchard* in performance, as well as the Cambridge *Shakespeare in Production* edition of *Romeo and Juliet* and *The Cambridge Introduction to Chekhov*. He is Director of the Shakespeare at Winedale program at UT Austin, where he and his students have staged thirty of Shakespeare's plays.

SCOTT L. NEWSTOK is associate professor of English at Rhodes College, where he co-ordinates the Pearce Shakespeare Endowment. He joined the Rhodes faculty in 2007 after teaching at Oberlin College, Amherst College, and Gustavus Adolphus College, as well as holding the Mellon Post-Doctoral Fellowship in the Humanities at the Yale University Library. He has published a monograph on Early Modern English epitaphs, produced a scholarly edition of Kenneth Burke's Shakespeare criticism, and co-edited (with Ayanna Thompson) a collection of essays on *Macbeth* and race.

PATRICIA PARKER is the Margery Bailey Professor in English and Dramatic Literature and Professor of Comparative Literature at Stanford University. Author of *Inescapable Romance: Studies in the Poetics of a Mode* (from Ariosto to Wallace Stevens) for Princeton University Press (1979), *Literary Fat Ladies: Rhetoric, Gender, Property* (Routledge, 1987), and *Shakespeare from the Margins* (University of Chicago Press, 1997), she has also co-edited numerous critical volumes including *Shakespeare and the Question of Theory* (with Geoffrey Hartman; Routledge, 1985) and *Women, "Race," and Writing in the Early Modern Period* (with Margo Hendricks; Routledge, 1993). She is currently at work on studies of race, gender, and multilingualism in Shakespeare and his contemporaries.

ELIZABETH PENTLAND is associate professor of English at York University in Toronto, where she teaches courses in Shakespeare, contemporary adaptations of Shakespeare, early modern political theory, and English travel literature. Her published and forthcoming work includes essays on Elizabeth I (in *Representing Elizabeth I in Seventeenth-Century England*), Shakespeare's Illyria (in *Twelfth Night: New Critical Essays*), *Hamlet* (in *Shakespeare Bulletin*; *Proceedings of the Ninth World Shakespeare Congress*), and Christopher Marlowe (in *Stages of Engagement*). Current projects include a book on the literature of the French civil wars in England and a related essay on Mary Sidney.

MICHAEL SAENGER is associate professor of English at Southwestern University, and is the author of two books, *The Commodification of Textual Engagements in the English Renaissance* (Ashgate, 2006), and *Shakespeare and the French Borders of English* (Palgrave Macmillan, 2013), as well as numerous articles on the Renaissance, modernism, and intertextuality, and has been a finalist for the Southwestern University Teaching Award. He is currently working on a study of *The Spanish Tragedy* in relation to national affect, and teaches on Shakespeare, early modern gender, and the history of reading.

PHILIP SCHWYZER is professor of Renaissance literature at the University of Exeter. He is the author of *Shakespeare and the Remains of Richard III* (2013), *Archaeologies of English Renaissance Literature* (2007), and *Literature, Nationalism and Memory in Early Modern England and Wales* (2004), and co-editor of *Shakespeare and Wales: From the Marches to the Assembly* (2010).

GARY K. WAITE is professor of history at the University of New Brunswick. His research focuses on early modern religion, heterodoxy, and its persecution, especially in the Low Countries. Recent publications include *Reformers on Stage: Popular Drama and Religious Propaganda in the Low Countries of Charles V, 1515–1556* (2000), and two books on the intersection of the Reformation and the witch-hunts: *Eradicating the Devil's Minions: Anabaptists and Witches in Reformation Europe, 1535–1600* (2007, 2009), and *Heresy, Magic and Witchcraft in Early Modern Europe* (2003). He is currently working on views of Jews and Muslims in seventeenth-century Europe, and has published several articles and chapters from this research.

ROBERT N. WATSON is the Neikirk Distinguished Professor of English at UCLA. His books include *Shakespeare and the Hazards of Ambition*, *Ben Jonson's Parodic Strategy*, *The Rest Is Silence: Death as Annihilation in the English Renaissance*, several editions of Jonson's plays, and *Back to Nature: The Green and the Real in the Last Renaissance*, which was named both the year's best book on early modern literature and the year's best book of ecocriticism. His poetry has appeared in the *New Yorker* and other journals. He has received Guggenheim, NEH, and ACLS fellowships, and various awards for innovative teaching and public service.

INTERLINGUICITY, INTERNATIONALITY, AND SHAKESPEARE

Introduction

MICHAEL SAENGER

Our encounter with the Renaissance inevitably involves a gap of language. This is obvious to any student who buys a Shakespeare textbook, but it is equally true, if we understand visual codes as a kind of language, for any tourist in the Sistine Chapel. That gap was traditionally set aside in literary criticism, as historicist critics saw as their task the reconstruction and instruction of the languages (visual, iconographic, musical, spiritual) by which Renaissance creativity is best understood – that is, the terms by which it was originally received.

Since the advent of New Historicism, of course, it is rare to find any criticism that ignores the extent to which the present shapes our perception of the past. The present collection looks at the idea of language in a new way. We live in a world where languages, both in the narrow sense of verbal systems and in the broader sense of genres and epistemologies, have become more mobile than ever before, producing translations, transplantations, and cohabitations of all sorts. In very different ways, the early modern period saw profound linguistic transformation. In the sixteenth century, languages were both stabilized and destabilized by a series of factors: the expansion of print culture, the social and textual convulsions spurred by the Reformation, the consolidation of nations and national historiography, the mercantile interest in translation, and the movement of refugees in Europe.[1] The sheer density of the interchange and cohabitation in the early modern period can hardly be overstated; one sixteenth-century teacher of French in London felt it was necessary to instruct his students in regional French dialects such as Picard and Walloon. He reasoned that because he knew his students would converse with French speakers from these regions in their daily life in London, he wanted to ensure that they would understand the dialectical differences, and thus be able to maintain a path toward Parisian fluency.[2] The fact that French was both so present and so multiple in England implies that we should rethink what we mean when we speak of French, and therefore also what we understand to be the language of London. Such a reconsideration offers new ways of viewing Renaissance culture, and also our own, in part because linguistic change, admixture, and valuation are so important to both periods.

When languages encounter one another, they both *symbolize* things and *mean* things, and the essays in this collection consistently attend to the ways in which languages carry cultures with them, or at least appear to do so. This volume begins with a revision of the way in which we connect Shakespeare's *Love's Labour's Lost* to Continental discourse in and about Navarre, and it ends with a study of how modern performances handle linguistic multiplicity when "foreign" languages inhabit the New Globe Theatre. The volume thus is concerned with the international resonances of that play as well as the international resonances of an increasing majority of modern performances. Indeed, many of the contributors to this collection have eyes on both periods, and put significant thought into how, on the one hand, our own point in history can either clarify or restrict our perception of the linguistic stress, commerce, and growth of four centuries ago, and, on the other, how a more subtle understanding of early modern linguistic borders can elicit new ways of seeing the multilinguistic and multicultural present. In both Shakespeare's period and ours, the experience of being between languages, and between nations, was an important element of lived experience.[3]

One of the basic premises of this book is that the integrity of languages has been significantly overestimated. We are often encouraged to think of languages as having histories that are relatively linear. Predominantly monolingual printing conventions, academic departmentalization, and national tongues have encouraged us to think of languages as essentially separate systems, with occasional friction and overlap. If we begin with this assumption, linguistic change tends to be characterized as either abrupt or gradual. The abrupt shifts are occasional moments of fusion or fission, such as the conjunction of Old English and Old French in England after the Norman Conquest,[4] or the fission of the Romance languages after the fall of Rome. The emphasis on what are seen to be abrupt moments of change has the effect of overstating linguistic integrity on either side of those shifts, as if Middle English was suddenly born in 1067. The focus on autonomous, gradual change appears to be an alternative view. In fact, however, regardless of whether change is internally generated and slow or externally generated and fast, the illusion of linguistic integrity and autonomy can easily be reaffirmed by either paradigm in linguistic and literary historiography, because both of these options occlude the experience of language, which is frequently promiscuous and volitile. For example, many natives hear words that are "in" the language as foreign to them, and many people, in varying degrees, speak and hear a kind of hybridized tongue that maintains genuine engagement with what we tend to think are multiple languages.[5]

It is particularly important here that the illusion of linguistic integrity can actually be reinforced by some discussions of gradual linguistic change. For example, if we focus on linguistic incursions or innovations, such as the inkhorn controversy in Elizabethan England or the seepage of American English into modern Japanese, we have a natural tendency to posit a cultural and linguistic integrity that preceded these marginal intrusions – and usually recovers from them, partly because we tend to take at face value the ideas of novelty and foreignness that undergird these controversies. This effect is particularly pronounced in literary studies, because despite a variety of deaths experienced by "the author" in post-structuralism, figures such as Shakespeare inevitably function as linguistic and cultural lodestones, appearing to naturalize or even to sacrilize the "English" in which they wrote. If we focus on relatively local internal evolution or migration of individual words, we tend to emphasize the life of a given language in its *longue durée*, rather than the socially experienced overlap of languages in such cities as London and Amsterdam, and the theatrical overlap of different ways of hearing and understanding, often a central subject of Shakespearean comedy.

Of course, the authors here do not wish to ignore the existence of English as a language, Shakespeare as an author, or literary studies as a discipline, but the essays that follow often view all three of these boundaries with some suspicion. After all, before the institutionalization of English academics, the idea of a language called English was experienced only when other languages were contrasted with it, and thus when there was an external contrast or confluence of words; this is underscored by the fact that "to English" was an Early Modern verb meaning to translate into that language. The problem of linguistic unity is particularly evident in the study and performance of Shakespeare. As Paula Blank discusses in her essay here, we must negotiate a linguistic gap every time we read or teach Shakespeare. Are we speaking the same English? How do we process the way his words are heard now? English itself could, in 1600 or 2013, be viewed either hypostatically or deconstructively; that is, it could be viewed as a language that harmonizes divergent root systems, ambiguities and dialects, or conversely, it could be viewed as a category of words that only strives for coherence as it plays host to rhetorics, dialects, and root systems that not only do not get along, but often come close to being mutually incomprehensible.[6] In his essay for this volume, Robert N. Watson characterizes the language of *Troilus and Cressida* in terms that could be extended to English more broadly, with its porous boundaries and internal divisions: "This is, and is not, English." The mixture of fear and arousal that Watson hears in the rapidly expanding English language of this time parallels the similar lust for, and fear of, gold that Daniel Vitkus has located in the moral allegory of Spenser as well as in the colonial experiments of Raleigh.[7] Both words and money were fundamentally international and essential to the burgeoning prosperity of England.

The title of this collection posits that languages have never really been as separate as we often understand them to be, and that in fact the normal condition of people, texts, and social space is one of "interlinguicity," which we take to denote a condition where multiple languages continuously cohabit systems of meaning. Following principally on Derrida,[8] I offer the concept of interlinguicity as a way of understanding the social experience of language in the early modern period as well as our own, as I have explored elsewhere.[9] We always exist in multiple languages, even if we believe ourselves to be monolingual, because no language itself can ever be monolingual. Verbal systems have always constantly mixed with one another and every language bears the ghosts of its own past as well as both avowed and concealed borrowings from its neighbours. Any site of citation or translation, then, does not *create* an engagement with multiple languages, but rather makes apparent the fact that such a condition was already inherent in the original, and remains alive in the translated text. Concomitantly, if languages cannot help but overlap, they also cannot help but be internally divided, an effect which is most pointedly present in the enduring audibility of the

Germanic substrate and the French superstrate in English, but which has also been thoroughly explored in Paula Blank's work on dialects in England, one of which was imaginative writing.[10] In his study of the language of Shakespeare, Russ McDonald observes that Elizabethan England was "a culture that was extremely self-conscious about its language,"[11] and this consciousness often manifested in concerns about neologisms, lexical and rhetorical affectation, dialectical strife, and foreign citation. Understood in this way, encounters between different linguistic systems are not exceptional but rather habitual, and though they might be particularly evident in what Sir Philip Sidney called the "mingled tongue"[12] of English, the condition of being between languages – that is, the condition of interlinguicity – is an inevitable condition of human thought. The term "interlinguicity" asks us to consider more carefully the fact that languages inevitably overlap, and thus that people, plays, and cities exhibit profound hybridity.

A similar assertion could be made about nations. The term "interlinguicity" is new; "internationality," on the other hand, is not, although it is more commonly used in historical studies than in literary ones. We employ "internationality" to refer to a space that displays an overlap or absence of national identification, whether that identification is understood as fictive or actual. Internationality, in other words, is a way of understanding a group of people, whether actors or not, who have layered, incoherent, or conflicting ideas of what nation they inhabit. The words "interlingual" and "international" are familiar adjectives to address a variety of ways in which borders are crossed, whether those borders are literary, sociological, or political. Inasmuch as these are adjectives, however, they are limited because they all describe an object – a page, a pun, a person, a scene, a city. I want to suggest that the nominal form of these words would be useful in addressing the ways in which languages and communities were defined in early modern Europe. What I mean to suggest is that there are *qualities* of internationality and interlinguicity that manifest in various pages, puns, people, scenes, and cities. Such a shift in perspective allows for, among other things, a different view of how people, plays, and languages are defined; in essence, it asks us to see moments of interpermeation between languages and between nations not as exceptions to the rule of monolingual, national consciousness, but rather as a dominant norm of the early modern world – to which nations and "languages" were a relatively marginalized exception. As Derrida suggests in his influential essay "What Is a Relevant Translation?" an interlingual pun can be seen as a momentary curiosity, but it can also be seen as a moment that unveils the fact that languages have never been either intact or separate.

The final element of the title of this book is the most iconic traveller between the Elizabethan period and our own, a name indeed that at times is used as a personification of the English language. His retrospective iconicity belies a profoundly multilingual writer: Shakespeare may be more translated than translating, but not by that much. Having travelled from a relatively monolingual Stratford to an increasingly multilingual London, he learned French and, perhaps just as importantly, developed a keen ear for the various linguistic layers that inhabit English. While most of the authors in this collection address Shakespeare, they do so with fundamentally different methodologies, and it would be evidently perverse to reinscribe England and Shakespeare as the sole subjects of inquiry into interlinguicity; several of the authors make a concerted attempt to look beyond the Bard, and beyond the borders of England. Even if it remains true that Shakespeare is a particularly interesting subject (in a variety of senses of the phrase), he was very much engaged in broader tensions and histories, and he still is. As several of the authors here address, Shakespeare was clearly eager to integrate, in varying degrees, neologisms, Latin, French, Italian, Spanish, and Welsh into his plays. In doing this he was entirely typical of other dramatists of his time, and in fact of London as a whole.

"Translate" comes from the Latin "move across," and translations inevitably move between cultures and locations as well as across verbal systems. Interlingual texts enact the motion of such transfer without offering any illusion of completing that process. During the early modern period, the traffic in translation intensified; as Peter Burke suggests, "a few large cities became centres of translation, in particular Venice, Paris, London and Amsterdam."[13] This traffic fostered an increased presence and visibility of the cohabitation of languages, here called "interlinguicity." Before Britain had an empire, London was a mercantile boomtown, thriving in large part because of its inclusion of multiple languages and its corresponding fluency in international trade. There was a French Church and a Dutch Church in the city, but there were also teachers of languages such as Arabic and Chinese.[14] Such increasing competencies, like the economic connections that also began to encircle the globe, did not erase localities at that time, any more than more recent connectivity erases them now. The translation of material between nations was shaped by, and helped to shape, spiritual, linguistic, and national perceptions of culture, as Peter Burke has consistently explored.[15] Recent studies of early modern English national identity-formation have been enriched by a renewed attention to how national and linguistic models of identity were created and troubled by macaronic texts, visible translations, and border-crossings, whether real or imagined,[16] and for some time Patricia Parker and others have attended to the ways in which multiple languages can inhabit a sentence and even a word.[17] Historically minded literary critics, such as Marianne Montgomery, have drawn attention to the ways in which England's neighbours, and the languages of those neighbours, were persistently characterized and gendered in drama, amounting to "disguise through speech."[18] This was equally true in other discursive fields; Claire McEachern observes that those who resisted the unification of England and Scotland argued that although the two countries shared a language in the narrow sense, they differed in their legal systems and in their customs. In the former, the Scots were too French, and in the latter, too Irish.[19] The Scots were thus seen, at least by some, to be linguistically but not culturally translatable.

The work of criticism and that of history are different, of course, and there has been something of a gap between Derrida and Burke – that is, between models of the productivity of translation and studies of the cultural history of early modern textual interchange. Foreign languages animated the commerce of Europe as well as the commerce of the Shakespearean stage, even as countries began to consolidate power along linguistic, confessional, and national lines. Three distinct subjects of research have been very active lately: literary critics have explored multilingualism, historians have explored how language defined communities, and performance practitioners have adapted Shakespeare into an ever-increasing array of meanings and languages, feasting on the ability of the Bard to be translated, transferred, and otherwise energized by the languages, conflicts, and cultures of an evidently nonpolar world. Alexa Huang has offered the notion of "localities" as a way of theorizing the various ways in which social context can create meaning in translated Shakespeare performances,[20] and in Sonia Massai's formulation, "Such locations include neighbourhoods, cities, regions and sub-regions, linguistic, religious and political ecumenes, along with national identity and traditions, as equally significant determinants of cultural production."[21] This book aims to join these productively divergent threads of history, literary criticism, and performance criticism around the twin concepts of intersecting languages and cohabiting nations.

To an extent, all languages are interlinguistic, inasmuch as they are fractured into dialects and carry etymologies from other languages and other times. Further, all nations are international, in the sense that any nation almost always is founded on the danger of erasure or the memory of disintegration. Borders are rarely if ever consistent between the "real" political boundary, marked by military and legal control; the "rhetorical" boundary, whereby England laid claim to France long after its armies had departed; and the kind of imaginative boundaries that are so central to Shakespeare's plays. The space between languages, like the space between nations, offered great risk and reward in bustling international early modern trade, and was processed simultaneously in a variety of incompatible registers: moral, linguistic, confessional, nationalistic, eschatological, and proto-capitalistic. Richard Helgerson has influentially offered a way of reading Renaissance poetic depictions as driven by the urge to align the English language with an emerging sense of national pride,[22] but others have put more emphasis on the ways in which the staging of multiple languages might undermine the notions of a stable English language and nation. We live in another set of spaces between languages, which offers different risks and rewards; any effort to cite, recover, or translate Shakespeare involves confronting the fluidity of language, even within English.

Language is at once internal and external, synchronic and diachronic, our own and not our own. Most words are commonly recognized as belonging to one language or another, and yet many languages, especially English, are always in the process of creating and appropriating new words – a topic here explored by Robert N. Watson. Those imported words (including names, as Elizabeth Pentland explores here) arrive with strategically inflected meanings drawn from various externalities, such as international history, divergent theologies, and foreign affectations. Thus a surprisingly large number of words are understood by many speakers of English, and yet simultaneously felt as "foreign" in one way or another. Patricia Parker has discussed the trope of metaphor as a kind of translation of sense, where one word is taken from its proper "home" and moved to an alien place. The fact that "meta-phor" is the Greek equivalent of "trans-late" only reinforces her point. Parker's quotation (and translation) of Cicero's discussion of metaphor could easily be applied to the presence of foreign language speakers (whether staged or actual) in London: "the metaphor ought to have an apologetic air, so as to look as if it had entered a place that does not belong to it";[23] and of course, our modern era has not ended this kind of linguistic valuation. The way in which the description of speech can be likened to ritual humility evinces the degree to which place is felt linguistically, whether foreigners are present or not.[24] This layered sense of foreignness in the English language had a societal analogue in the English class system. In her wide-ranging study of the effect of immigration on London in the early modern period, Lien Bich Luu notes that the influx of refugees, in large part spurred by religious strife, profoundly enriched the English economy, introducing new skills and industries that were key to the transformation of England during that time from an "economic backwater" to a leading European power. Luu notes, however, that England's progress was hindered during this period because many of those immigrants became frustrated and ultimately were more attracted to states that allowed them an easier path to citizenship, such as the Dutch Republic; "the guiding principle in England was that natural-born subjects should receive preferential treatment."[25] Shakespeare was as multilingual as his London, and like his city he was fundamentally affected by foreign dynamics.

A century ago, the question of Shakespeare's relation to other languages was frequently framed in terms of evaluating his degree of engagement with Latin sources and in tracing the presence of Continental authors and royal figures in his plays.[26] Since then, literary scholars of early modern culture have followed the lead of historians more generally, looking for "history from below," finding linguistic back-currents of various kinds, and illuminating the richly multiple languages of early modern England. As our view of England has become more complex and multivocal, so the figure of Shakespeare has been recognized to embody much of this complexity; his uses of Latin (throughout his career), French (throughout, and particularly in *Henry V*), and Welsh (in *1 Henry IV*) are now viewed not as momentary anomalies, but rather as indications of a profound interest in linguistic alterity. It is then deeply ironic that such a multilingual author would later come to personify the greatness, and hence the integrity, of English. Shakespeare wrote in London's 'language,' which was not simply 'English' any more at that time than it is now.

There is a general tendency of research in the field of Renaissance studies either to focus on Shakespeare or to ignore him. This tendency encourages an awkward insularity: in literary studies of Shakespeare, other contemporary figures and other disciplinary perspectives play a supporting role. The authors of the present volume do not all focus on Shakespeare and they employ diverse methodologies. This heterogeneity is especially important because the collection is primarily about language, which is so inherently social, promiscuous, and historically determined. If Shakespeare is a narrowing presence, language is a broadening one, and the potential scope of material germane to the ideas of interlinguicity and internationality is vast. Inasmuch as these ideas pertain to history as well as literature, the potential scope for methodology is also wide. My basic intention is, on the one hand, to view interlinguicity and internationality as important ideas worthy of study in their own right, and, on the other, to offer Shakespeare as something of an anchoring presence. In so doing, I hope to resist the tendency to draw the field of study too tightly around the literary study of that one author. The use of such an anchoring presence allows for threads of connection based on methodology and subject matter, and the diversity of work related to Shakespeare encourages interdisciplinarity. The overarching question the book seeks to answer is: how did linguistically marked social encounters affect the early modern international world, and how have they functioned since then in Shakespearean adaptation?

Two modern examples might be helpful here. Grigori Kozintsev's 1964 tour-de-force *Hamlet* is, of course, mainly in Russian. Filmed at the height of the Cold War, the movie repeatedly frames Hamlet's distrust of authority in terms that resonate with Marxist historiography; Hamlet stalks Elsinore as Lenin paced St. Petersburg. In this movie, when Claudius gives his infamously perfidious introductory speech (1.2.1–39), Kozintsev begins the speech as an orally delivered proclamation, then cuts to nameless courtiers who recite snippets of the speech in their own languages as they leave the palace. The courtiers translate the speech into German and French; as they do so, the actual meaning of Claudius's words, which was already

Hamlet, Mogilev Regional Puppet Theatre, directed by Igor Kazakov

weak, becomes so requoted as to be nullified, as it is spliced and moved into different tongues. Clearly, that is Kozintsev's point. The authority that Claudius represents in his film is transnational; the King is the Tsar, and the Kaiser, and the Roi. This internationality offers Hamlet an opportunity, as he does throughout the film, to observe peasants toiling, and thus implicitly to ally his struggle with theirs; the king's guilt, in turn, becomes metonymic of the royal oppression inherent in his office. Kozintsev's interlinguicity here uses *Hamlet* to speak to his own place and time. In this moment of translation, Shakespeare is essentially absent.[27]

Almost fifty years later, Igor Kazakov's Russian-language production of *Hamlet* for the Regional Puppet Theatre in Mogilev, Belarus, in 2013 is quite different in style, but once again language plays an important role. In Belarus, the Russian and Belarusian alphabets are visible throughout urban life, and here as in many places in the world, English letters are also legible, though frequently in a disconnected form, as brand names or as phrases on t-shirts. In the image provided here, Kazakov costumes Hamlet, performed by Yurka Divakov, as a superhero with an "H" on his chest, a letter that does not exist in a similar form in either the Belarusian or the Russian alphabets. The production was performed in Russian, so the presence of that English letter, in such a central position, was out of place, but then so was Hamlet, dressed as a superhero in a performance populated by puppets and puppet-human hybrids. The English language was present, and so was Shakespeare, but only as a citation, as a t-shirt quotation. Shakespeare's Englishness, like that English letter, enters as a part of a distended, appropriated, hallucinatory collage, not unlike the quasi-human figures of Rosencrantz and Guildenstern on either side of Hamlet, who are partly puppets and partly human costumes on oversized hangers (portrayed here by Sergey Sergeenko and Igor Rakitskiy, respectively). Kozintsev was modernist, and Kazakov postmodernist, but both versions testify to the enduring power of linguistic boundaries to speak to larger and wider issues – perhaps even the inevitability and omnipresence of such connections between gaps in language and broader structures of meaning.

"You speak a language I understand not."
The Winter's Tale, 3.2.78[28]

The first section of essays crosses national and generic boundaries, discussing the localities of Wales, Navarre, and the Netherlands, and rhetorical frames such as apologist historiography, religious polemic, collaborative citation of foreignness, and satire. Each of these essays investigates the ways in which texts are used to articulate the intention and meaning of a community and those of its neighbours, predecessors, and antagonists. The idea of "language" can be understood literally (e.g., Dutch, English, Italian, etc.) or it can be understood more metaphorically, to include apocalyptic, nationalistic, symbolic, or poetic *ways* of speaking. In either conception, heterogeneous language can bring people together or push them apart. Elizabeth Pentland examines how the names and cultures of Navarre and Spain echo through Shakespeare's very interlinguistic *Love's Labour's Lost*. Pentland examines and complicates the international background of that play; for her, the royal aspirations and gynophobia of Shakespeare's courtiers are linked to the elite and popular history of what Parker here calls "the linguistic borderland of Navarre." Next, Philip Schwyzer examines the presence and the meaning of Welsh in England; though Wales no longer functioned as a separate kingdom, its language retained, and continues to retain, a stubborn strangeness. His exploration of Welsh in *1 Henry IV*, in its original and more recent performances, as well as in plays by Shakespeare's contemporaries, points to the presence of the Welsh language in England as both familiar and foreign. Finally, Gary Waite explores how, during a period when many sects ascribed satanic agency to their foes, the Dutch Republic resisted this tendency, to a remarkable degree. The inscrutability linked to Spiritualism became a way of managing competing conceptions of faith. In this social history of the perception of demonic agency in the Netherlands we get crucial insight into the social definition of religious integrity in this profoundly mixed urban environment. These essays, then, develop local examples to investigate some ways in which the friction of different kinds of language helped to shape the perception of social identity and agency in Europe in the early modern period. All of these encounters between languages can be seen to complicate identities of various kinds, such as the Christian (Waite), the English literary text (Schwyzer), and the idea of Navarre (Pentland). These essays use both historical and literary approaches to consider how meaning was located in interlinguistic encounters. Foreign spiritual and verbal languages *mean* something, quite apart from how they might be translated, a point that is emphasized in the quotation above. When Hermione says this to Leontes in *The Winter's Tale*, she is not just refuting his charge of adultery, but also rejecting his entire method of constucting it. The fact that 'language' could so comfortably be used by Hermione as a term for a tyrant's rage attests to the deep mobility of the term, a mobility that hints at the fundamental instability of other languages, such as English, as well as pseudo-languages, such as salvific rhetoric and international legitimacy.

The second section of essays emerges from the peculiar nature of English. Because of its historical and inherent hybridity, descending primarily from Germanic and French sources, English has always been prone to lexical expansion and syntactic and aural ambiguity. These features can breed expansiveness and inclusivity, but they can equally create a gradated lexicology, wherein some words are more English than others. English carries with it into the medieval period a particularly dense set of stresses, between legitimacy and illegitimacy as well as between orality and textuality, and these tensions play out through intralinguistic conflicts and ambiguities. Scott Newstok and Robert N. Watson each address the expansiveness of English; for Newstok, the figurative marriage between Anglo-Saxon and Latin roots at the heart of the English lexicon persists as a syntactic rhythm that Shakespeare echoes and develops in his plays, whereas Watson examines the dynamic trade in neologisms that was as active as other markets in early modern London, a trade that is enacted most famously in Shakespeare's plays. For Patricia Parker and Lauren Coker, the sound of words becomes a central focus. In Shakespeare (and, for Coker, in Webster as well) words have a slippery relationship to other languages and indeed to English itself. Whether one views the management of such sounds as an artistic project or a patriotic one, any attempt to control how words are spoken and heard is daunting. Paula Blank concludes this section with an important turn in the understanding of the often overlooked relationship between our language and that of Shakespeare. We cannot hear the same words Shakespeare did (a point developed also by Watson), both because they have become more strange and because they have become more familiar. The language of Shakespeare's time has become "Shakespeare's language" in ways that cannot easily be retracted.

Finally, two essays engage, in very different ways, the transformations with which the modern world has welcomed, repositioned, and contested Shakespeare's texts. These essays examine two divergent kinds of adaptation, in German prose and in dramas staged in many languages. In both of these essays, as in several of the previous studies, the authors are concerned with how different languages and national positions are configured and 'heard.' The goal of these essays, and that of the adaptations they analyze, is neither to celebrate the revivification of an original Shakespeare, nor to celebrate his postcolonial demise, but rather to attend to the multiple ways in which Shakespeare crosses linguistic and national boundaries. Brian Gingrich examines an important German adaptation of *Romeo and Juliet*. The lovers' story had already crossed many borders before Shakespeare wrote his play, and by the nineteenth century, it had become emblematic not just of love, but also of literary genius and even national meaning. Alexa Huang's essay, on the other hand, explores how ascriptions of meaning play out in performative environments, such as a Cantonese *Titus Andronicus* coming to the reconstructed Globe Theatre in London. Huang's vision of the London Globe in 2012, as a site of cultural and linguistic contestation and opacity, is strikingly reminiscent of Gary Waite's vision of Amsterdam in 1600. Both Huang and Waite provide socially historicized readings of texts that mark distinct fields of communal agency. The interest of this volume is partly in the role Shakespeare plays in these intersections, and partly in the more general condition of interlinguicity, which often feels new, but is not.

But back to the elephantine Shakespeare in the room. The outsized presence of Shakespeare in literary criticism has had both salutory and deleterious effects; on the positive side, Shakespeare's intentionality and international appeal are compelling, and the complexities of his plays and their aftermath have led Shakespeareans to develop some very sophisticated models of literary theory, which often bridge postmodernism with philology. On the negative side, Shakespeare has been so thoroughly studied as to be isolated from the rest of the cultures and writers of his own time. Although modern Shakespeareans are quick to scoff at the Romantics' idea of Shakespeare as a solitary genius, they often replace this notion with a different kind of outsized intentionality, in the manner of Marjorie Garber, who has suggested that "Shakespeare makes modern culture."[29] This conception of a virtually omnipotent bard resembles Coleridge's impression of Hamlet's relation to Elsinore: Coleridge wrote that Hamlet "sees through the very souls of all who surround him."[30] For Coleridge, Hamlet was a syecdoche and personification of Shakespeare's own relation to the world, but of course Coleridge was seeing Shakespeare in fundamentally Romantic terms. Similarly, Garber freely acknowledges the extent to which modern revisions of Shakespeare diverge from their originals, but overlooks the notion that, for modern culture, citation does not always carry meaning with it. Shakespeare often functions as a quarry from which stones are taken to build things that have essentially no relation to their source. The solution, at least in part, to this recurring problem, from a critical point of view, is simply to combine studies that focus on Shakespeare with studies that focus elsewhere.

If only because the present collection focuses on the ideas of language and national borders, it is particularly urgent that it attend to different fields of agency. For example, Dutch culture could be noted only as it might inform Shakespeare's allusions to the Dutch,[31] modern Shakespearean performances could be read in terms of their relation to Shakespeare's originals, and the Welsh text in *1 Henry IV* could be viewed as fundamentally irrelevant to the "play." In all these cases, our authors go in other directions, considering Dutch communitarian definition during Shakespeare's life, seeing modern Shakespeare performance as a multicultural encounter, and viewing *1 Henry IV* as, essentially, a collaborative play. Such reconsiderations are certainly not meant to ignore the presence of Shakespeare as a creator, and indeed several of our authors are quite concerned with Shakespeare's literary intent. Rather, the entire volume seeks to trace patterns of linguistic boundaries and to explore how they also mark nations and, in the widest sense, authors. Shakespeare stands at the centre of this collection but not in each of the essays. His presence helps to narrow the field of view to a manageable scale, but not to reinscribe an updated bardolotry. Holland is more relevant to Shakespeare than, for example, linguistic communities in the contemporary Levant, but this collection could easily include similar analyses of Scotland and northern France, if the size of the resulting book were no limit. Indeed, it is our hope that the kind of research practiced here, though not unitary in methodology, is both sufficiently coherent and sufficiently incomplete to spur similar new work.

One example may suffice here to attest to the potential for such interconnections: Shakespeareans are very familiar with the moment when Othello turns to Iago, once he realizes that he has been deceived, and says, "I look down towards his feet, but that's a fable" (*Othello* 5.2.292). Shakespeareans are accustomed to understanding this moment, when Othello considers and rejects the notion that Iago is a devil, as a reflection of a profound psychological development of the origins of malice, and also as indicative of a culture that was increasingly characterized by skepticism, even as it was haunted by ghosts onstage and off. But this same moment could productively be connected to the language of confessional difference, and Waite's essay usefully informs us that in the Netherlands of Shakespeare's time, religious drama "encouraged audiences to think less in terms of a corporeal devil and more in terms of human agency and responsibility." Thus Othello's understanding of the language of malice is part of a wider European economy of spiritual agency.

Languages often – perhaps, always – assign symbolic meaning to each other, especially when they maintain long states of cohabitation. Latin functions gnomically in English, Welsh sounds strange, and French sounds refined. These meanings are clearly derived from social history. All linguistic encounters – indeed, all dialectical encounters too – are asymmetrical, and one language is often portrayed as earthy and another as evidentiary, one as manly and the other as effeminate, or even one as godly and another as satanic. The concept of interlinguicity denotes a critical recognition of the interpenetration of languages. It does not involve ignoring these hierarchies, but rather it frames them with the notion that languages always cohabit social space. If a page, a person, or a city contains multiple languages, it then displays interlinguicity, and such a categorization encourages us not to rush to sort the languages into the categories of native and foreign, principal and borrowed, ancient and new, communicative and citational, familiar and strange, though we may easily see how these contrasts were felt at the time. Those dynamics may well be found in the text, but to understand such a text, person, or social space in terms of interlinguicity involves allowing for the possibility that there is no definite single language that the text is *in*. There are, instead, a host of competing codes that cohabit the page, person, or city, and constantly vie for agency and value. Internationality is an extension of this concept to the idea of nations, and it is particularly important because the Renaissance plays so often begin in foreign places, and those introductory scenes often lead to still more and more new locations. That mobility was a key pleasure that the theatre sold, and it meant that audiences could never be sure precisely where they were. That indecision, here called internationality, could be seen as a pervasive characteristic of early modern social space, made particularly evident in the theatre. According to Bradin Cormack, "As history-making, the interlinguistic pun or macaronic exchange reaches beyond the vernacular's immediate temporality to open it onto its own history and so make the vernacular differently available to itself as history and culture."[32] The authors of this collection extend this line of thinking outward beyond puns and citation, in recognition of the pervasive issue of linguistic multiplicity and its effects on society, memory, and art.

Interdisciplinarity and diversity of focus are pervasive in the book. Philip Schwyzer is focused on text in *1 Henry IV* that is only implied in stage directions, and thus essentially not by Shakespeare. Coker's essay is about Webster as much as Shakespeare. Huang and Gingrich are not really concerned with what Shakespeare did but rather with what others do to (or with) Shakespeare. Gingrich's and Huang's essays underline the fact that, even when the object of critical study is to some degree Shakespeare's words or the outlines of his plots, adaptive encounters at linguistic borderlands can often involve profound appropriations that give primacy to a different set of actors, and a different set of authors. One of the most important goals of this collection is to take seriously the consequences of thinking about language and community across borders. Holland was the greatest source of immigrants to London, so Waite's exploration of Dutch social history is pertinent to the use of similar rhetorics of social differentiation in England. Gingrich's essay extends to the volume's interest in Continental communities, whether in Switzerland, Navarre, or Holland, both in Shakespeare's time and in the penumbra of Shakespeare's influence.

This study thus presents cultural history at the beginning and performance studies at the end, with Shakespeare operating as a kind of rich and polysemous bridge. Shakespeare is a useful figure to play this part, because he was so embedded in his own time and is also so interwoven with our own. Indeed, while the subjects listed above adumbrate a field that could not possibly fit within these covers, Shakespeare allows for a more manageable and clearly necessary task: while there has been an increasing level of interest in linguistic matters in relation to Shakespeare, that interest has focused either on the early modern period or on recent receptions, and these two fields of study need to be connected to one another. Even as "Shakespeare" has come into focus as a multivocal, interlinguistic social presence, he has often still operated as the straight man in the ever-expanding world of Shakespearean adaptation. While methods of using Shakespeare have varied so widely that it is often not clear that Shakespeare is still meaningfully present in a given adaptation, there has, undeniably, been a vital dialectic between the art of Shakespeare and the life of the modern world, with all of its interconnections, tensions, and performativities. Indeed, perhaps the very profusion of media and languages in the modern world has helped to generate a countervailing image of Shakespeare as the "original," the very English author whose text wanders around the world, like a confused Viola, wondering "What country, friends, is this?"[33] While scholars have been avidly pursuing this interlinguistic early modern Shakespeare on the one hand, and the multivocal poststructuralist Shakespearean avatars on the other, there has been little effort to bridge the gap between these fundamentally coherent trends. This collection aims to perform that role, and it does so partly by giving Shakespeare only a limited centrality, in recognition of the fundamentally shared world both of his time and of ours.

PART ONE

The Meaning of Foreign Languages

Shakespeare, Navarre, and Continental History

ELIZABETH PENTLAND

This essay considers the relationship between the Franco-Spanish setting of *Love's Labour's Lost*, the academic ambitions so famously articulated by its king in his opening speech, and the gender politics that undergird so much of its comedy. Moving beyond the narrowly focused topical readings that have dominated historicist criticism of the play, my aim instead is to explore its broad-ranging allusions to Navarre's history; to link the play's preoccupation with problems of legitimacy, inheritance, and succession to an array of French, English, and Spanish sources that placed the kingdom of Navarre at the centre of such anxieties and debates in the sixteenth century. There are two principal narrative strands at work in this transnational and multilingual "conversation" about Navarre: a looking back to the realm's famed "French" past, and bitter controversy over its annexation by Spain in 1512. Reading *Love's Labour's Lost* against the backdrop of this literature opens up rich new interpretive possibilities for the play that reflect Navarre's geographical, political, and cultural situation between two major European powers – Spain and France – during this time. My purpose here is to lay out the principal contours of this transnational discussion, since it remains largely unexplored by critics of the play, and to suggest how the play translates some of this material – often parodically – into the stuff of romantic comedy or satire. In so doing, I hope to open the way for new interpretive approaches to this "insistently topical"[1] play.

The kingdom of Navarre, once the seat of a flourishing medieval court, and associated in the sixteenth century with learned women such as Marguerite of Navarre or Jeanne d'Albret, would seem an appropriate setting for a "little academe" of the sort imagined in the opening scene of the play – except that the men of Navarre intend, rather absurdly, to exclude women from their court during the three years they plan to devote to their scholarly exercises. Shakespeare's more educated audience members would have enjoyed the irony in seeing the King of Navarre try to banish women from his court, given their pivotal role in his kingdom's history. It was well known, however, that the king of Spain had driven out Navarre's queen in the early sixteenth century. Ferdinand's academic pretensions would not have seemed out of place, either: Navarre's "scholarly" associations, in Shakespeare's time, were multiple and transnational in character, linking this tiny and contested kingdom not just to the literary accomplishments of the French Renaissance and the literature of the French Reformation, but also to scholars famed for their service to the Spanish court under Ferdinand II and his successors.

Much has been written about the French resonances of *Love's Labour's Lost*, and especially its topical references to figures associated with Henry of Navarre and the French civil wars during the final decades of the sixteenth century. Most recently, Gillian Woods has commented on the "insistently topical" names Shakespeare gives to the main male characters in the play, once again in order to link them to contemporary French counterparts.[2] But the tradition of reading Shakespeare's play as "French" goes back at least as far as Sidney Lee's essay on the subject, first published in 1880.[3] Far less has been said, however, about the play's Spanish resonances, and Shakespearean scholars have been slow to explore the significance for the play of Navarre's Franco-Spanish history.[4] Instead, the play's setting has been read, persistently, as an unambiguously French space by critics who ignore the fact that in Shakespeare's day the greater part of the kingdom of Navarre was under Spanish rule – a fact that any informed Elizabethan would certainly have known. It is true, of course, that for three hundred years, Navarre *had been* French (and a small portion of its territory still was) – ruled first by the Counts of Brie and Champagne and later by the Counts of Evreux and Foix. From 1512 onward, however, the kings and queens of Navarre laid claim to the realm in absentia, and held court not in Navarre itself but in the neighbouring principality of Béarn. It seems to me problematic that so many readings of the play depend upon a reading of

"Navarre" that not only elides this history but also conflates the kingdom of Navarre with an adjacent French territory that in fact went by another name altogether. Navarre, which is clearly identified as a Spanish province or realm on many of the period's maps, had its own history and its own set of legal traditions that have direct bearing on Shakespeare's play, especially with respect to its treatment of gender.

In our search for source material or historical analogues in the life and exploits of Henry of Navarre, or in events roughly contemporary to Shakespeare's own life, we have overlooked significant transnational conversations about Navarre that were playing out in the period's popular literature, histories, and political tracts. If we look beyond the writing about Henry of Navarre, we find that the topic most often discussed in relation to the kingdom of Navarre in the 1580s and 1590s was its annexation by Spain in 1512. But even as the political controversy raged over Spain's conquest of Navarre, the popular literature of Shakespeare's time recalled the Franco-Navarrese court under some of its most illustrious, and its most notorious, rulers: the fifth volume of François de Belleforest's *Histoires Tragiques*,[5] for example, features the story of Gaston de Foix's tragic dealings with the infamous fourteenth-century king of Navarre, Carlos II ("Charles the Bad"), who ruled from 1349 until his death in 1387. Belleforest's source for this story, Froissart's *Chronicles* (which we know Shakespeare consulted in writing *Richard II*), makes frequent mention of Navarre's kings and nobles during this dramatic period in Navarre's history.

Most studies of *Love's Labour's Lost* read the play against the contemporary backdrop of the French civil wars, but Froissart's famous account of the Hundred Years' War offers up a wider set of interpretive possibilities. In it, we see the fourteenth-century king of Navarre actively taking part in the warring and diplomacy of the period, visiting and fortifying his estates in Normandy, negotiating with the king of France over a disputed land claim, and eventually marrying a French princess. Froissart explains, at one point, that

> kyng Charles of Nauarr … who was in base Normandy … was behated with the frenche kynge bicause of certayn landes that he kept and claymed them as his enheritance the whiche the frenche kyng denied: for the whiche theyr counsayles had ben often

> tymes to guether: But they coulde neuer make agrement bitwene them and so the matter hanged styll, eche of them takyng good hede of other.[6]

While Shakespeare's Navarre does not appear to be "behated" with the king of France, Froissart's account of this dispute seems, nevertheless, to find its analogue in the play when the Princess of France arrives at his court to negotiate, on behalf of her ailing father, the release of some lands in Aquitaine. Indeed, as the realm's subsequent history suggests, Navarre itself would become subject to competing claims of "enheritance" by French and Spanish monarchs, beginning in the late fifteenth century – an issue that finds its way into the play not just through the aforementioned diplomatic negotiations, but also through Navarre's attempt to banish women from his court, and through the subsequent "siege" of said court by the Princess of France and her attendants. Indeed, as we shall see, the women's siege of Navarre in the play resonates not with a single historical event or source, but with several recorded attempts by French forces to recover Navarre in the sixteenth century – all of them unsuccessful.

Much like Shakespeare's Navarre, the Franco-Navarrese court was repeatedly associated with learned princes in the fifteenth century, and experienced a period of cultural renewal under Carlos II's son and successor, Carlos III ("Charles the Noble," r.1387–1425), who styled himself "*el Nuevo Salomón*"[7] and built a splendid castle in the town of Olite, just south of Pamplona. This palace, built within the walls of the medieval town, and overlooking the wide plains of Navarre, was a favourite royal seat until the early sixteenth century, but fell into decline after Navarre's annexation by Spain in 1512.[8] Shakespeare's play seems to invoke one or both of these famous kings when the Princess of France refers to Navarre's father as "Charles" in 2.1. It is tempting, moreover, to imagine the royal court at Olite, and the "wide fields" (2.1.93)[9] adjoining it, as the setting for Shakespeare's play. However, another famous "Charles," the Prince of Viana, was heir to Navarre (by way of his mother) in the fifteenth century. This Charles was described by the French jurist Pierre de Belloy as

> vn des plus sages & lettrez Princes de son temps, ayant esté bien nourry aux lettres grecques & latines, tellement qu'il traduit du Grec en Espagnol, les Ethiques d'Aristote, il fut d'abonda[n]t,

> fort versé en l'histoire, & se trouue encores de luy vn abrege, & chronologie des Roys de Nauarre, ses predecesseurs iusques à son pere.[10]

Charles, Prince of Viana, never actually ruled Navarre, however: his ambitious father, John II of Aragon, deprived him of the crown. The Prince of Viana's reputation and his family ties may be significant for the play, however, since this Charles was half-brother to Ferdinand II of Aragon (1452–1516), who was John II's son by his second wife, Juana Enriquez. Sixteenth-century critics such as Belloy described her as "l'vne des plus ambitieuses, & malitieuses creatures qui fut pour lors,"[11] and argued that this marriage had brought about "la ruine des legitimes Roys de Nauarre" (Belloy, 83).[12]

Shakespeare's King of Navarre is provocatively named "Ferdinand" (in the play's paratexts, at least), and his father is "Charles" – names that recall Navarre's rich political history, the scholarly fame of its princes, and Spanish attempts to disrupt or redirect the Navarrese succession beginning in the late fifteenth century. In fact, it was the Spanish king Ferdinand II who conquered Navarre in 1512 and displaced the realm's legitimate rulers, Catherine of Foix and her consort Jean d'Albret. In 1516, Spanish Navarre passed to Ferdinand's French-speaking grandson, Charles V, who ruled as regent for his mother, Juana of Castile ("Juana la Loca"), until her death in 1555. In the play, however, Ferdinand *succeeds* Charles in another instance, perhaps, of what Patricia Parker has called its "preposterous reversals."[13]

Other names in the play, too, recall figures associated with Navarre's Spanish or Franco-Spanish past, and especially with its traditions of female inheritance, dynastic marriages, and disputed lines of succession. The name "Joan" – first invoked disparagingly at the end of Act 3 with Berowne's remark that "some men must love my lady and some Joan" (3.1.201–02), and then again, twice, in the closing song's references to "greasy Joan," who "doth keel the pot" (5.2.903; 912)[14] – resonates powerfully (and ironically) with the dynastic history of Navarre. The joke is that in England "Joan" was – as so many editors of the play point out – a "proverbial name for a lower-class woman,"[15] whereas in Navarre it was commonly associated with royalty. Carlos II was the son of Juana II (Jeanne or Joan) de Navarra (r.1328–49), and his consort was Juana de Valois (1343–73; sister of Charles V of France).[16] Froissart alludes briefly to a "marryage ... made bytwene Charles of Nauer and kyng Henrys doughter called Jane / a right fayre lady," incorrectly identifying the aforementioned French "Jane" – Juana de Valois – as a princess of Castile.[17] Her son was Carlos III ("the Noble"), and in 1403, their daughter, Juana de Navarra (Joan of Navarre, 1370–1437), became the second wife of Henry IV of England (and thus stepmother to that most famous of English kings, Henry V). Furthermore, as we have seen, the name Joan was controversially associated with the court of Navarre in the fifteenth century through the figure of Juana Enriquez, the meddlesome and ambitious second wife of John II of Aragon (who usurped the throne of his own son, Charles).

In the sixteenth century, there were two famous Joans associated with Navarre: on the French side, Jeanne d'Albret (or Jeanne III of Navarre), Henry of Navarre's mother and queen regnant of Navarre from 1555 to 1572 (whose death, of a suspected poisoning, was dramatized by Christopher Marlowe in *The Massacre at Paris*); and on the Spanish, Juana la Loca (Joan or Joanna the Mad, 1479–1555), daughter and heir of Ferdinand and Isabella, sister to Catherine of Aragon, and mother to Charles V (1500–58). Jeanne d'Albret "protested vehemently" against her first marriage to the Duke of Cleves in 1541, and "had to be physically carried to the altar."[18] Although Juana la Loca was legally queen of Spain for nearly a half century, she was confined to a convent soon after her husband's death, while her father and then her son ruled as regents in her place.[19] Juana's married life was unhappy: her husband, Philip of Burgundy, was notoriously unfaithful; she herself was (as her epithet suggests) mentally unstable and tormented by jealousy. Legend has it – as early as the sixteenth century – that she eventually succumbed to a kind of "love madness," showing excessive devotion to her husband after his death. To be sure, the "Joan" of Shakespeare's song is as proverbial as any "Tom," "Dick," or "Marian," but it seems to me that Jeanne d'Albret's unwillingness to marry, and the twin problems of infidelity and jealousy that plagued Juana la Loca's marriage, could not be more pertinent to this play, in which the women express their misgivings about promises "made in heat of blood" (5.2.790). *Love's Labour's Lost* ends with marriages deferred and a song in which the heated passions of Spring give way to the harsher realities, the icy cold, of Winter. It is in this context, of cooling or cooled passions, and of sober second thought, that "greasy

Joan doth keel the pot," pouring in something cold to keep the contents from boiling over.

Navarre's efforts in the play to banish women from his court, and to silence them, would have struck Shakespeare's audiences as absurd. The playwright's contemporaries would have been aware of the prominent role women had played, for several centuries, in the history of Navarre. In the sixteenth century, for example, Navarre was associated with learned women such as Marguerite de Navarre (1492–1549), queen consort of Henry II, and her staunchly reformist daughter Jeanne d'Albret. Marguerite, especially, was known for her patronage of literary figures like Rabelais and Marot and as the writer of *The Heptameron* and an earlier religious poem, the *Miroir de l'Ame Pecheresse* (1531; translated into English by Princess Elizabeth in 1545). Moreover, the realm had long been associated with female inheritance and rule, having originally come into the possession of the French nobility by way of a woman, Blanca or Blanche of Navarre (1177–1229). Historical accounts make clear that the right of Navarre originally passed to the Counts of Champagne and Brie by way of Blanche, "sister to Sanctius the eight, and daughter to Sanctius the seaventh," as Shakespeare's contemporary, Gabriel Richardson, explains.[20] Richardson confuses one Sancho for another: she was, in fact, the younger sister of Sanctius VII (also known as "Sancho the Strong"; 1154–1234), whose name sometimes appears as "Sampson" in English works. Blanche married the Count of Champagne, and their son, Theobald IV, became the first "French" king of Navarre in 1234. Thereafter, from the thirteenth century until well into the sixteenth, the title to Navarre was repeatedly inherited by and through women in the absence of direct male heirs – a tradition that distinguished this realm from France, where the Salic Laws were invoked on several occasions to prevent foreign claims to the crown. Twice in the sixteenth century, the title of Navarre was claimed by women: Catherine of Foix or Catherine of Navarre (1468–1517) inherited the crown after the death of her older brother in 1483; her granddaughter, Jeanne d'Albret or Jeanne III, ruled from 1555 until her death in 1572. In Shakespeare's time, Henry of Navarre claimed the kingdom of Navarre by right of his mother, Jeanne d'Albret, and the kingdom of France through his father, Antoine de Bourbon. For, as Richardson explains, Navarre had for five hundred years, up to the time of Sancho VII, "been still continued in the line masculine. After his decease sans issue it first fell to the right of women, transported over the mountaines into France; where, transmitted from one French family vnto another, it hath rested vnto our times, and the vnion thereof with that kingdome" (Richardson, Aa3v). Navarre was, for sixteenth-century readers and audiences, historically identified with learned women who exercised their "right" to rule and to inherit, and who made good use of their tongues and their pens.

It also seems relevant to a play like *Love's Labour's Lost*, which opens with the King's decree that "no woman shall come within a mile of my court" (1.1.119–20), that toward the end of the fifteenth century, the right of women to inherit the crown of Navarre came under dispute. Contemporary historical accounts report that when Catherine of Foix succeeded her brother in 1483, her uncle (John of Foix) tried, unsuccessfully, to claim the throne for himself by invoking the French Salic Laws; his actions brought a civil war to Navarre that lasted until 1492. Some writers, such as Pierre de Belloy, argued that the king of Spain, Ferdinand II, was ultimately behind this attempt to strip the young queen of her right. When that failed, Ferdinand sought to secure by her marriage to his young son a Spanish, instead of a French, heir for Navarre, but in 1484 Catherine was married instead to a French nobleman, Jean d'Albret.[21] Later, in 1512, Ferdinand (now married to John of Foix's daughter, Germaine)[22] invaded Navarre and captured all of the territory to the south of the Pyrenees, including the capital city, Pamplona. Catherine and her husband fled into France, retaining only the small portion of their former kingdom on the north face of the Pyrenees; thenceforth, Ferdinand and his successors in Spain also claimed the title "King of Navarre." Ferdinand legitimized his claim to Navarre by arguing that Jean d'Albret had been excommunicated, and thus deprived of his right to rule, but French critics such as Belloy countered that the title belonged to Catherine, not Jean – the papal bull had named the wrong person and was thus without legal standing. In each case, Ferdinand's attempts to redirect the Navarrese succession depended upon either the denial of women's inheritance rights or an insistence upon the husband's claim *de jure uxoris*.

As I think this account makes clear, the name "Ferdinand," although it is significant only to printed editions of *Love's Labour's Lost* – appearing in speech prefixes and stage directions, but never uttered in the play's dialogue – resonates in important ways with the history of Navarre, for it was Ferdinand II of Spain who conquered the kingdom in 1512, banishing, in the process, Navarre's queen and bringing to an end some three hundred years of French rule. The play's opening speech, delivered by a fictional king of Navarre named "Ferdinand," therefore takes on a special kind of irony when he addresses his men as "brave conquerors" – not of Navarre itself, it turns out, but of "the huge army of the world's desires" (1.1.10). Moreover, the King's decree in this scene, that "no woman shall come within a mile of my court" (1.1.119–20), is an "excommunication" of sorts, since the penalty – "on pain of losing her tongue" (1.1.122–3) – like the decree, is designed not just to banish women, but also to silence them. The legislation, criticized by Berowne as a "dangerous law against gentility," clearly means to deter any and all communication between the sexes by stating: "if any man be seen to talk with a woman within the term of three years, he shall endure such public shame as the rest of the court can possible devise" (1.1.128–31). This fictitious Ferdinand's "excommunication" of women from his court suggests that in the play the struggle for control of Navarre is comically refigured as Navarre's effort to govern himself. The King's proclamation would have recalled, for Shakespeare's audiences, one of the most controversial events of the 1512 "War of Navarre": the excommunication, by Pope Julius II, of the kings of France and Navarre, a decree that paved the way for Spain's invasion of Navarre that summer.

This history was part of a larger transnational "conversation" in the 1580s and 1590s about Spain's geopolitical ambitions – a conversation that also frequently touched on Henry of Navarre's dynastic claims, the Armada, and the dispute over Portugal's succession. In *Albion's England* (1597), for example, an epic poem that is exactly contemporary with the earliest surviving quarto of *Love's Labour's Lost*, William Warner drew a straight line between the invasion of Navarre in 1512 and the attempted conquest of England by Philip II's "invincible" Armada seventy-six years later.[23] The poem argues that Spanish "ambition" for universal empire – witnessed, as Warner points out, by a "Mot" (or motto) claiming "*the World sufficeth not*" – had already led to the conquest of territories in Europe, Africa, and the New World. No sooner had Castile, "by what right or wrong so-eare"[24] (Q1r), wrung the diadem of

Navarre from its rightful king, and stolen Portugal with "brybed Traytors, fraude, and force" (Q1r), but his aim turned "hether," to England:

> The great *Nauarrois*, Sampson,[25] stauld[26] the first *Castilian* King:
> But badly *Castile* quits[27] his loue whence did that honor spring:
> And from his Line by trecherie the Diademe doth wring.
> So, by what right or wrong so-eare, *Spayne* clouteth Crownes together
> And aimeth, euen from *Portugale*, as is supposed, hether. (Q1r)

Ironically, Warner suggests, the "first *Castilian* King," Ferdinand I, Count of Castile (c.1015–65), had owed his position to his father, "Sampson" (Sancho III of Navarre, also known as Sancho the Great, c.992–1035). Five hundred years later, it was another "Castilian" king, Ferdinand II,[28] who had "requited" this "love" by wringing the crown from the royal line of Navarre. In this manner, Warner continues, "*Spayne* clouteth Crownes together." Now Spain has set its sights on England, Warner admonishes, aiming "even from *Portugale*, as is supposed, hether."[29] Just as the memory of Navarre's conquest "haunted" later accounts of the Spanish Armada, so, in Shakespeare's play, does a braggart named "Armado," the object of much pointed satire, haunt the court of Navarre, entertaining the men with his fantastical tales of Spanish chivalry. I shall return to this figure later in the essay.

Shakespeare's comedy engages broadly, and fancifully, with elements of Navarre's past. The plot and the characters are fictitious, and yet the allusive energies of the play suggest an awareness of the realm's rich history and its place in the political debates of the time. Since Shakespeare's contemporaries were more familiar with the "conversation" about Navarre than we are today, it is worth reconstructing it here, at least in its main points. Prominent French, Italian, and English accounts of the conquest – and the range of opinions is impressive – emphasize how, in 1512, Pope Julius II colluded with Ferdinand II of Spain to deprive Jean d'Albret and his wife, Catherine, of their kingdom. The Italian historian Francesco Guicciardini's remark that it "hath bene a perpetuall desire in the ancient kings of *Spaine*, to impatronize themselues vpon the realme of *Nauarre*"[30] is echoed by several writers, including Richard Sergier, who comments that Ferdinand "long before had gaped for that kingdom,"[31] and Belloy, who claimed (citing the Spanish historian Esteban de Garibay) that Ferdinand and his father, John II of Aragon, had long ago decided that "il falloit à quelque prix que ce fust, ioindre le Royaume de Nauarre au reste de l'Espagne, & à la premiere occasion qui se presenteroit, en chasser les Comtes de Foix, François de coeur, & de nation, qui s'estoient venus planter là, pour tenir vn canton d'icelle."[32] These accounts conflate Ferdinand's worldly and erotic appetites, since he "desires" the realm of Navarre and "gapes" for it; it seems ironic, then, that the King's opening speech in this play is all about conquering one's passions or desires instead.

An act of excommunication, which had political as well as religious consequences for Christian monarchs even after the Reformation, had been instrumental to Ferdinand's conquest of Navarre in 1512. Theoretically, any king or queen who was excluded from the communion of the Church also lost his or her right to rule.[33] André Thevet, the French cosmographer, argued that the pope had excommunicated the king of Navarre, and deprived him of his realm, "sans occasion" – that is, "without reason" or "without just cause."[34] Other authors explain, however, that Julius II's bull of excommunication was payback for Louis XII's Italian wars (Guicciardini, 517).[35] Most writers, however, concur with Thevet that the king of Navarre was punished simply for his loyalty to the French king. As Guicciardini explains: "the king Catholike, who had set his eyes vpon that realme, required the king of *Nauarre* to stand neuter betweene the French king and him: and to suffer to passe through his realme, his souldiers that were to enter *Fraunce*." The French king knew "of what importance for the defence of the Duchy of *Guien*, was the realme of *Nauarre*" (Guicciardini, 517),[36] and, as Henry Wotton explains, when Louis XII asked Jean d'Albret to assist him by refusing passage to the Spanish armies, Albret, his vassal, was legally obliged to comply: "the king of *Navarra* could not without manifest loss and forfeiture of this kingdom unto the French king, deny or resist his Commandment."[37] Refused passage by the king of Navarre, Ferdinand II promptly appealed to his ally the pope, who excommunicated the king of France, subjecting "aswell his person as whosoeuer were his adherents, to all the paines of heretikes and schismatikes, giuing sufferance to euery one to occupy their substances, estates, and all that appertained vnto them"

(Guicciardini, 517). The Calvinist writer and jurist François Hotman reports that the king of Spain then

> turned his forces prepared against the French king, against the king of Nauarre: and this was the cause that Ferdinando did cast out the king his neighbour: though he did also pretend another, bicause both the king of France, and those that did aid him, were pronounced accursed by the popes edict, and their kingdoms were made common. (Hotman, 307)

In a play that artfully avoids the religious controversies associated with Navarre, and with Henry of Navarre – indeed, avoids the question of religious difference altogether – we see instead an attempt to exclude women from a different sort of "fellowship" or community. Gender, in other words, replaces religion as the site of political struggle in this play.

Since Jean d'Albret had declared himself loyal to the king of France, his realms, like those of the French king, were "made common" in the eyes of the Church – available to be occupied by anyone who might so choose. The Spanish king, having conquered Navarre, was thus able to claim that he had been "rightfully and iudicially impatronized of it by the authority of the Sea Apostolike" (Guicciardini, 517). The significance of these events, as François de Belleforest observed in his *Grandes Annales* (1579), was that the kingdom of Navarre

> reuint aux hoirs de Iean d'Arragon pere de l'heritiere de Nauarre, mais non habile à venir à ceste succession, pour n'estre du sang direct de ceste couronne: & furent reunies les Prouinces de Nauarre & de Castille soubs vn mesme Prince trois cens soixante dix-huict ans apres qu'au temps du Roy Sanche dit le Grand, ces seigneuries furent separées, & données à diuers Princes.[38]

The "excommunication" of women in Shakespeare's play, it seems to me, parodies this historical "casting out" of the realm's female heir, Catherine, by her male rival, Ferdinand II. John II ("the Faithless") of Aragon had become ruler of Navarre *de jure uxoris* (by right of his wife), but worked to divert the succession away from his first son, Charles (the Prince of Viana). Ferdinand was John's son by his second wife, Juana Enriquez, and so not – as Belleforest points out – in the direct line of inheritance. Catherine of Foix, who was in the direct line, had a far stronger claim to the throne. Historical and legal precedents were also on her side. It is not a little ironic, then, that Boyet should describe Navarre as the "sole inheritor" not of the kingdom but of "all perfections that a man may owe" (2.1.5–6).[39] As in Navarre's opening speech, questions of inheritance, succession, and ownership or indebtedness that one might readily attach to the play's setting – or (in print versions, at least) to a king named "Ferdinand" – are recast, here, in terms of individual moral virtue or self-discipline.

Shakespeare treats Navarre's attempt to "excommunicate" women from his court as foolish and laughable – indeed, the inevitable failure of his decree underwrites much of the play's comedy. Even before they sign the decree, the courtiers realize that they must be "forsworn 'on mere necessity'" (1.1.151), as the Princess of France will be arriving shortly "in embassy … / About surrender up of Aquitaine" (1.1.131, 134) and they will, of course, be forced to speak with her. Just moments later, Costard is brought in by the Constable, with a letter from the "magnificent Armado" explaining that the clown has been caught consorting with a buxom dairy maid named Jaquenetta. And this is only the beginning of Navarre's troubles: in 1.2 we learn that Armado, too, is in love. Even before the French princess arrives at the gates, it is clear that the King's decree is in peril. And once the courtiers have met their matches, as it were, Ferdinand's all-male regime is doomed. Indeed, the fun will be in watching it fall.

Aware of Navarre's rich history, the play suggests that the kingdom is (or perhaps was) a kind of "Promised Land" for women. In 3.1, the clown, Costard, privy to the men's oath-breaking, likens Navarre to the besieged city of Jericho when he pointedly asks Berowne, "how much carnation ribbon may a man buy for a remuneration?" (3.1.142–3). Having just received payment of three farthings from Armado, for whom he has promised to deliver a love letter to the milkmaid, Jaquenetta, Costard is met by Berowne, who is about to approach him with a similar task. The clown acknowledges Berowne's greeting by asking the courtier about the price of red ribbon. Costard's question recalls the siege of Jericho by the Israelites in the Book of Joshua. The biblical story opens as Joshua, preparing to cross the Jordan into the Promised Land, sends two of his men ahead to spy on the walled city of Jericho. Upon entering the city, the spies come to the house of a harlot named Rahab, who offers them lodging and hides them from the king.[40] Rahab's sympathies are with the Israelites, for she says to Joshua's spies: "I know that the Lord hath giuen you the land, and that the feare of you is fallen vpon vs, and that all the inhabitants of the land faint because of you" (2:9). In recognition of her service to them, Joshua's men promise to spare her household when the city falls. As they depart, they say to her:

> Beholde, when we come into the land, thou shalt binde this corde of red threde in the windowe, whereby thou lettest vs downe, & thou shalt bring thy father and thy mother, & thy brethren, and al thy fathers housholde home to thee.
>
> And whosoever then doeth go out at the dores of thine house into the streat, his blood shal be vpon his head, & we will be gylteles: but whosoeuer shal be with thee in the house, his blood shal be on our head, if anie hand touche him. (2:18–19)

The destruction of Jericho unfolds a few chapters later, the walls of the city famously collapsing before the shouts and the trumpets of the Israelites: "So the people shouted, when they had blowen trompets: for when the people had heard the sounde of the trompet, they shouted with a great shoute: and the wall fel downe flat: so the people went vp into the citie, euerie man streight before him: and they toke the citie" (6:20). The city is destroyed, and all that is in it, but as promised, Rahab and her family are spared: "So Ioshua," we are told, "saued Rahab the harlot, and her fathers housholde, and all that she had, and she dwelt in Israel euen vnto this day, because she had hid the messengers, which Ioshua sent to spie out Iericho" (6:25).

Costard's sly question about "carnation ribbon" is more than a passing reference to this story, since it suggests an elaborate parallel between the biblical siege of Jericho and the "siege" of Navarre, in *Love's Labour's Lost*, by the French princess and her ladies-in-waiting. Costard's joke announces that Navarre's gynophobic regime is about to fall. The allusion suggests, furthermore, that the women of the play are like the Israelites, heirs to this "promised land" of Navarre. Sure enough, Berowne's "certaine treason" (4.3.186) is quickly discovered, but not before Navarre and his followers succumb, one by one, to the erotic charms of the French women. Upon learning that every one of them has, despite himself, fallen in love, Ferdinand asks Berowne – who has already shown "How well he's read to reason against reading" (1.1.94) – to "prove / Our loving lawful and our faith not torn" (4.3.280–1). Overpowered by their desire for the French women, Navarre's regime of scholastic austerity is undone not by forces from without, but by weakness and, as Jericho was, by "treason" within its gates. Thenceforth, the men resolve to woo the women, the gates of Navarre are flung open, and the Princess of France and her ladies, forced until now to camp in the field beyond the city walls, are at last invited in. As Berowne urges his companions,

> First from the park let us conduct them thither;
> Then homeward every man attach the hand
> Of his faire mistress. In the afternoon
> We will with some strange pastime solace them,
> Such as the shortness of the time can shape,
> For revels, dances, masques, and merry hours,
> Forerun faire Love, strewing her way with flowers. (4.3.348–54)

The attempt by Navarre and his men to justify, retrospectively, their transgressions in the play resonates powerfully with the kingdom's history, and especially with the king of Spain's request that a history be written that would justify, after the fact, his 1512 conquest.

In the 1590s, even though Ferdinand II had conquered most of the realm decades earlier, a Frenchman, Henry of Navarre, retained the title of "King of Navarre." Nevertheless, through much of the sixteenth century, the titular kings and queens of Navarre held court not in Navarre but in neighbouring Béarn, and some critics refused to recognize their title, referring to Henry of Navarre disparagingly, for example, as the "Prince of *Bearn*" or simply the "*Bearnnish man*."[41] As the polemical works of the 1580s and 1590s – and plays such as Christopher Marlowe's *Massacre at Paris* (1593) – suggest, however, Henry of Navarre's supporters in England and France continued to hope that he would one day succeed in recovering his lost territory. As Warner put it in his 1597 poem, "*Nauar* hath meanes to haue *Nauar*" (P8v). Similarly, we hear Marlowe's Pleshé fantasize that the armies of the "true Religion" would soon make way for the crowning of Navarre's "rightfull Lord and Soueraigne," Henry, at Pamplona:

> The vertues of our true Religion,
> Cannot but march with many graces more:
> Whose army shall discomfort all your foes,

And at the length in Pampelonia crowne,
In spite of Spaine and all the popish power,
That holdes it from your highnesse wrongfully:
Your Maiestie her rightfull Lord and Soueraigne.[42]

The parodic "siege" of Navarre in the play, by the ladies of France, resonates with discourses that circulated in the 1580s and 1590s about the recovery of Navarre by its rightful heirs (who also happened to be French). The suggestion of this play, which was performed for Elizabeth I, might even be that it sometimes takes a woman to do a man's job.

The French had tried more than once in the sixteenth century to recover their lost territory. François Hotman, a partisan of Henry of Navarre, reported for example that in 1512, "the king of France, being not ignorant that the senior ought to deliuer his vassall from the danger of that event ... sent his armie to recouer *Pompiopolis*, ouer which he set as captaine *Dunosius* chiefe gouernor of Aquitania, and duke of *Longouilla*" (Hotman, 303).[43] While critics point to more contemporary events (and the French civil wars in particular), it is also possible that accounts of this early sixteenth-century campaign inform the play's depiction of bickering among the French delegation to Navarre. According to the account in Belleforest's *Grandes Annales* (1579), the 1512 expedition was led by a French prince, François, Duke of Valois (later François I), accompanied, on account of his youth, by the more experienced Dukes of Bourbon and Longueville (François II d'Orléans, 1470–1512). Ultimately, Belleforest reports, this expedition failed because of infighting among the senior nobility: it seems Bourbon and Longueville could not agree as to who was actually in charge (Belleforest, 1397r). Belleforest comments, moreover, that "si est-ce qu'il fut impossible de rien faire de bon, d'autant que ceste ialousie allant en croissant, empescha aussi le seruice du Roy, & l'aduancement du Nauarrois" (Belleforest, 1397v).[44] The play offers a comic analogue to this ignominious moment in the verbal sparring among Boyet and the ladies of France in 2.1 (after they, too, lay "siege" to Navarre), and the Princess's remark that "This civil war of wits were much better used / On Navarre and his book-men, for here 'tis abused" (2.1.224–5). To enjoy this parody, it is not necessary to find more than a passing resemblance between the events described by Belleforest or Hotman and the scenario staged in the play; no special knowledge of these events or persons would have been needed by Shakespeare's Elizabethan or Jacobean audiences.

Despite having laid siege to the walled city of Pamplona in 1512–13, the French were eventually compelled to withdraw – and were reportedly mocked, as they did so, by the Castilians (Belleforest, 1397v). Later campaigns to take back the lost territory of Navarre also proved unsuccessful: in 1521 French forces, led by Andrew of Foix on behalf of François I, captured the Navarrese town of St Jean de Pied-de-Port, and as in the previous campaign reached Pamplona before being turned back. Shakespeare's play parodies the French attempts to retake Navarre by staging, instead, a "siege" of Navarre's court by the Princess of France and her attendants. In Act 2, soon after their arrival, Boyet announces to the Princess that the King of Navarre will not admit her to his house, but "rather means to lodge you in the field, / Like one that comes here to besiege his court" (2.1.85–6). Although the women gain the upper hand in the play's battle of wits, they are in the end, like the French forces that had besieged Navarre earlier in the century, compelled by circumstance to withdraw.

Shakespeare's Navarre is an historical fiction, an anachronistic space that recalls, simultaneously, the realm's French past, its conquest by Spain, and its contested status at the close of the sixteenth century. If we look beyond topical readings that foreground the (Béarnaise) court and politics of Henry of Navarre and instead focus on the significance of the play's setting, Navarre, we can more easily account for the presence, alongside the French courtiers, of characters named "Ferdinand," "Armado," and even "Jaquenetta" (a feminized variant of the French Jacques, the English James, and the Spanish Iago).[45] Elizabethans who knew their history, or followed the reports and pamphlets about Henry of Navarre, would have been aware, for example, that the conquered portion of Navarre had been formally joined to the kingdom of Castile on 25 July 1512 – "le jour de S. Jacques" (the feast day of St. James).[46] The fact is mentioned by French and Spanish chroniclers alike, beginning with the standard account of the Navarrese war by the Spanish scholar Antonio de Nebrija, the *Belli Nauariensis Libros Duos* published in 1545.[47] Nebrija not only mentions the feast of "diui Iacobi Zebedei" (Saint James, son of Zebedee), but he also points out that 1512 was a jubilee year for Spain ("erat annus Hispani iubilei") – that is, a year in which these particular celebrations fell on a Sunday.[48] François de

Belleforest's *Grandes Annales* (1579), one of the most detailed French accounts of the conquest, and a work that was well known in England, also mentions "la feste de S. Iacques":

> Tout cecy fut passé le vingt & quatriesme de Iuillet mille cinq cens douze, qui estoit vn samedy, auquel entra dedans le Comte de Lerin Connestable de Nauarre: & l'endemain le Duc d'Alue, qui estoit la feste de S. Iacques Patron d'Espaigne, la feit son entrée comme Lieutenant du Roy de Castille, au nom duquel il prit possession due Royaume de Nauarre: & fut ceste-cy la premiere fois que iamais Pampelonne laissa son Roy naturel, pour se rendre au Castillan, Arragonnois, quoy qu'il y eut eu de grandes, & cruelles guerres entre Nauarre, Arragon, & Castille. (Belleforest, 1396)[49]

Saint James, whose remains lie at Compostela in Galicia, was, as these authors point out, the patron saint of Spain ("Patron d'Espaigne"), and his name was closely associated not only with the famed pilgrimage route that passes through Navarre – the famed Camino de Santiago de Compostela – but also with the Reconquista (as "Santiago Matamoros," or "Saint James the Moorslayer") and the project of Spanish unification undertaken by Ferdinand II and his first wife, Isabella. The name given to Shakespeare's buxom dairymaid, Jaquenetta, cannot but ironically recall Navarre's historical and geographical association with this figure.

In Shakespeare's time, Spanish soldiers were famous, both in print and on the English stage, for invoking the name of "Santiago" or "S. Jacques" as their battle cry. In *The Spanish Colonie* (1583), for example, the earliest English translation of Bartolomé de Las Casas' *Brevísima relación de la destrucción de las Indias*, they are heard to cry out "*Saynttiago*, let vs amongst them, & upon them sirs."[50] Similarly, the knights in Thomas Kyd's *Soliman and Perseda* (ca. 1590) – incidentally, the only extant English play before *Love's Labour's Lost* to feature a character named "Ferdinand" (or "Ferdinando")[51] – are each asked by the Prince of Cyprus: "Vpon the onset of the enemy, / What is thy motto when thou spurres thy horse."[52] The Englishman replies with "Saint George for England, and saint George for me"; the Frenchman with "Saint Denis is for France, and that for me," and the Spaniard declares: "Iaques, Iaques, is the Spaniards choice" (Kyd, A4v). It is rather comic, then, and not a little telling, that Navarre and his men invoke neither Saint Denis nor Saint Jacques as their patron when they enter the fray in 4.3. Instead, upon discovering that they have all secretly "perjured" themselves by falling in love with the French women, the men of Navarre promptly embrace their new roles as "affection's men-at-arms" (4.3.286), and with an enthusiastic "Saint Cupid then! And, soldiers, to the field!" and "Advance your standards, and upon them, lords!" (4.3.340–1), they resolve to do the very thing they had so solemnly (and so recently) abjured – to "woo these girls of France" (4.3.345). Readers of Las Casas might have heard a parodic echo here of the Spaniards' battle cry (above) as they ambushed "the flower of the nobilitie of all the state of *Motensuma*" in New Spain (Las Casas, D4r). In *Love's Labour's Lost,* however – a play that is ever so conscious of its national and martial resonances – war is love (or love is war), the patron saint of these "soldiers" is Cupid, and the "flower of the nobilitie" they seek to conquer is female and French. In a different way, Shakespeare spoofs the Spaniards' "love" for their patron saint in Armado's infatuation with that "base wench," Jaquenetta.

That the conquest of Navarre in 1512 coincided so neatly with the feast of S. Jacques (or Saint James) linked this event securely to Ferdinand's other wars, to the expulsion of the Moors and the Jews from Spain at the end of the fifteenth century, the project of Spanish unification, and the conquest of the Americas. As Belleforest remarks in another work, the *Harangues Militaires* (1572), "L'Espaignol ... poursuiuit [la guerre] de Nauarre auec plus d'animosite qu'il n'auoit fait celle de l'infidelle, qu'il remit en ses terres, & dechassa un Chrestien de son patrimoine."[53] Shakespeare's contemporaries also drew connections between the history of Navarre, narratives of Spanish unification and expansionism, and the Armada of 1588, so it should not surprise us that a braggart figure like the "magnificent Armado" should "haunt" the court of a "brave conqueror" named Ferdinand. This "refinèd traveler of Spain" (1.1.160), described by the king as a "child of fancy" (1.1.167), amuses the courtiers of Navarre with his rhetorical excesses and his tales of "the worth of many a knight / From tawny Spain, lost in the world's debate" (1.1.171–2). As Ferdinand remarks to his men, "How you delight ... I know not, I, / But I protest I love to hear him lie, / And will use him for my minstrelsy" (1.1.173–5). Clearly an object of satire, this pompous Spaniard and his "vain tongue" would almost certainly have recalled for English audiences Spain's conquering rhetoric on the eve of the Armada. The historian William Camden remarks, for example, that "*Don Bernardin de Mendoza* vainely and falsely printed a Poeme in France of a triumph before the victory."[54] A contemporary pamphlet, *The Masqve of the League and the Spanyard discouered* (1592), also refers, punningly, to "the Ambassadour *Mendoza*" as the "*Lyar of Spaine*."[55] In Shakespeare's play, the presence of Armado at the court of Navarre serves to juxtapose the imagined *end* of Spanish aggression – the attempted invasion of England by Philip II in 1588 – with an event that, for many writers, marked the *beginning* of Spanish expansionism in Europe – the conquest of Navarre by Ferdinand II.

Like the Armada, the 1512 conquest of Navarre was associated with a famous Spanish "liar" – at least according to French critics who wrote about the event in the 1570s and 1580s. The renowned "grammarian," Antonio de Nebrija, was also famous in the sixteenth century for his account of the War of Navarre, written for Ferdinand II in celebration of the Spanish conquest of 1512 and published posthumously in 1545. French critics of Nebrija, including François de Belleforest and Pierre de Belloy, accused the scholar of lying, and of "abusing history" with his tract, which sought to justify Ferdinand's actions long after the fact. Nebrija, known today for having written the *Gramática de la lengua castellana* – the first grammar of the Spanish language, which he dedicated to Isabella I of Castile in 1492 – figures prominently in late sixteenth-century English and French political writing as an apologist for Ferdinand II's conquest of Navarre. His *Belli Navariensis Libros Duos* became the standard account of the "War of Navarre," and the target of much criticism on both sides of the English Channel. French writers, especially, attacked the work as a cynical attempt by the Spanish king to justify, retrospectively, actions that violated the principles or conventions of international law. Belloy, for example, argues that Ferdinand, knowing the injustice of his conquest of Navarre, and aware of the dangerous precedent he had set, commissioned Nebrija to write a history of the war that would bolster, retrospectively, his *legal* claims to the realm:

> Voilà pourquoy aussi Ferdinand, iugeant bien en soy, qu'il auoit violé la iustice, & commune alliance des Princes, & que outre le blasme que la posterité luy en donneroit, par son mauuais exemple, pourroit auoir occasionné vn plus puissant que luy,

> à le payer de mesme ou plus forte monnoye ... Voulut & commanda ledit Ferdinand, à Anthoine Nebrisse, qui viuoit allors, de rechercher & metter par ordre les raisons qui se pourroient apporter, pour la telle quelle deffence de ceste incursion, & les publier, comme il a fait, auec ce qui s'est passé en Nauarre apres la guerre faite par ledit Roy Iean 3 pour le recouurement du Royaume. (Belloy, 103r)[56]

Belloy takes great pains in his treatise to dismantle Nebrija's arguments, referring to him contemptuously as "Monsieur le grammarien" and asking which rule of grammar it was that served to justify Ferdinand's behaviour. Significantly, Belloy, a jurist, sought to refute Nebrija's claims on the grounds that Julius II's bull of excommunication in 1512 had named the wrong monarch: legally, he argued, the kingdom was the inheritance not of Jean d'Albret but of his wife, Catherine of Foix:

> La seconde raison de Nebrisse est, que le Roy Iean de Nauarre auoit esté declaire schismatique, par le Pape Iules 2. & ses terres mises en proye, au premier vsurpateur d'icelles, demeurans les subiets du Royaume, deschargez du serment de fidelité. A cecy il y a de belles responses premierement le Royaume de Nauarre n'estoit pas du Roy Iean, car c'estoit la succession de la Royne Catherine sa femme, laquelle Ferdinand qui portoit titre d'oncle à ladite Princesse, deuoit conseruer & garder, contre tous ceux, qui eussent voulu luy faire tort, mais ie croy que le Pape n'a pas entendu excommunier & donner en proye les biens d'vne pauure femme, qui ne luy auoit iamais fait desplaisir. (Belloy, 103v–104)[57]

As far as Belloy was concerned, Ferdinand's claim to Navarre on the basis of Jean d'Albret's excommunication had no legal validity.

Belloy's contemporary, François de Belleforest, is similarly scathing in his appraisal of Nebrija's work, calling him, among other things, a liar, a pedant, a smooth talker, and a "Grammairien gastehistoire" (Belleforest, 1394v).[58] Characterizing the Spanish scholar as a dilettante when it came to the writing of history or the interpretation of the divine and common laws of nations, Belleforest concludes his discussion by urging his readers to "rebuff" this "chatterbox" (or "bauard") (Belleforest, 1395r). Nebrija's reputation in France – and in England as well – thus served, in Shakespeare's time, to associate the court of Ferdinand II with pedantry and propaganda, just as the fictional court of the fictional "Ferdinand" is in Shakespeare's play. For some readers, at least, Shakespeare's "Ferdinand" must have satirically recalled the conquering Spanish king, characterized by his opponents as a patron of "liars" who called upon his courtiers (or his "bookmen") to produce, in the aftermath of Navarre's capture, "some flattery for this evil" (4.3.283). Indeed, the court of Shakespeare's fictional Ferdinand is full of figures who seek to justify, *post facto*, their transgressions: in 1.1, just as Dumaine tries to reason his way out of the oath he has sworn, the "rational hind,"[59] Costard, using a rhetoric of substitution and displacement,[60] tries to evade the letter of the law when, in direct contravention of Navarre's recent edict, he is caught with a woman: "I was taken with none, sir, I was taken with a damsel" (1.1.275–6); "This was no damsel neither, sir, she was a virgin" (1.1.278); "If it were, I deny her virginity. I was taken with a maid" (1.1.280–1). While he doesn't escape punishment altogether, his verbal wrangling does result in a reduced sentence. In 1.2, Armado, also in danger of breaking his oath, looks to Moth to supply "some mighty precedent" for his love of "that country girl" Jaquenetta (1.2.112–13). And even before Berowne is commissioned by his fellows to "prove / Our loving lawful and our faith not torn" (4.3.281), to provide "some authority how to proceed / Some tricks, some quillets, how to cheat the devil" (4.3.283–4), and some "salve for perjury" (4.3.285), we are witness to the self-important chattering of that pedant Holofernes, whose long-winded *excursi* into the finer points of Latin grammar must have recalled, like a devastating caricature, not just his namesake in Rabelais, but also that other, infamous grammarian, Nebrija. No single character in the play should be read as "Nebrija" but several of them, in one way or another, recall the Spanish grammarian's project of retrospective justification, and each is, in his way, a "type" with historical ties to the play's setting, Navarre.

Shakespeare's play, I would suggest, signals its awareness of Navarre's complex cultural and political history in both its plot structure and its language – not least, as we have seen, through its use of names. While several of these names (Navarre, Berowne, Longaville, Dumaine) have long been identified with contemporary French political figures, the allusive range of the play suggests that Shakespeare was invoking several periods in Navarre's history at once. Even the comical Pageant of the Nine Worthies in Act 5, organized and directed by the pedant, Holofernes, is adapted to the Navarrese context of its performance. Critics have noted that the Pompey the Great is not usually counted among the Nine Worthies, a group that traditionally included Julius Caesar, Alexander the Great, Hector, Joshua, David, Judas Maccabeus, Godfrey of Bouillon, Charlemagne, and King Arthur. Costard's appearance as "Pompion[61] the Great" (5.2.501) or "Pompey surnamed the Big" (5.2.545), however, draws a great deal of attention within the play, Boyet and the others gently mocking the clown's performance. Audiences and readers might assume that the inclusion of the Roman general Pompey among the Worthies is yet another error on the pedant's part (he's already proven himself a lousy grammarian by this point in the play): Shakespeare's contemporaries, certainly, would have recognized the mistake. But Pompey's historical connection to Navarre makes his inclusion in the Pageant ironically appropriate in this instance, since, as several writers observe, he was credited with founding the capital city, Pamplona. François de Belleforest, for example, alludes to "la cité de Pampelonne, chef du tout le royaume Nauarrois (Colonnie ancienne des Romains, & fondée par Pompée le grand)" (*Harangues* 1296), and François Hotman refers at least twice to "the principall citie of the kingdome named Pompiopolis" (303; V8r). Mercator's *Atlas*, which also makes reference to Ferdinand's invasion of Navarre ("which hee long gaped for"), notes that the "chiefe Citie of *Navarre* is now commonly called *Pampelona*, some call it *Pompeiopolis*, as if it were built by *Pompeius Magnus*."[62] Costard's performance as Pompey is comical in and of itself, but the clown's wit (and Shakespeare's) would be all the more apparent to playgoers who knew their Roman history.

This rich array of allusions suggests an awareness of Navarre's history that extends beyond the borders of that "nook of France" that critics have long assumed to be the setting for Shakespeare's play. The play's ironic references to past figures associated with the kingdom of Navarre and to its capital, Pamplona – under Spanish rule when Shakespeare wrote his play – work against the assumption that *Love's Labour's Lost* is simply a "French" play obliquely concerned with the civil wars or capitalizing on the popular reputation of Henry of Navarre. But the play does more than allude to Navarre's ancient and medieval past: it also stages clever parodies of historical events that remained contentious for French and English writers throughout Shakespeare's lifetime.

"*The Lady speaks in Welsh*": *Henry IV, Part 1* as Multilingual Drama[1]

PHILIP SCHWYZER

From the earliest quartos and the First Folio down to modern scholarly editions, printed texts of Shakespeare's plays have observed what seems a common-sense distinction between speech (presented mainly in roman type) and non-verbal action (indicated by italics). Spoken lines not only account for by far the larger part of any Shakespearean text; they are also regarded as more reliably authorial, and more essential to the dramatic work. Sparse and laconic in most plays, and smelling more of the promptbook than the poet's study, stage directions generally confine themselves to telling us in few words who is entering, leaving, sleeping, or dying. Clearly distinguished as they are, lines and stage directions may each on occasion be called upon to do the work of the other. Not infrequently, speech may be used in addition to or instead of stage directions to indicate physical movement. ("Look where it comes again!" "See, it stalks away."[2]) Much more rarely, a stage direction may indicate the enunciation of words not included amongst the play's lines. The major example of this latter phenomenon in Shakespeare's *oeuvre* occurs in the latter part of Act 3, scene 1, of *Henry IV, Part 1*:[3]

> *Glendower speaks to her in Welsh, and she answers him in the same.* (3.1.193)
> *The Lady again in Welsh.* (3.1.199)
> *The Lady speaks again in Welsh.* (3.1.207)
> *Here the Lady sings a Welsh song.* (3.1.240–1)

These unique stage directions present a series of conundrums. Do these Welsh speeches count amongst the play's "lines"? (That is, does Lady Mortimer, who may speak and sing for several minutes on stage, have any lines in the play?) Is speech in Welsh to be understood as language, or rather as a form of physical behaviour, comparable to entrances, alarums, and excursions? Are the Welsh Lady's unspecified words and song an integral part of the literary work, or are they a dangerous Derridean *supplement*, at once compensating for and laying bare the play's linguistic lack? In either case, what are the implications for our perception of Shakespeare as sole and original author of *Henry IV, Part 1*? Might these stage directions, which depart from Shakespeare's normal practice as well as that of his contemporaries (a number of whom had no objection to scripting Welsh dialogue), point the way to a more complex understanding of the "English," "Shakespearean" text?

Shakespeare was not habitually shy in the face of foreign languages. Liberal sprinklings of Italian are found in early plays such as *Love's Labour's Lost* and *The Taming of the Shrew,* and several of the plays, most notably *Henry V* and *The Merry Wives of Windsor*, include passages in French. Shreds of Latin, of course, pervade the canon. The use of a stage direction to indicate lines spoken in another tongue occurs nowhere in Shakespeare's works outside of *1 Henry IV* (though he does occasionally use stage directions to indicate inaudible speech in English, as at *Richard III* 3.2.107). Nor do the dramatic works of Shakespeare's contemporaries afford more than a small handful of instances of this kind of stage direction. In *The Second Part of, If You Know Not Me, You Know Nobody* (1606), "*the Queen entertaines the Ambassadors, and in their severall languages confers with them*."[4] This stage direction seems to call for an exchange of pleasantries in French, Italian, and German which might well be accomplished in a matter of seconds; the dialogue would almost certainly not stretch to the several minutes necessary for Glendower and Lady Mortimer to say and sing everything that Shakespeare's scene requires of them. The omission of the song itself from the printed text of *Henry IV, Part 1* is arguably not quite so unusual. Munday's *John a Kent and John a Cumber* and Middleton and Dekker's *Chaste Maid in Cheapside* both call for a "Welsh song" whilst failing to provide the Welsh lyrics. In the latter case the words of an English song are included in the printed text, suggesting perhaps that all that is called for is a song in the Welsh style.[5] Lady Mortimer, by contrast, explicitly "speak[s] no English" (3.1.189).

One obvious explanation for Shakespeare's failure to provide the dialogue called for in the stage directions is that he simply did not know enough (or any) Welsh. Yet linguistic ignorance did not prove a stumbling block for a number of Shakespeare's contemporaries. Welsh was in fact one of the non-English languages most frequently heard on the London stage. At least eighteen extant plays and masques by Dekker, Middleton, Jonson, Shirley, and others include passages in Welsh.[6] Whilst in many cases the Welsh element is limited to a few words – *taw son* (be quiet) and *digon* (enough) were clearly amongst the phrases most familiar to London audiences – some works contain much more extended dialogue in Welsh. Most notable amongst these is *Patient Grissil*, by Thomas Dekker, Henry Chettle, and William Haughton, performed in 1599, in which the irascible Sir Owen and his equally feisty love Gwenthyan woo and quarrel in Welsh to the amusement of their Italian companions.

> SIR OWEN: *Belly the ruddo whee: wrage witho, Manda gen y Mon du ac whelloch en wea awh.*
> GWENTHYAN: *Sir Owen gramarcye whee: Gwenthyan Manda gen y, ac welloch en Thlawen en ryn mogh.*
> FARNEZE: *Mandage Thlawen,* oh my good widdow gabble that we may understand you, and have at you.
> SIR OWEN: Have at her: nay by Cod is no have at her to, Is tawge in her prittish tongue, for is fine delicates tongue, I can tell her Welsh tongue is finer as greeke tongue.
> FARNEZE: A bakte Neates tongue is finer than both.[7]

Although the play's Welsh is wildly and absurdly misspelled ("*Belly the ruddo whee*" for *Ble 'roeddech chwi* [Where were you?]), this is nonetheless unmistakably an attempt to write intelligible Welsh dialogue along phonetic lines. Whether the lines are Dekker's own composition (he shows an interest in Welsh in other plays, but not on the same scale), or were cooked up with the help of Welsh-speaking actors, is unknown. What is clear is that Dekker and the players thought it not unfeasible to include extended sections of Welsh conversation in the play. Although these passages might be fully intelligible only to a small proportion of the London audience, they were also calculated to flatter and amuse the larger body of English speakers. Even if some of the more grotesque errors in the play's Welsh can be laid at the door of the scribe or compositor, there is clearly an intention to make comic hay of the language, for instance by making Welsh words sound like English terms for body parts (*belly*, for instance).[8] This is comparable to the fun that Shakespeare has with the Francophone Katherine's speech in *Henry V*, which keeps lapsing into obscenity as she misinterprets the English names for body parts. Yet Shakespeare was clearly not inclined to have similar fun with (or at the expense of) Lady Mortimer.

Patient Grissil was performed by an acting company which included a minority of Welsh speakers and a majority with no knowledge of the language; the audiences before whom it was first played would have been of a similar linguistic complexion. Admittedly, it is difficult to achieve a reliable estimate as to the numbers of native Welsh speakers in early modern London. As the Welsh were not legally foreigners, they were not subjected to the same degree of monitoring by civic and parish authorities as were the French or the Dutch. Yet there is clear evidence that Welsh speakers were to be found both amongst the professions – most notably the law – and in most of the trades. In the perhaps overly sanguine view of Geraint Dyfnallt Owen, "in the febrile world of commerce and trade, there was hardly one sphere of activity into which Welshmen did not penetrate. The various guilds of merchant tailors, drapers, glovers, coopers, dyers, haberdashers and others, contained a strong Welsh element."[9] This "Welsh element" was, almost by definition, Welsh-speaking. (The penetration of English into the heartlands of Wales was at a very early stage, and the Welsh word for language, *iaith*, was also a familiar term for "the people.") Although few of the city's English speakers made an effort to learn Welsh, most would have been acquainted with its sound, and would have known someone to approach should they require translation into or out of the language. The comparison sometimes made between Welsh, as the native language of Britain, and Native American languages in the United States is thus very wide of the mark.[10]

There is, then, nothing very surprising about the presence of the Welsh language in *Henry IV, Part 1*. What sets Shakespeare apart from his literary contemporaries is only his failure to script it. Did Shakespeare simply care less about the sound and sense of Welsh than did Dekker or Middleton? Or does his reticence indicate a greater measure of respect for a language which, where it features on the English stage, is usually the subject of derisive laughter?[11] Whatever the case, Act 3, scene 1 of *Henry IV, Part 1* as Shakespeare conceived it requires fairly extensive passages of Welsh dialogue; if he wished to stage anything more than a comic medley of *digon*s and *taw-son*s, the playwright would have had to rely on the assistance of one or more native speakers. The most probable assumption is that the Welsh speakers who scripted the dialogue between Glendower and Lady Mortimer were the actors who played these roles. A number of members of the Chamberlain's Men, including Augustine Philips and Robert Gough, have names that might well suggest a Welsh origin, whilst the presence of at least one boy actor capable of speaking Welsh in London in the late 1590s is attested to by Dekker's *Patient Grissil.*[12] These Welsh-speaking actors might have improvised their Welsh parts afresh for each performance. However, there is good reason to suppose that the Welsh lines were scripted and included in the company's book of the play. The actor playing the English-speaking Mortimer would have had to take extra care to learn his cues, three of which are in Welsh; the inclusion of the Welsh lines in the promptbook would also have permitted later actors to attempt the parts of Glendower and his daughter, whether or not they spoke Welsh. The Welsh of the promptbook would thus most probably have been a phonetic transcription, resembling in that respect the Welsh of *Patient Grissil,* though presumably without the same intentionally comic effect.

Although the inclusion of Welsh lines in the promptbook belonging to the Chamberlain's Men seems probable enough, we will never know whether they were recorded there or what they were. The first quarto of *Henry IV, Part 1*, from which all later quartos and the Folio text ultimately derive, includes few stage directions and does not appear to be based on the promptbook. It seems, rather, to have derived from Shakespeare's own manuscript, or from a scribal copy of that manuscript.[13] Although we are thus prevented from knowing what lines of Welsh were spoken on the Elizabethan stage, the likelihood that the quarto derives from a pre-performance text invites us to understand the stage directions of 3.1 in a different light. Arguably, phrases such as "*the Lady again in Welsh*" do not constitute stage directions at all, but are rather Shakespeare's notes to the players that a Welsh speech by Robert Gough or Augustine

Philips must be inserted into the promptbook here. To put the point more strongly, the text of *Henry IV, Part 1* that has come down to us represents the play in an unfinished form, lacking as it does those passages of Welsh dialogue that Shakespeare had entrusted to one or more co-authors.

From the later seventeenth century down to the present, performers of the play have necessarily relied on printed texts, rather than on the long-lost promptbook of the Chamberlain's Men. As a result, they have had access to only part of the play: the part by William Shakespeare or, in other words, the English bit. There is nothing to suggest that performers in the eighteenth and nineteenth centuries regarded this as any great loss. From the Restoration to the late Victorian era, an English-only version of *Henry IV, Part 1* held the stage, with the part of Lady Mortimer or indeed the whole of Act 3, scene 1 being omitted from performance. As John Heraud remarked ruefully in 1865, "For the convenience of theatrical arrangements, the great Glendower scene is generally omitted in acting."[14] Although the change of setting and the introduction of several new characters and costumes might be counted amongst the scene's technical inconveniences, chief amongst them is the requirement that two actors speak in Welsh. Samuel Phelps' 1864 Drury Lane production of the play was hailed for its inclusion of the neglected scene, though it is not clear what arrangements if any were made for the enunciation of Welsh.[15]

Ironically, though not altogether surprisingly, the first twentieth-century production of the play known to have included Welsh dialogue was mounted not in England, nor indeed in Wales, but in Germany. For his 1912 production of *Henry IV, Part 1* at the Deutsches Theater in Berlin, Max Reinhardt commissioned a passage of Welsh dialogue written specifically for the scene. The process whereby this Welsh text was obtained and preserved would ultimately involve the participation of several of the leading European Shakespearean scholars and Celticists of the day. Reinhardt initially approached the great German Shakespeare scholar Alois Brandl, who discussed the matter with his English colleague, C.H. Herford. Herford led Reinhardt and Brandl to Edward Anwyl, Professor of Welsh at the University of Wales, Aberystwyth, who was able to supply a suitable Welsh text. (Anwyl may well have been the author as well as the purveyor of the passage, though he does not seem to have sought any credit.) About a decade after the Reinhardt production, the linguist Max Forster of Leipzig University set about correcting and restoring Anwyl's Welsh text, which survived only in a version badly mangled by a German typist. Forster, himself a student of Celtic languages, was aided in this enterprise by two native Welsh speakers, Thomas Jones of Nefyn, then a theology student at Leipzig, and Bodfan Anwyl, brother of the late Edward Anwyl. The resulting passage of Welsh dialogue, printed by Forster in his 1924 article "Die kymrischen Einlagen bei Shakespeare," is both fairly lengthy and surprisingly lurid; Lady Mortimer's lines, in which she insists on her willingness to face death and pleads for her husband's strong embrace and his kisses sweeter than honey, would require a good deal of stage time even without her song. Forster himself acknowledges that the passages of dialogue printed in his article are probably too long for performance.[16] (The acknowledgment is suggestive of the impatience that English-speaking audiences in particular are likely to experience at this point in the play, a point to which I will return later in this essay.)

Although the Reinhardt/Anwyl/Forster passage may have been too long in its original form, it has proven enduringly influential in providing the basis for the Welsh text favoured for the last half-century by the Royal Shakespeare Company. This text, first recorded in a promptbook of 1964, has been regularly recycled in RSC performances.[17] It was also used by Megan Lloyd in a United States college production of the play in 2000, as described in her book *Speak It in Welsh: Wales and the Welsh Language in Shakespeare*.[18] Whilst clearly influenced by Forster's text, the RSC version is shorter and more restrained in its language and imagery, and is set out on the page as verse rather than prose. Relatively brief as it is, the Welsh text is sometimes cut further, as it was in the version of the play screened as part of the BBC series *The Hollow Crown* (2012).

Even the briefest version of the Welsh lines necessary for a performance of 3.1 is too long to quote in full in this context. Therefore, as a way of indicating the range of linguistic, stylistic, and dramatic options open to those who undertake the task of devising Welsh dialogue for the play, I will quote here only the initial exchange between Glendower and his daughter (the passage that generally marks the first eruption of Welsh into the auditory world of the play), in three different twentieth-century versions (Forster's text, the RSC version, and a shorter version used by Roger Gross in a University of Arkansas production in the early 1990s). The translations that follow each version are my own.

Version A (Berlin, 1912 / Leipzig, 1924):
MORTIMER: Good father, tell her that she and my dunt [sic] Percy / Shall follow in your conduct speedily.
GLENDOWER: Bydd resymol a dewr; nid oes dim arall yn bosibl i ni: rhaid i'r milwyr fyned ymlaen, a bydd i ti a'th fodryb Percy ganlyn gyda myfi; a chei weled Mortimer drachefn.
LADY MORTIMER: Mae fy nghalon yn torri; nis gallaf ei ollwng oddiwrthyf. I'r rhyfel yr â, a pwy all ddweyd y caf ei weled eto. Fy nhad, gadewch i mi fyned gydag ef: nid oes arnaf ofn na dychryn.
GLENDOWER: Na, amhosibl. Rhaid yw iti aros yma.
LADY MORTIMER: (*firmly and defiantly*) Na wnaf. Mi af gydag ef; nid oes dim a'm rhwystra; mi ruthraf trwy farwolaeth ei hun i'w ganlyn.
GLENDOWER: She is desperate here; a peevish self will'd karlotry [sic], one that no persuasion can do good upon.[19]

[GLENDOWER: Be reasonable and brave; nothing else is possible for us: the soldiers must go on ahead, and you and your aunt Percy will follow with me, and you will see Mortimer again.
LADY MORTIMER: My heart is broken; I can not let him depart from me. He goes to war, and who can tell whether I shall see him again. My father, let me go with him. I have neither fear nor dread.
GLENDOWER: No, impossible. You must stay here.
LADY MORTIMER: I will not. I will go with him; nothing can hinder me, though I rush through death itself to follow him.]

Version B (Stratford-upon-Avon, 1964):
MORTIMER: Good father, tell her that she and my aunt Percy
Shall follow in your conduct speedily.
GLENDOWER: Bydd ddewr, fy merch.
Rhaid i filwr ateb ei alwad.
Cei ddilyn yn fy ngofal i gyda'th Fodryb
Persi, ac fe weli dy Fortimer annwyl yn fuan eto.

LADY MORTIMER: Ond pwy wyr na welaf mohono byth.
O, fy nhad, gadewch i mi fynd gydag ef.
Nid oes arnag ofn yn wir.
GLENDOWER: Na, nid lle i wragedd yw rhyfeloedd, fy ngeneth i.
Rhaid i ti aros a chanlyn gyda mi.
LADY MORTIMER: Nis gallaf aroshebddo.
Mae'n rhaid i mi gael mynd, a chaiff neb fy ngwahardd chwaith.
GLENDOWER: She is desperate here; a peevish self-will'd harlotry…[20]

[GLENDOWER: Be brave, my daughter.
A soldier must answer the call.
You have to follow in my care with your aunt
Percy, and you will see your dear Mortimer again soon.
LADY MORTIMER: But who knows whether I will ever see him.
O, my father, let me accompany him.
GLENDOWER: No, wars are no place for women, my little girl.
You must wait and follow with me.
LADY MORTIMER: I cannot remain without him.
I must go, nor can anyone prevent me.]

Version C (Arkansas, 1994):
MORTIMER: Good father; tell her that she and my aunt Percy
Shall follow in your conduct speedily.
GLENDOWER: Na wyla, fy mhlant i. Ddof gyda thi, pan ddychwela'r
Boneddiges Perci.
LADY MORTIMER: Ni arhosaf i, ar-ol fynediad f'annwylaf Arglwydd.
GLENDOWER: She's desp'rate here, a peevish self-will'd harlotry,
One that no persuasion can do good upon.[21]

[GLENDOWER: Weep not, my children [sic]. I will go with you, when Lady Percy goes back.
LADY MORTIMER: I will not stay, after the going of my dear Lord [sic].]

There are significant differences between these passages in terms of both style and content. Though most of the stylistic differences may not be easily detected by English readers, some of them at least could be audible in performance even to those with no knowledge of Welsh. The version composed for Max Reinhardt's production is in good literary Welsh of the early twentieth century, with only a few small errors which may result from poor transcription. (We should remember the damage wrought by the typist on the 1912 version, and note as well the misspellings of English words in the version printed by Forster: "dunt" for "aunt," and "karlotry" for "harlotry.") Yet, as noted above, there is little attempt to achieve an elevated or "Shakespearean" tone; the characters speak in prose, and Lady Mortimer in particular seems to have been lifted from the pages of a rather racy Edwardian novel. In the RSC version, by contrast, the language and imagery are more restrained, and the lines are set out as verse. Specifically, the author seems to have arranged the lines in a form that an English ear might recognize as blank verse, which has no close equivalent in traditional Welsh poetry. (There is just a hint of *cynghanedd*, the repetition of consonantal patterns across the caesura characteristic of bardic poetry, in a line like "O, *fy n*ha*d*, *gad*ewch I my *fyndgyd*ag ef.") More than either of its predecessors, Version C seems to be reaching for an elevated literary tone worthy of the Shakespearean context, though this attempt is rather undercut by errors in grammar and vocabulary (including the surprising use of the plural in Glendower's addressing of Lady Mortimer as *fy mhlant*, "my children").

Perhaps with the challenge of matching Shakespeare's style in mind, some productions have chosen to give Glendower and his daughter dialogue cobbled out of pre-existing Welsh poetry, rather than scripting new lines appropriate to the context. Thus, directing the play for the English Shakespeare Company, Michael Bogdanov drew on "bits and pieces of Welsh poetry from the eleventh and twelfth centuries ... constructing a scene in Old Welsh which we then worked back into contemporary Welsh."[22] Appearing as Lady Mortimer in the RSC Histories Cycle (2006–08), the Welsh musician and vocalist Sianed Jones adapted some of her lines from the very contemporary poetry of Mererid Hopwood (winner of the bardic chair in the National Eisteddfod, 2001).[23] Through the adaptation of ancient or modern Welsh poetry, such performances seek to match Shakespeare's English bard for Bard.

Nonetheless, only Welsh dialogue written for the play, as the original passages in the Chamberlain's Men's promptbook must have been, can address and resolve certain fundamental questions about the scene. The most intriguing of these involve Lady Mortimer's relationship with her husband, who cannot understand her words, and with her father, who interprets between them. In Forster's version of the passage, Lady Mortimer in her initial exchange with her father speaks the language of desperation ("I will rush through death"), whilst his speeches to her quickly become impatient and peremptory ("No, impossible"). In this version, Glendower's ensuing English description of her behaviour as "peevish, self-willed harlotry" becomes dramatically intelligible. Lady Mortimer's heightened erotic language in her subsequent address to her husband allows the Welsh auditor to recognize that, in translating her words for the benefit of his son-in-law, Glendower is doing his best to tone down their overt passion and sensuality. In the RSC version, Glendower is more patient with his daughter, though also more condescending; in this version, his description of her behaviour as "harlotry" might involve a half-embarrassed shrug acknowledging his failure to control her. RSC Glendower's translation of his daughter's invitation to Mortimer to lie upon the rushes is problematic, however, as he appears responsible for introducing "wanton" (3.1.209) imagery into what is in fact a fairly modest speech on her part. There is no doubt that shorter versions of the dialogue create significant problems for Glendower as a character. This point applies to Version C in particular, where he is required to lose all patience with his daughter's peevishness after little or no provocation, and to dwell perversely on the erotic pleasures offered by Lady Mortimer to her husband when she has barely hinted at them. In dramatic terms, then, the long Version A is most successful in resolving the question of why Glendower responds to his daughter's Welsh speeches as he does, and in giving Lady Mortimer a dramatically intelligible, if somewhat overdrawn, personality.

So far, this discussion has largely ignored the elephant – or rather, the Anglophone – in the room. As dramatically logical as Forster's version may be, how much incomprehensible Welsh dialogue is an English-speaking audience likely to absorb without shuffling and resentment? Having employed the comparatively short Version C in a University of Arkansas production, Roger Gross affirmed, "it is worth the trouble to learn to speak these lines. They make the scene pure magic."[24] There are various anecdotal reports of successful stagings involving the Welsh-language passages and song.[25] Yet such responses are not universal by any means. An enthusiastic academic review of a 2006 production of *Henry IV, Part 1* at the Stratford Festival of Canada acknowledged, "The only time I felt time hang heavy in the production was in Laura Condlln's singing in Welsh near the end of 3.1. Her voice was good, but the song and Welsh dialogue seemed to go on too long."[26] The perception of dramatic "inconveniences" that dogged the scene in times past has not evaporated in the twenty-first century. A dramatic passage which, in Bogdanov's estimation, "really says everything that needs to be said about racial, cultural, linguistic tolerance" is still capable of provoking intolerant responses from those who wonder whether it needs to be said at all.[27]

What is at stake in such responses? That audiences might on the whole prefer to listen to dialogue in a language they comprehend is surely understandable. Yet the notion that absolute comprehension is the prerequisite for enjoyment of a Shakespearean performance is open to question. In almost any audience, many of those present will experience passages at least as long as the Welsh dialogue in *Henry IV, Part 1* as a kind of English music, appreciating the sonority without necessarily grasping the precise linguistic sense. The difficulty posed by the Welsh passages in performance has, I would argue, less to do with the fact that many of us do not understand them, and more with the challenge they pose to the notion that Shakespeare's works are the natural birthright and property of English speakers. Even where we do not understand it, Shakespeare's English is telling us something about ourselves, and about the role of English in the world. The Welsh of Act 3, scene 1 is telling us something different. Terence Hawkes has commented that Welsh in the play functions as "the sign of a foreign force that resists incorporation ... an obstacle to the cultural and ideological project of constructing a unified entity called 'England' or 'Great Britain.'"[28] The unsettlement of the Elizabethan audience member is arguably so much the greater today, when Shakespeare is the standard-bearer for a language that proposes to conquer not only the British Isles but the world.

If *Henry IV, Part 1* is an English play, and Shakespeare its sole author, then the Welsh passages heard in performance are, at best, a patch, covering over an awkward and potentially scandalous gap in its textual fabric. Where Welsh is conceived of as a patch or plaster, bridging the space between genuine Shakespearean moments, it will perhaps always merit the damning review of Polonius: "This is too long" (*Hamlet* 2.2.478). But what if we were to alter our understanding of *Henry IV, Part 1* so as to recognize it as a multilingual, co-authored work, of which only the English portion has survived?

In that case, the composition and performance of Welsh dialogue ceases to be a business of embarrassed cobbling across a gap, and becomes instead a matter of the restoration and completion of a damaged, partial text. When the play is understood from this point of view, dramatic logic becomes the only factor determining the length of the Welsh speeches and song, and the question of who the play is "for" essentially evaporates. As multilingual productions become increasingly common and acceptable, we may yet see an authentic production of this long truncated play: *Henri IV, Rhan 1* (Cymraeg gan E. Anwyl, gyda Saesneg gan W. Shakespeare).

Where Did the Devil Go? Religious Polemic in the Dutch Reformation, 1580–1630

GARY K. WAITE

A significant element in the early modern construction of national (or proto-national) identities was the sixteenth-century Reformation, which broke the myth of Europe as "Christendom" united under Christ's earthly agent, the pope. The process of confessionalization that the Reformation subsequently inspired saw princes in the second half of the century align their people's religious identity with these emerging national identities. Each realm therefore adopted one of the new formal confessions of faith, whether Lutheran, Reformed (Calvinist), or Catholic. No prince adopted a Mennonite doctrinal statement, although these too were produced.[1] In 1555 the Peace of Augsburg established the principle that the faith of a prince was the religion of his people, hence political boundaries were also religious ones, and religious zeal and passions inflamed political conflicts. The resulting wars of religion were particularly vicious thanks to this blend of confessional identity and growing national sentiment.[2] Throughout, the demonizing and dehumanizing of the opponent – usually depicted as the religious other – was a critical tactic in defining one political-religious group against the other. Shakespeare's drama was composed during this era of religious and political turmoil, one which most people believed was a result of the devil's raging, in both the religious divisions of the day and in the notorious witch hunts. One therefore would expect references to the devil to appear in Shakespeare's drama, and one is not disappointed. Yet, across the Channel in the Dutch Republic, which was, like England, in a state of war against Catholic Habsburg Spain, there seems to have been a distinctly different approach to utilizing the devil in religious debates. This chapter seeks to examine and explain this provocative distinction within the broader context of religious and national identity formation.

Central rulers also sought to purify their realms of internal religious dissent. Persecution was heaviest in the Habsburg-controlled Low Countries and Holy Roman Empire, although France, the Swiss Cantons, and England sought to keep pace. Identifying heterodox religion as a form of sedition helped a great deal. Those suffering the most in this early campaign were the Anabaptists, who, unlike Martin Luther or John Calvin, had no prince or magistrate to defend them, and they accounted for some two-thirds of all known judicial executions in Europe.[3] Half of these deaths were in the Low Countries, where Anabaptists were involved in one of the most notorious events of the century: the apocalyptic kingdom of Münster, 1533–35.[4] While most of those Anabaptists who survived its collapse gave up militancy, the myth of Anabaptist sedition and madness lingered for decades.[5]

By the middle of the century, many urban magistrates and some princes tried to allow some measure of religious alterity within their boundaries, although for the most part Anabaptists were excluded from any accommodation. Some kings went so far as to allow one alternate faith under a number of restrictions, as in the Holy Roman Empire and France.[6] As they crafted their new national identity, the Dutch took a rather different approach to religious accommodation. While Holland defined its struggle for independence as one against Spanish Catholic hegemony – epitomized in the black legend of the Spanish Inquisition – it did so without enforcing confessional unity among its own citizens. Instead, when they established a national Reformed Church, the States General and Prince William of Orange in 1579 adopted "freedom of conscience" as a founding principle of their Republic and, most remarkably, did not require membership in the state church. In this chapter we will examine this development through the popular press, especially in the use of demonizing language associating others with the devil. It will reveal that, in stark contrast to neighbouring realms such as England or the Spanish Netherlands, Dutch writers generally avoided such rhetoric, even in their heated arguments over theology and confessional identity. Instead, the few appearances of the devil in Dutch pamphlets were mostly set in foreign lands. It is as if the Dutch Republic had expelled Satan from its own boundaries. This de-demonizing, as it were, is revealed also in the Republic's approach to witch trials. We will first review the role of demonizing language in the Reformation before examining in closer detail its use, or more appropriately, its absence, in Dutch popular literature during the confessional age.

Language is a powerful tool that can inspire heights of fame or folly. In Reformation Europe, it was the means to motivate people to support or oppose religious and social reform, and was complicit in great acts of cruelty and destruction, as preachers on all sides – Catholic, Protestant, and the radical sects – railed against their opponents, whom they castigated as agents of the devil. Such rhetoric was evident not only in sermons and treatises, but in literary and dramatic genres ranging from the seriously didactic to the comedic.[7] The German Reformer Martin Luther was an expert at manipulating opinion through the oral sermon and the printed tract, although not all of the results were intended: in 1524–25, emboldened by Luther's slogans of the "freedom of the Christian" and "godly law," tens of thousands of commoners rose up against their lords in the German Peasants' War.[8] In his effort to disavow responsibility, Luther used intemperate language, especially in his May 1525 pamphlet "Against the Robbing and Murdering Hordes of Peasants," which encouraged lords to slay the rebels like dogs.[9] Losing much of his popular support, Luther found a firm ally in the princely authorities. These increasingly utilized the new Protestant identity to strengthen their grip on their territories against the centralizing efforts of the ultra-Catholic Holy Roman Emperor, Charles V.[10] Other rulers, such as Henry VIII of England and Francis I of France, sought similarly to unite their nations under a single faith and suppress alternatives, whether that effort accepted some measure of religious reform (Henry VIII) or rejected it entirely (Charles V). In all regions of Europe, the stakes were high.

Heightening this already tense situation was the propensity of Reformers and their opponents to characterize this struggle as an apocalyptic one, believing that all sides were engaged in a cosmic struggle pitting the allies of Christ against the minions of the devil in the Last Days.[11] For Lutherans and the Reformed, the pope was the Antichrist, while Catholics associated the Reformers with Satan's efforts to destroy Christendom. All polemicists especially demonized the radical Anabaptists as the devil's spawn, although Catholics and

Lutherans used more demonizing rhetoric against this small, persecuted minority than the Reformed.[12] By the middle of the century, fear of the devil and anxiety over divine wrath were widespread. In Lutheran Germany, printers produced dozens of devil books linking each vice to its particular demon.[13] At the same time and place, angry denunciations over the removal of the exorcism rite from baptism led to a sudden rise in demonic possession cases.[14] Across the Holy Roman Empire, both Catholic and Protestant rulers became deeply anxious over a demonic witch conspiracy, leading to the execution of thousands of accused witches.[15] The devil was, it seemed, everywhere, and stronger than ever.[16]

In this context, one expects to read demonizing rhetoric in polemical treatises, and its absence necessarily requires comment. The Dutch produced no known demonologists supporting the witch hunts, only writers who opposed them; very few pamphlets on witchcraft; and very little use of demonizing rhetoric against the religious other.[17] As Hans de Waardt has noted, after 1594 in Holland, "it was virtually impossible to torture a person indicted for witchcraft," a remarkably early date for this development among a nation's judicial elite and intelligentsia. The last execution for the crime was in 1608, and the last formal trial led to an acquittal in 1614.[18] How then do we explain the devil's absence in Dutch polemics and courts?

The devil had, however, been a major participant in Dutch polemics in the first half of the sixteenth century. As the Habsburg and local authorities sought to suppress the Reformation, whether Lutheran, Anabaptist, or Calvinist, they accused these groups of being in league with the devil. The language of demonizing directed against Anabaptists and by Anabaptists against their persecutors is strong and clear.[19] In his anti-Anabaptist mandates, Charles V explicitly linked Anabaptists to the devil and insurrection, finding support in Catholic polemicists who found medieval precedents for the new Anabaptist heresy in the Waldensians and in the Luciferans who allegedly worshipped the devil himself.[20] By 1540 hundreds of Anabaptists had been executed by the region's secular courts, and while many urban magistrates argued that the heresy mandates interfered in their jurisdiction, at times they were more than willing participants.[21] With the start of the war against Spain around 1568, the region's notables made these heresy mandates a *cause célèbre* justifying taking up arms against their hereditary ruler. In the process, the rebel leaders, William of Orange, and the notables who would form the States General crafted an unusual approach to national religious identity that was essentially Spiritualistic.

Spiritualism was an approach to religious reform and identity that was fashioned out of two major streams: the late medieval mystical and devotional movements of the Rhineland, and the practical need to survive the persecution with "true beliefs" intact.[22] Spiritualists depreciated doctrinal confessions and external rites in favour of an inner religiosity. Advocates could put on a public face of orthodoxy while keeping their real heterodoxy secret, a practice called Nicodemism after Jesus's secret disciple, or Libertinism by opponents such as John Calvin, who preferred his followers to either stand up publicly for the faith or move to a Protestant realm.[23] Holland's most prominent Spiritualist perfectly illustrates these dual developments: a heavily persecuted Anabaptist leader with mystical tendencies, by 1540 David Joris was a Spiritualist who explicitly denigrated external religiosity, doctrinal confessions, and ritual in favour of a religion of the conscience.[24] Other Dutch Spiritualists, such as Hendrik Niclaes, who knew Joris and founded the Family of Love, became prominent across the Low Countries, and similarly included members of the elite, such as the prominent Antwerp printer Christophe Plantin (c.1520–89). The Familists were also present in England, including some members of Queen Elizabeth I's household.[25]

Many Netherlanders desired this persecution's end, if only for the sake of good business. Such appeals were made by the magistrates of Antwerp, for example, in response to Charles V's insistence that Judaisers among the Portuguese Nation merchants be prosecuted. They argued instead that these should be left alone not only for economic reasons, but also because no one could know the inner heart. Prince William of Orange similarly argued that the Netherlands' economic prosperity required religious tolerance and the ability to welcome merchants of different faiths.[26] In the Chambers of Rhetoric (*rederijkerskamers*), urban merchants, shopkeepers, and artisans composed and performed many plays evidencing a strong desire for religious accommodation and peace intended to encourage civic harmony and good business.[27] These amateur literary societies were, as Arjan van Dixhoorn has put it, creators of knowledge within their urban communes, a function that went well beyond the crafting of entertainment and contributed to the scientific, political, and religious discourses of their day.[28] In their religious drama the devil played only a small role as playwrights (factors) increasingly turned to the allegorical Vices to portray evil tendencies, an approach that encouraged audiences to think less in terms of a corporeal devil and more in terms of human agency and responsibility.[29]

While the Chambers of Rhetoric had been most prominent in the Southern Netherlands before the start of the Revolt, censorship there soon became the norm, in sharp contrast to the northern provinces. For example, one of Joris's more interesting innovations was his notion that the devil did not exist apart from the individual's inner evil nature, a posture not dissimilar to the *rederijkers*' Vices portraying inner evil inclinations of humans as external characters.[30] Joris's father had been an actor with the Chambers of Rhetoric, and as an artist Joris himself would have an affinity for the Chambers, which in many cities were affiliated with artists' guilds.[31] By 1600 the focus on battling the devil within each person had become a popular theme in Dutch publications.[32]

As Stuart B. Schwartz notes, quasi-Spiritualistic attitudes, encapsulated in the popular phrase "each person can be saved in his or her own law," were common even in arch-Catholic Spain.[33] Hence, the desire to tolerate those of alternate faiths was widespread, but could be fulfilled only with governmental support, which the Dutch Republic provided. Not all Dutch religious leaders were enamoured of the idea, and many Calvinist preachers fought vigorously against Catholicism and the Spiritualists, decrying toleration as an inherent subversion of a coherent national identity. Most residents who were in favour of religious reform, however, wanted one that would be more broadly inclusive than what the hard-line Calvinists sought.[34] Despite these efforts to shape the Republic's religious identity, its Regents refused to enforce religious conformity and offered instead its *schuilkerken* criterion, wherein non-Reformed sects worshipped in the fiction of the private space of a "hidden church," a policy that was applied to Catholics, to Mennonites, and, after 1600, to Jews.[35] Until about the middle of the seventeenth century, in fact, a sizeable proportion of the population did not openly belong to any denomination.[36] Many of the political and merchant elites clearly appreciated the tendency of Spiritualism to blur confessional distinctions to ease trade and political alliances with religious others. Joined with such merchant pragmatism and a principled defence of freedom of conscience, Spiritualism became mainstream. This is evident in the popularity of the second-generation Spiritualist Dirck Volkhertsz Coornhert, who briefly served as secretary to William of Orange.[37] As De Waardt has revealed, some of the jurists and professors who in 1593 and 1594 declared against the application of both torture and the water test in witchcraft cases were associated with the Family of Love, while the Dutch physician Johan Wier, author of the anti–witch-hunt *De Praestigiis Daemonum* of 1563, was also a Spiritualist who corresponded with Joris.[38] What distinguished the Dutch expression of tolerance from many other variants across Europe was the fact that the former was supported by the elites, reaching up to Prince William of Orange, whose courtier Emmery de Lyere publicly championed Spiritualism against the invective of its Calvinist enemies.[39]

The ease with which the Dutch abandoned diabolical conspiracies should therefore not surprise us. A quick scan of titles of the Knuttel collection of Dutch pamphlets reveals a pronounced absence of works directly relating to the devil or witchcraft, especially compared to the popularity of the subjects in England and Germany.[40] Almost all demonizing rhetoric was applied to the hated Spanish Inquisition.[41] Even efforts to outlaw dissident religious groups such as the Mennonites did not require the devil's assistance; when the government of Groningen issued a placard on 7 September 1601 forbidding any practice of religion aside from the Reformed, it used no demonizing language. Its tone was moderate compared to the anti-Anabaptist placards of the previous Habsburg government.[42] This proclamation moreover elicited a strong negative response by pamphleteers fighting for freedom of conscience.[43] Similarly, when Amsterdam's magistrates became aware in 1603 that members of the Portuguese Nation – Iberian Conversos – had reverted to Judaism, the most vociferous complainer was the Calvinist Abraham van Coster (Costerus), who in his *History of the Jews* (*Historie der Joden*) of 1608 calls the Jews impure blasphemers of God. He does not, however, follow the well-trodden path of associating them with the devil, nor does he even recommend expulsion.[44]

Soon anxieties over Judaism were swallowed up in 1609 with the publicity over the signing of the twelve-year Peace of Antwerp. When on 9 April King Philip III of Spain ordered the signing of this truce with Dutch heretics, he hoped to burnish his reputation as "defender of the faith" by commanding on the same day the expulsion of the Moriscos – Muslim converts to Christianity – from

Valencia.[45] Philip III's tactic worked, as Dutch publications celebrating or condemning the peace swamped the few publications on the expulsion.[46] That said, the Dutch showed some sympathy for the plight of the expelled Moriscos, in 1609 providing refuge for a number of them, and discussing with them issues theological and diplomatic. Several writers also expressed empathy for Conversos and Jews, who as it turned out proved helpful allies in this Christian-Muslim interaction.[47]

1609 was indeed a watershed in many ways, and many writers were aware of the potential dangers involved in peace with a country whose ruler was generally perceived as a tyrant. This is illustrated especially in a treatise by a conservative Mennonite elder, Pieter Jans Twisck, *Religion's Freedom: A Short Chronicle Describing the Freedom of Religion against the Forcing of Consciences*.[48] If anyone had the right to demonize Catholic and Protestant oppressors both, it was a Mennonite whose coreligionists were still suffering from harassment and oppression elsewhere. In *Religion's Freedom*, Twisck argues strongly that the secular authority has no right to interfere whatsoever in matters of faith, and he cites a number of predecessors and contemporaries to support this.[49] His praise of the posture of William of Orange and the Dutch Regents on freedom of conscience is fulsome, and he extends this right to Catholics as well as sectarians.[50] While condemning the efforts of the popes to "bewitch" the secular magistrates to enforce their decrees, he notes many examples in Catholic realms of resistance against this papist magic, and he does not tar all Catholics with the same brush.[51] He also includes incidents of tolerance toward Jews, Muslims, Conversos, and Moriscos in a positive light.[52] He concludes this work with a plea for members of all religious groups – Muslims, Catholics, Orthodox, Lutherans, Calvinists, and Mennonites – to get along in a friendly manner, and when seeking to convince the other of their errors in religion, to do so without slander or pressure.[53] There is no place whatsoever for demonizing language in Twisck's writings.

Despite such examples of interreligious engagement, the pause in the war with Spain seems to have encouraged some leaders of the Dutch Reformed Church to turn on each other, as the simmering theological differences within the national church boiled over into open conflict between the moderate Reformed who followed the theology of the recently deceased Jacobus Arminius (1560–1609) and those Calvinists who sided with Franciscus Gomarus (1563–1641), who promoted a doctrine of complete predestination that excluded any human role in salvation. In 1610 the Arminians presented to the Regents a five-article remonstrance that set out how they differed from their hard-line brethren; they therefore became known as Remonstrants, and their Gomarist opponents as Counter-Remonstrants, after their own document. These theological disputes became interwoven with the politics of the day, especially on the question of whether or not to continue the war against Spain. Charges of treason followed, and some of the prominent Remonstrant leaders who advocated peace were arrested. While Holland's Regents were decidedly in favour of the Remonstrant position on religious toleration, Stadholder Maurice of Orange (r.1585–1625) soon sided with the Counter-Remonstrants as the best means to restore religious harmony. After the execution for treason of the liberal statesman Johan van Oldenbarnevelt in 1619, Remonstrants were officially outlawed and, like Catholics and Mennonites, had to hide their worship in *schuilkerken* until 1630. Even as Counter-Remonstrants resisted the efforts of these groups to regain public status for themselves, they did not resort to demonizing their opponents; this was in stark contrast to their coreligionists elsewhere, such as English Puritans, Scots Presbyterians, or Swiss Reformed, all of whom engaged in the practice of vilifying their Catholic and radical Protestant opponents by associating them with the devil.[54] Occasionally a catastrophic event, such as the assassination of the Protestant-friendly Henri IV of France by a Catholic zealot in 1610, did inspire propaganda linking Jesuits to a treasonous conspiracy inspired by the devil.[55] Even so, none of these publications depict the Jesuits as a diabolical sect in the way polemicists had portrayed the Anabaptists in the previous century; nor did the States General make membership in this religious order a capital offence, as had Elizabeth I in 1582, nor did it follow her parliament in making refusal to attend the state church punishable by execution, as England's Conventicle Act of 1593 did.[56]

While I cannot claim to have perused more than a handful of the hundreds of the publications in the Remonstrant versus Counter-Remonstrant battles, the lack of demonizing language in the titles of any of them is indicative. Most of the dozens of such works on predestination from the second decade of the seventeenth century are dense theological treatises filled with nuanced interpretations of scriptural citations.[57] At this stage in the debate, the harshest term used against the opponent was "innovation"; Remonstrants too had to ensure that their advocacy of some measure of free will in salvation was not confused with the "spirit of error," the Anabaptists. Even when counteracting the Mennonite errors, however, most Reformed writers avoided the easy path of demonizing them, but applied their reasoned analysis of scriptural passages to convince and persuade.[58]

Many Calvinist preachers felt themselves under attack from multiple sides and rejected their Regents' approach to toleration. Gaspar Grevinchoven (d.1606), Reformed pastor at Rotterdam, for example, was engaged in polemics against both "new Lutherans" and Antwerp's Jesuits.[59] His dyspeptic treatise complains about "the freedom of sects" and the harm this causes the true "church of God."[60] Heresy, it claims, is a cancer that spreads superstition, idolatry, hypocrisy, and sedition, as seen with the Münster Anabaptists who proclaimed freedom of religion yet forced all residents of Münster to be rebaptized.[61] A godly government should not tolerate such false prophets, but support the Reformed preachers to oppose them.[62] Despite Grevinchoven's aversion to allowing sects religious freedom, the only figure he suggests was directly inspired by the devil was Muhammad.[63] Instead, when Grevinchoven rebuts the aspersions made against Christ that he was a blasphemer who "had the devil in him,"[64] he implicitly condemns the tactic of demonizing the opponent. He furthermore renounces those who spread evil rumours against others, since such false reports may indeed be inspired by the devil.[65] Grevinchoven thereby explicitly rejects the tactic of demonizing the opponent.

In their rejection of Catholic superstition, exorcism, and religious magic, Dutch Reformed writers moved Satan into the biblical background, or reserved him only for the most extreme cases of Spanish Catholicism and Libertine innovation.[66] One of the very few pamphlets published in the Dutch Republic dealing explicitly with diabolical pacts or sorcery was in fact written by an outsider, the Moroccan Jew Moses Pallache, nephew of Samuel Pallache, Muslim Morocco's agent in Holland. In this work Pallache demonizes an upstart claimant to the Moroccan throne in order to promote the interests of the incumbent and the Pallaches' patron Mulay Zaydan.[67]

The one target of Reformed writers that did tend to bring out language of demonizing and pollution was the Spiritualists, as seen in the anonymous 1614 diatribe *Answer to the Foreword and Afterword placed before and after the printed book of Sebastian Castellio*.[68] The Castellio work referred to was his famous 1554 book against the execution of heretics, *Concerning Heretics: Whether they are to be persecuted*, which itself had been inspired by the execution in Calvin's Geneva of Michael Servetus the year before.[69] Our Reformed author takes enormous offence at the scandalous charges against Calvin by the unknown editor of Castellio – who may have been Coornhert or one of his circle.[70] He therefore describes the Libertine ideas as the dirt and filth of wandering spirits which have as their fountain the "hellish pool of all the venomous vapours of the devil."[71] The anti-trinitarian Socinians – officially outlawed in 1639 – and the Rosicrucians elicited similar responses from the orthodox, as seen in a rhymed pamphlet by an I. Verhaghen which claimed the secretive (hence implicitly foreign) sect or "plague" was both deceived by the devil and had become his instrument to enlarge his hellish kingdom.[72] Such demonizing was made easier by the reputation of Rosicrucians for possessing occult knowledge.

The conclusion of the Twelve Years' Truce in 1621 inspired some pamphleteers to return to apocalyptic language to discourage the Regents from signing another peace treaty with Spain, since if the Spanish crown was allied with the papal Antichrist, a treaty would be an act of treason against God.[73] Even so, the incendiary description of the enemy as bloodthirsty tyrants does not mention the devil.[74] In the 1620s Dutch printers also produced an increasing number of works on the religious and political situations in the Holy Roman Empire, England, and France, condemning especially the persecution of Reformed citizens in both realms, but these are largely translations of works originating outside of the Republic.[75] In 1620 and again in 1622, Dutch Calvinists depicted the Bohemian revolt against Habsburg Austria – which started the Thirty Years' War – in apocalyptic terms as a war between God's oppressed people, the Protestants, and those of the Antichrist, the pope.[76] In a 1622 treatise seeking to uncover when the true church would be delivered from the Antichrist's "yoke of tyranny," an anonymous Calvinist preacher interprets the secrets of the book of Revelation to his own day.[77] Despite the current polemical situation, he includes good Hussites and Lutherans among those in the true church and hopes that the Anabaptists and Libertines would "open your eyes" and return to God's community.[78] Compared to the 1596 treatise on the Apocalypse by the English Puritan George Gifford, our anonymous pastor's musings on the radicals are mild in the extreme, since he does not follow Gifford in aligning such sectarians with the devil and with the papal Antichrist, nor does he apply epithets such as "filthy monsters," the "synagogue of Satan," or "damnable atheists" to them.[79] The growing market for works on affairs external to the Dutch Republic was addressed also by our conservative Mennonite, Pieter Jansz Twisck, who in 1620 published his two-volume *Chronicle of the Decline of Tyranny*, which emphasizes that the devil's work was in forcing the conscience, hence it is institutions such as the Inquisition or governmental heresy mandates that are demonized, rather than the religious others.[80] Throughout this decade, other Dutch writers would follow suit, depicting the devil's agents as external to the Dutch Republic itself and as instigating the repressive religious policies of the Habsburgs.[81]

In their efforts to win the Remonstrants back to the Reformed Church, Dutch Calvinist writers continued to steer away from demonizing language, preferring instead to convince their erring brethren through scriptural interpretation and reason.[82] By the 1620s they had clearly realized that demonizing language had lost its ability to motivate the Dutch populace. This was a remarkably early development, as Calvinist preachers in other parts of Europe were quite happily warning their flocks of the diabolical dangers around them, whether in Catholicism, radical sects, or blatant witchcraft.[83]

In all of the works consulted, the devil was either ignored or essentially expelled to Rome, Bohemia, or Spain; he had become a far less prominent player in the various debates and conflicts within the Dutch Republic itself. Catholic anti-Protestant propaganda continued to apply demonizing rhetoric, such as, for example, a Spanish anti-Protestant work that was translated into Dutch and allegedly printed in Granada in 1632. This pamphlet recounted a couple of "miracle stories" counteracting the iconoclasm of the Protestant heretics and proving the Catholics to be members of the true church. The first story relates a gruesome account of a Calvinist minister of 's-Hertogenbosch whom the author describes as "this preacher of the Devil." While this man was enflaming his congregation of heretic soldiers with "gruesome blasphemies" to destroy a beloved icon of Christ, the "Devil began a very intense pain in the preacher's intestines" so that "they burst before the eyes of all the bystanders" and landed on the floor. This affirmed, the writer insists, not only that the preacher's "damned soul spit out into the Devil's hands," but also his body, for "as most of the people recounted as the truth," the preacher's body suddenly disappeared, with the presumption that he had been taken bodily into Hell.[84] The author's second story involves an entire legion of demons that Protestant soldiers unleashed upon the community in the effort to wrest the city from Catholic control.[85]

While a commonplace of Catholic polemic, such literal evocations of Satan were rare in the extreme in the Dutch Reformed pamphlets that we have surveyed here. Northern Dutch discourse – including Calvinist, Remonstrant, Doopsgezind, and Spiritualist – was remarkably different from that of their neighbours, both Catholic and Protestant. Perhaps most telling is the relative absence of the devil in Northern Netherlandic publications between 1580 and 1630, which was the height of the major witch-hunts and of the publication of demonological treatises elsewhere, such as the Spanish Brabantine Martin del Rio's *Disquisitionum Magicarum Libri Sex* (Louvain, 1599/1600).

The Dutch Republic was, however, no model of religious peace and harmony, as it suffered from its share of intolerance and conflict. Despite the fulminations of some Calvinist preachers reported in unpublished synod minutes and correspondence demanding that the state act to suppress the radicals, public discourse was generally civil, and within the fiction of private space most dissenting sects were allowed to prosper. Judging from the works consulted here, in their public press presentations the Reformed had essentially expelled the devil from the United Provinces, assigning his activity primarily to Catholic Spain or Bohemia.

As noted, such restraint contrasts with the nasty invective spilling from the quills of Calvinists elsewhere, which often enthusiastically associated enemies with the devil.[86] What was specific to the Dutch context? First, the merchant ethic and prosperity of the Dutch society helped, although it must be acknowledged that the English were developing a similarly strong merchant culture.[87] Second was the contribution of Spiritualism, which, while not acceptable to the Counter-Remonstrants, infused the attitudes and polemics of their Remonstrant opponents and of many of the Republic's civic leaders, whose public versus private sphere solution to informal toleration was Spiritualistic, with its outer versus inner religiosity.[88] Third, it is possible that the vehemence that Calvinist writers reserved for "Libertines" was in fact an indication of the attractiveness of

Spiritualistic notions within the Reformed community. Spiritualism's depreciation of the devil helped in the Dutch Republic's ending of witch trials, and would lead ultimately to the logic of the Reformed minister Balthasar Bekker's *De Betooverde Weereld* of 1691, which denied the existence of a real devil.[89] Fourth, by adopting the slogan "freedom of conscience" the Regents had set the tone for their citizens, most of whom regarded other Christians as erring brethren rather than as heretics in league with the devil. As they sought to appeal to a broad audience, Dutch Reformed writers followed in general terms this new paradigm of freedom of conscience, if not of worship, whatever they might have thought in private. Finally, tired of being demonized by Catholics, Reformed pastors seem to have adjusted their language accordingly. In the Dutch Republic, the devil was relegated to a biblical past or exiled to Spain. The contrast with the demonizing of the other in neighbouring regions could not be clearer.

PART TWO

Difference within English

Loving and Cherishing 'True English': Shakespeare's Twinomials[1]

SCOTT NEWSTOK

Therefore, you Clowne, abandon – which is in the vulgar, leave – the society – which in the boorish is company – of this female – which in the common is woman; which together is, abandon the society of this female, or, Clowne, thou perishest; or, to thy better understanding, diest …

Touchstone, *As You Like It* (5.1.43–8)[2]

I want to remember and recall a peculiar lexical feature of Early Modern English which tends to be forgotten and neglected: the curious prevalence of synonymous word pairs, collocated with an 'and.' Following the Norman invasion (and the consequent intermingling of French, English, and Latin in the court, law, and market), 'English' writers frequently deployed synonymous terms emerging from both major roots of the language, what Dr Johnson would later categorize as "*Roman* and the *Teutonick*: under the *Roman* I comprehend the French and provincial tongues; and under the *Teutonick* range the *Saxon, German*, and all their kindred dialects." Others have characterized these roots as *Latinate* and *Germanic*, *classical* and *vernacular*, even *foreign* and *native*. All such categories are necessarily heuristic, and historically porous; linguists are quick to remind us that Church Latin began contributing to the Anglo-Saxon lexicon as early as the fourth century. Yet English remains "the only great European language firmly and extensively based on a system of double derivation," creating what could be seen as an "arbitrary principle unique to the language."[3] As I shall explore, this habit of pairing two near-synonyms from different root systems could be seen as arbitrary or quite significant, depending on the context in which such a pairing, here called a 'twinomial,' occurs. This essay will first assess the pervasive presence of twinomials in English and how they have been understood, both in the early modern period and since. Then, I examine one particularly interesting locus of this trope and its potential importance in Shakespeare's *Henry V*.

The trope I focus on here is both common in and fundamental to English, particularly in ceremonial contexts. Perhaps the most resonant early modern example derives from "The Form of Solemnization of Matrimony" in the 1559 *Book of Common Prayer*. The groom is instructed to give his troth to the woman by promising "to *love* and to *cherish*." (The bride plights a third, submissive vow: "to love, cherish, and *to obey*.") Instances of these kinds of nearly tautologous combinations of words pervade the *Book of Common Prayer*; in fact, the first words of this vow are "[t]o have and to hold." But what I find particularly intriguing about the combination of *love* and *cherish* is that these two words, (nearly) synonymous, derive from what Richard Mulcaster termed the two 'heds' of English: *love* has a Germanic etymology, and *cherish* a Romance etymology. There are dozens of these found throughout the *Book*; in the Matrimonial ceremony alone we discover cadences such as "lusts and appetites," "help and comfort," "perform and keep," "token and pledge," "loving and amiable," and "sanctify and bless."

We remain familiar with these kinds of pairings through their continuing prevalence in legal formulae (to the great irritation of modern-day stylistic reformers of the law). Early modern "wills and testaments" are thick with them (even cross-cast ones, such as being "of perfect mind & good remembrance" [1588]). Among many bilingual synonyms coupled in legal discourse, particularly probate law, we can include:

acknowledge and confess (OE: OF)
act and deed (F/L: OE)
deem and consider (OE: F)
fit and proper (OE: F)
free and clear (OE: OF)
give, devise, and bequeath (OE: OF: OE)
goods and chattels (OE: OF)
had and received (OE: F)

in lieu, in place, instead, and in substitution of (F: F: OE: OF/L)
keep and maintain (OE: F)
made and provided (OE: L)
maintenance and upkeep (F: E)
mind and memory (OE: OF)
new and novel (OE: OF)
pardon and forgive (F: OE)
right, title, and interest (OE: OE: F)
shun and avoid (OE: F)
will and testament (OE: L)[4]

Existing rhetorical and linguistic terms imperfectly describe this lasting phenomenon: *hendiadys* or *pleonasmus* (George Puttenham's "Twinnes" and "Too Full Speech" [1590] – both having to do with different kinds of repetition); 'binomials' (which too broadly refer to *all* word pairs); 'doublets' (words derived from the *same* source at different points in time [e.g. 'regal'/'royal']); 'bisociation' (which is getting close – indicating synonymous terms derived from dual roots, but not necessarily collocated in close *conjunction*).[5] Other phrases have been suggested by linguists: 'mixed pairings,' 'diglossic conjuncts,' 'sister words,' and so forth. In hopes of marking them as a unique phenomenon worthy of further critical attention, I propose a new term for these redundant word pairs: 'twinomials,' appropriately conjoining Germanic (*twi-*) and Latinate (*-nomial*) roots, with the additional felicity of punning on Puttenham's "Twinnes." While they begin appearing soon after the Conquest, and are noticeably present in the work of figures such as Marjorie Kempe and Geoffrey Chaucer (who, for instance, poetically joined the synonyms "mind and memory," now treated as legally non-synonymous), twinomials flourished in the sixteenth century. But did they *mean anything*?

There are many long-standing objections made by early philologists[6] (who argued about this phenomenon from roughly the 1880s to the 1920s) and later linguistic and stylistic studies (which returned to the subject starting in the late 1960s) against isolating what I am nominating as 'twinomials,' most of which are exhaustively (and skeptically) catalogued by Janel Mueller in her examination of Caxton's "word pairs."[7] Overall, they question whether such pairings are *unique* to English (they are not; the practice of doubling goes back at least to the Hebrew Bible,[8] and Old English oaths are replete with emphatically duplicated synonyms[9]); whether they are invariably rooted in *both* Germanic and Romance lines (again, they are not; even the strongest advocate of "Romance-Germanic synonymic pairs," Jürgen Schäfer,[10] acknowledges that while they are significantly "more frequent, [they] by no means eclipse pure Romance or Germanic pairs");[11] and whether they are used *deliberately* by authors for *specific* rather than haphazard effect.[12] These objections certainly mitigate any desire to extrapolate generalizations from bilingually rooted pairs to all such synonymous pairs. Yet Mueller goes too far in denying the utility of identifying twinomials as a valid subset of synonymous collocation. One would not disregard the value of examining a *species* in isolation because its traits do not fully account for all other *species* within its *genus*. The strenuousness of the desire to dismiss the clear prevalence of twinomials (not unique to Mueller) further confirms the need for such a neologism to help distinguish the unique utility that category entails – a utility that can be observed in Tudor practice and even occasionally in theory.

Renaissance writers contemplated such twinomials with an attitude that alternated between nativist chauvinism and uncertain defensiveness. Sir Thomas Elyot justifies the addition of his "strange terms" as a nationalistic project to "*augment* our Englyshe tongue," approved by Henry VIII himself: "His Grace also perceyued that throughout the boke there was no terme new made by me of a latine or frenche worde, but it is there declared so playnly by one mene or other to a diligent reader, that no sentence is therby made dark or harde to understande." Elyot conveys this pedagogical *glossing* through the conjunction *or*, rather than the usual *and*, making clear that he will "*devulgate* or *sette fourth*" words "which be borowed of the latin tonge for the insuficiencie of our owne language."[13] Such verbal importation was by no means unproblematic for Tudor writers yearning for Spenser's "Kingdom of our own language" (1580). Richard Mulcaster, who insistently uses twinomials out of a pedagogical impulse for clarity, uneasily posits a civic analogy between the "enfranchisment" of "manie foreners" (that is, foreign words) to "stranger denisons" who become similarly naturalized and bound "to the lawes of our cuntrie" – the terms and people thereby "become *ours*."[14]

This kind of assimilationist rhetoric was inverted in Ascham's critique of (Hall's) "Indenture English" (1568), with the proposal that his "strange and inkhorne tearmes" be translated, in effect, into

English, and that all "superfluous and idle" passages be "wede"d out. (With appropriate irony, both "strange and inkhorne" and "superfluous and idle" are themselves twinomials; apparently their inevitability demands scrupulous excision.) The cleaned text would leave us "halfe as moch as it was in quantitie, but twise as good as it was both for pleasure and also commoditie" – an arithmetic of halving and doubling that owes much to the old *res et verba* debate. This peculiar mode of bilingual redundancy, which had for the most part been practiced without notice in previous centuries, began to be weighted with new assertions of English nationhood, to the extent that even Chaucer was blamed for the "corruption" of English from its original Saxon "purity."[15]

Thus we find that behind the contentious issue of twinomials lies a deeper bias about what exactly a 'pure English' would mean in the first place: need it reach back beyond the medieval period entirely? The process of Englishing the Bible, for instance, often pivoted on whether or not a word rooted in the Germanic or Romance languages would be used, even if inconsistently – More attacked Tyndale for using "seniors" or "elders" instead of "priests"; "congregation" instead of "church"; "love" instead of "charity." Two extreme points in this debate are caricatured by Bishop Gardiner and John Cheke. Gardiner proposed that translators actually *keep* certain essential terms in Latin – *Christus, Dominus, Spiritus Sanctus, ecclesia, episcopus, caritas, gratia.*[16] Cheke, on the other hand, in a letter appended to Thomas Hoby's 1561 translation of Castiglione's *Courtier*, held that "that our own tung should be written clean and pure, unmixt and unmangeledwith borrowing of other tunges,"[17] leading to his beguiling "Saxon" version of Matthew's Gospel, replacing *lunatic* with *mooned*, *centurion* with *hundreder*, *prophet* with *foresayer*, *crucified* with *crossed*, *resurrection* with *gainrising*, and *founded* with *groundwrought*. In an age when people were executed for their theological stances, the precise implications of lexical choices were desperately important. We might consider the twinomials present throughout the *Book of Common Prayer* as a canny linguistic compromise on Cranmer's part to a contentious doctrinal crux.[18] Early modern debates about "national languages" (and, indeed, today's "English-only" proposals[19]) remain blind to a fundamental hybridity still extant in twinomial pairs.

The tendency to welcome this redundancy is perhaps the most compact example we can find of Erasmian *copia verborum* – the copia of words for similar things or concepts. In fact, it is such "plenty" that Richard Carew cites as proof of "the excellencie of the English tongue"; he is even moved to praise "the long words that we borrow being intermingled with the short of our own store," as "mak[ing] up a perfect harmonie."[20] But the seventeenth century's renewed vigilance about the perceived split between *copia rerum et verborum* did not look very kindly on such copiousness, particularly in the philosophies of language by writers such as Bacon.[21] Their focus on language as communication rather than rhetorical persuasion contributed to an eventual disdain for and decline in the use of twinomials within developing rationalist discourses.[22]

Shakespeare's twinomials could thus be linked to at least two sources of meaning. For one, bilingually rooted synonyms would seem more likely a manifestation of contemporary Tudor debates surrounding the "inkhorn" controversy, and for another, they might be heard as an echo of England's medieval entanglement with France.[23] Concerns regarding overly aureate *Latinity* would appear to have been more pressing on the lexical consciousness than a belated anxiety about the *Francophone* inheritance of the Conquest. It should be stressed that for many of the terms I have associated with Romance etymologies, the precise Romance source is not clearly knowable, even to modern linguists, as the OED's use of the phrase "akin to" attests. Even when these English Romance words were born, they almost certainly emerged from a sense that the Latin and French alternatives were nearly equivalent. But when those words were *heard*, especially onstage, the audible etymologies would have had a natural tendency to gravitate toward particular meanings, just as all words similarly form particular meanings when spoken onstage. The epigraph from Touchstone would better fit this Latinate evaluation, as would comparable passages from Armado or Holofornes; likewise the nonce "incarnadine" and its gloss ("making the green one red") that Shakespeare invents solely for *Macbeth*. In these instances, the syntagm does not conform to the twinomial formula x + y, and the Latinate neologisms convey a self-awareness of dual registers within the language, used sometimes for extravagant *pathos* but often to caricature pedantic bombast.

And what if the Romance words sounded French? Bradin Cormack has argued that *Henry V* presents a kind of "reverse conquest" of France, one that re-enacts yet again an anxiety about English autonomy (his term is "jurisdiction") that was constantly re-negotiated in English culture following the Norman invasion. Concentrating on the paradoxical status of the *Englishness* of English law being defended in the fifteenth and sixteenth centuries in spite of or even indeed *on account of* its *French* language, Cormack details the contortions that produce a kind of "'France-in-England' – an analytical category rooted ... in a continuous cultural development extending from 1066 forward."[24] For centuries afterward, every threat of invasion recursively refigured the scarring and foundational Conquest. We ought to read Renaissance English's relationship to cross-Channel *words* as comparably re-enacting a *verbal* conquest – yet with a crucial difference being that these more recent words were adopted "from within" rather than imposed "from without" – "a sort of delayed revenge for the Norman Conquest."[25] The emergence of Renaissance philological self-awareness in England entailed a series of attempts to come to terms with this foundational historical rupture that inaugurated the medieval period and the language that the Renaissance was to "augment" anew.[26] Linguistic resistance became triumphantly figured in a symbolic attempt to rewrite the historical fact of the invasion, as in "[The Normans] coming therewith [i.e. French] to our countrey, they *could not conquere the English language as they did the land*, howbeit as alredy I haue noted, they much mingled and tempred it with their French."[27]

The conflicting evaluations of twinomials which exercised philologists a century ago are still largely present with us today. Do they emerge out of mere habit or deliberate statement? Are they used for emphasis or out of anxiety? Are they applied for difference or similitude? Do they convey a redundancy or surfeit? These concerns resonate with the familiar analysis of "the dangerous supplement," as is inevitable whenever we add B to A. (This is not at all an unhistorical concern, since such a proto-philologist as William Camden himself described the "Norman" invaders as attempting to "*supplant*" the English language).[28] That is, we are led to question how necessary, equivalent, or superfluous the two terms are to one another.[29] The near-equivalence of the terms asks us to see how they differ; this is, after all, similar to how rhyme works, by making two words comparable by sound, and therefore different in meaning. Some might hear that difference in inkhorn terms, and thus resonant with a class distinction, as Touchstone does, and some might hear in the divergent etymologies echoes of the history of England, a history that caused this doubling in the first place.

Thus, to make a preliminary hypothesis, before the sixteenth century twinomials in English were present but largely unexamined;

during the sixteenth century they became subject to increasing scrutiny in conjunction with an emerging historical consciousness, and an anxious reconsideration of medieval inheritance; and after the sixteenth century they became relegated to ornamental practitioners of 'eloquence' and 'poetry,' evicted from communicative argument. Shakespeare began writing following a century of exchanges about the problematically multilingual English lexicon; is it not plausible that he might have consciously deployed twinomials, particularly in a play fraught with anxiety about the lingering effects of Anglo-French relations? I conclude with a brief glance at *Henry V*, where I want to inflect the long since conventional readings of the language politics of *Henry V* (which invariably concentrate on Katherine's language lesson, Pistol's French prisoner, and the meeting between King Henry and soon-to-be Queen Katherine at the close) with a renewed attention to twinomials. While some, such as Watson and Steinsaltz, distinguish how certain passages tend toward greater Latinity (e.g. Henry's nighttime meditations to himself) and others to greater 'English'ness (e.g. Henry's Agincourt speech), and while Cormack further unpacks the complicated conflation of Wales and French present in Pistol's exchange with "Harry *le roi*," so far as I know only Schäfer has even catalogued the more covert "French-in-English" that these twinomials entail. Twinomials here are rarely fully synonymous, yet they are frequently present, particularly in highly rhetoricized moments – thus Canterbury speaks of a "scrambling and unquiet time" that preceded the paradise that would "envelop and contain spirits" in Henry's body. Henry's "sweet and honeyed" rhetoric is present throughout the play – in his outrage against the traitors ("garnished and decked"); in his inspirational cry at Harfleur ("o'erhang and jutty"), in his contemplation on ceremony ("flexure and low bending"), and in his numbering of the dead at Agincourt ("gentlemen of blood and quality"). Schäfer identifies further pairs, albeit not usually conjoined with "and" – disqualifying many of them, in my view, from being twinomials since they lack the necessary collocation. I cite some of them, nonetheless, to further indicate the intricate bilingually rooted echo of English's medieval heritage that Shakespeare accomplishes throughout the play:

Canterbury: weak/faint (1.1.15/16)
Canterbury: wish/desire (1.1.40/41)

Canterbury: still/mute (1.1.49/50)
Canterbury: audience/hearing (1.1.93/94)
Canterbury: woman/female (1.2.39/50)
Canterbury: corrupt and naught (1.2.73)
King Henry: shook and trembled (1.2.154)
King Henry: kind/gentle (2.2.13/14)
King Henry: dear care / And tender preservation (2.2.57–8) (Schäffer calls this "the triple contrast – etymological, morphological and stylistic ... in which the Germanic monosyllable, the common word, is opposed to the Latinate polysyllable" ["Shakespeare's Synonymy Re-examined," 206])
Chorus: fleet/navy (3.0.16/18)
Dauphin: wild and savage (3.5.7)
Constable: robustious and rough (3.7.142)
King Henry: defunct and dead (4.1.21)
King Henry: perish/die (4.1.166)
King Henry: forehand and vantage (4.1.268)
Grandpré: still and motionless (4.2.50)
King Henry: company/fellowship (4.3.38/39)
Warwick: fight/battle (4.3.75)
Fluellen: [on Alexander's rage in comparison to Henry's] Why, I pray you, is not 'pig' great? The pig, or the great, or the mighty, or the huge, or the magnanimous are all one reckonings, save the phrase is a little variations. (4.7.16–19); Alexander, God knows and you know, in his rages and his furies and his wraths and his cholers and his moods and his displeasures and his indignations, and also being a little intoxicates in his prains, did in his ales and his angers, look you, kill his best friend, Cleitus – (4.7.31–5; Fluellen is interrupted)
Fluellen: wits/judgments (4.7.42/43)
Fluellen: witness and testimony (4.8.36)
Fluellen: verily and in truth (5.1.56)
King Henry: meeting/assembly (5.2.1/6)

The quotations above hint that twinomials are notably at play in a drama that directly concerns the English reconquest of France. But what is striking is that the character with the most tendentious, and therefore for this essay central, diversion into synonyms is Fluellen. Fluellen is, of course, obsessed with history, and not just history but precedent *qua* precedent, as a hovering presence in the present.

In 4.7 he is debating with Gower over Henry's order to kill the French prisoners, an order which resonates with the brutality of Alexander. Must all great kings also be so brutal? The fact that the speech so clearly is concerned with the extent to which Alexander does and does not match with Henry, and the extent to which being big does and does not match being great, all show how deeply Shakespeare is aware of the ways in which words point to etymologies that revive the past in the present. The roots of the words are showing, even under the comic veil of Fluellen's difficulty with the letters P and B. In fact, his accent causes us to pay *more* attention to his words, as we listen to what he says and try to *hear* what he means. The twinned synonyms resonate with two kings, and Fluellen is seeking to underpin his king with an old and antique past. The profusion of his synonyms, however, is almost as compulsive as a lawyer's. And because a lawyer's rhetoric often depends upon precedent, it is a rhetoric that is often, albeit invisibly, buttressed by twinomials, which linguistically associate law with a solid foundation, a basis that is both native and educated, both true and veritable. By nearly parodying this lawyer's habit, Fluellen draws attention to this subtle effect of the collocation. Indeed, it might be tempting to look for twinomials in *Henry V* as a direct reflection on Anglo-French history, because of the overall nature of the play. But here it can be noted that although these issues cannot help but be linked, Fluellen's quotation problematizes any direct reading of such a resonance. His Welsh nationality and his consistent concern with Roman and Greek precedents block any neat association of Romance words with a French past.

In an earlier scene, Fluellen attempts to lecture MacMorris:

> Fluellen: Captain MacMorris, I beseech you now, will you vouchsafe me, look you, a few disputations with you, as partly touching or concerning the disciplines of the war, the Roman wars, in the way of argument, look you, and friendly communication? (3.3.36–40)

There are no particular twinomials here, but what is apparent is that Fluellen's compulsive and voluble quest for antecedents is at best a distraction from war, and at worst a source for internal dissent – shortly after this he accidentally insults MacMorris and his "nation" (3.3.60–4). Fluellen's search for cultural memory may seem laughable, but he is also the character who nearly forgets, and then remembers,

Falstaff (4.7.38–42) and Bardolph (3.6.90–7), two characters whose departures from the Henriad constitute ambivalently felt erasures. Though he may be principally a source for comic relief and harmless contention on the battlefield, Fluellen also consistently reminds us of the troubles memories cause, and the ways in which the very words we use to address the present are indelibly marked with the battles of the past, even when we do not intentionally cite that past.

It is beyond the scope of this essay to comment on the wider scope of the play, and how these pairings may speak in other ways to a classical and medieval inheritance. However, since Fluellen so clearly makes the rhetorics of etymology and of history an issue, at the very least he attests to the untilled fecundity of this quintessentially English trope. By attending to the philological traces inherent in the fabric of English signification, we can gain new insight into the Renaissance imagination.

Shakespeare's Coining of Words

ROBERT N. WATSON

1.

That Shakespeare invented – or, at least, successfully promoted – more new English words than anyone else in history is a truth universally acknowledged.[1] But how and why did he do that? An otherwise superb exploration of "Some Functions of Shakespearean Word-Formation" identifies many technical purposes – "To ensure coincidence of metrical and lexical stress,"[2] for example – but does not attend to what were surely important functions for Shakespeare: to draw paying customers to his plays by appealing to their need for cutting-edge social tools, and to articulate the complexities of mood and consciousness that are a hallmark of his literary achievement. This double business – selling to a wide popular audience, while also serving a fathomless interior intellect – may seem contradictory, but the combination is surely essential to Shakespeare's greatness.

The shared life of the vernacular, granted new range and prestige across Europe by the printing press, was extended by the English stage; as poets, notably Spenser, reached backward for archaisms, perhaps to appeal to a fading aristocratic economy of patronage, playwrights pushed ahead. The Elizabethan theatre was a "knowledge marketplace,"[3] and a key commodity in that market was lexical. English was evolving rapidly, not only because print and trade were accelerating exchange with other languages (to which English has always been unusually receptive) and because social and technological revolutions were requiring new terminologies, but also because the disappearance of grammatical inflections in English allowed words to be easily converted from one part of speech to another, as Shakespeare liked to do, by what linguists call "zero derivation"[4] and Renaissance rhetoricians called *anthimeria*. As I have argued elsewhere, these new products were manufactured and sold by Shakespeare and his rival playwrights.[5] Dramatists were fighting for market share in a theatrical economy that was partly a store of new words and a lecture-demonstration of new ways of assembling them.

Demand must have been strong, because playwrights spent much less time demonstrating the product's successes than warning against the failures of rival versions; presumably they (like modern advertisers) could count on audiences to identify hopefully with the victors rather than with the fiascos. Or perhaps this negative emphasis reflects the ambivalent function of Elizabethan theatre as an instrument for re-negotiating status and hierarchy: while advertising the rhetorical means of social advancement, the plays also persistently implied that such uprisings were likely to fall flat. The same ambivalence is legible through Shakespeare's long reign as a worldwide cultural idol, proffered as a means of self-improvement for the working classes, but also wielded as a legitimator of traditional class distinctions. Listening to the mighty lines of Marlovian heroes, groundlings must have wondered whether they too would seem heroic, or instead simply ridiculous, if they marched through the world mimicking Tamburlaine's "high astounding terms."[6]

Many Renaissance authors noticed that England's colonial project was bound up with a struggle between languages; and a number of those authors found uses more profitable than Caliban's imprecations for the new vocabulary. With a remarkable persistence, the coining of words was associated with the coining of currency in this period.[7] Thomas Nashe even argues that the characteristic English monosyllables are like small change – making the Elizabethans into a nation of verbal "shop-keepers" – and that his more elaborate diction enables his countrymen to trade profitably in larger sums.[8] The familiar terms of monetary debate – will imports increase the national wealth, or deplete or dilute it? – pervade discussions about imported vocabulary, as does (on the spectrum from approval to disapproval) the terminology of profit, minting, mining, credit, borrowing, theft, and counterfeiting.[9] English commentators wondered whether the accelerating assimilation of the Welsh, Scottish, and Irish languages would "enrich" or contaminate" their own;[10] "enrich" occurs repeatedly in discussions of the Elizabethan lexicon, in the works of John Harington, Richard Sherry, and others. Sir John Cheke, in a letter appended to Thomas Hoby's 1561 translation of Castiglione's *Courtier*, warns that English should be wary of "borowing of other tunges, wherein if we take not heed bi tijm, ever borowing and never payeng, she shall be faine to keep her house as bankrupt."[11]

Predictably, nativist resentment often allied itself with class resentment, against the imported language used by sophisticated lawyers and world travellers to make the ordinary person feel worthless and helpless.[12] Audiences surely sided with Kent (whose facility for moving across social strata, in styles of speech as well as clothing, is remarkable) when that aggressively plain-spoken Anglo old-timer mocks the social-climbing smoothie Oswald's mannered speech in *King Lear* (2.2.101–10). The Marston-figure in *Poetaster* is warned against introducing "Some *Gallo-belgick* phrase" into his writing.[13] Writers faced a choice between a kind of jingoistic defense of established English, and a desire to profit – individually and collectively – by a globalized trade of vocabulary.

Others had a far rosier view of the exchange, however. Thomas Dekker's *Villanies Discovered by Lanthorne and Candle-Light* (1608) observes that English was once "poorest," but "those Noblest Languages lent her Words and phrases, and turning those Borrowings into Good husbandry, she is now as rich in Elocution and as Abundant as her proudest and Best-stored Neighbors."[14] "I marvaile," remarked another Elizabethan defender of neologisms, "how our English tongue hath cracke it credite, that it may not borrow of the Latine."[15]

If England would profit, the neologist wanted his finder's fee. Francis Meres claims that "the English tongue is mightily enriched" by writers such as Shakespeare, Marlowe, and Chapman;[16] but the writers were enriched in turn. In "The Excellencie of the English Tongue" (1595–96), Richard Carew (a defender of dialects) comments that "For our owne parts, we employ the borrowed ware so farre to our advantage that we raise a profit of new words from the same stocke, which yet in their owne countrey are not merchantable."[17]

Elizabethan and Jacobean playwrights were also determined to defend their neologistic practices to a more scholarly audience; they sold high rhetoric to the underclass, but sold themselves to the elite as national benefactors. Thomas Heywood's *Apology for Actors*

(1612) therefore claims that "our *English* tongue, which hath ben the most harsh, uneven, and broken language of the world, part *Dutch*, part *Irish*, *Saxon*, *Scotch*, *Welsh*, and indeed a gallimaffry of many, but perfect in none, is now by this secondary meanes of playing, continually refined, every writer striving in himselfe to adde a new florish unto it; so that in processe, from the most rude and unpolisht tongue, it is growne to a most perfect and composed language, and many excellent workers, and elaborate Poems writ in the same, that many Nations grow inamored of our tongue (before despised)."[18] Chapman's "Epistle to the Understander" of *Achilles' Shield* (1598) emphatically defends the importation of foreign words as enriching English. The Preface to Robert Parry's 1595 *Moderatus, or the Adventures of the Black Knight* claims that English vocabulary had recently become so copious that it "may compare with most of the richest tongues in all *Europe*."[19]

Throughout Western Europe, the growth of vernacular literatures and linguistic theory created a lively competition for the tongues and ears of the world. The verbal inventiveness of Elizabethan and Jacobean theatre could thus claim to be part of a patriotic project – perhaps making English the world language, as Alexander Gill proposed,[20] which must have seemed a much more distant fantasy in the 1590s (when Francis Meres failed to mention English in his list of the world's eight leading languages) than it does today.

A nation that had recently begun actively trying to replace Latin with English as the language of religion, and was similarly struggling to displace French as the language of high aristocracy and common law, must have been engaged in a lengthy, half-conscious struggle against its legacy as a colony rather than an empire. The connection between the linguistic project I have been describing and emerging Elizabethan nationalism, especially through Shakespeare's second history tetralogy, is explored (mostly in a New Historicist mode) by scholars such as Claire McEachern, Richard Griffin, and Stephen Greenblatt, far above my poor power to add or detract.[21]

But the modern assumption that nations and local populations produced languages may be wrong-way-round from a Jacobean perspective: Dekker speculates that, when the builders of the Tower of Babel scattered, "glad was he that could meet another whose speech he understood: for to what place soever he went, others (that ran madding up and down) hearing a man speak like themselves, followed only him: so that they, who when the work began, were all

Countrey-men, before a quarter of it was finished, fled from one another as from enemies & strangers. And in this manner did men at the first make up nations: thus were words coyned into Languages, and out of those Languages have others been molded since, onely by the mixture of nations, after kingdoms have been subdued."[22] Language sorts the world, and new words threaten – or are symptoms of a threat to – the old world order.

2.

Scholarship on Elizabethan and Jacobean drama has almost entirely overlooked a battle for market share in this sideline business of compiling and vending a fresh verbal repertoire at a moment when social advancement and humiliation were extraordinarily dependent on mastering the latest tricks of speech. Thomas Dekker's satiric 1609 "How a Gallant should behave himselfe in a Play-house" observed that "The *Theater* is your Poets Royal-Exchange, upon which, their Muses (ye are now turnd to Merchants) meeting, barter away that light commodity of words ... your *Groundling*, and *Gallery Commoner* buyes his sport by the penny, and, like a *Hagler*, is glad to utter it againe by retailing." That upwardly mobile commoner is advised to "hoord up the finest play-scraps you can get" in order to banter with gentlewomen.[23] In *The Return from Parnassus* (1599), Gullio values poets, especially Shakespeare, because he can "take some of there wordes and applie them to mine owne matters by a scholasticall imitation." Public-theatre dramatists therefore sought, like Chapman's Monsieur D'Olive, to "have my chamber the Rende-vous of all good wits, the shoppe of good wordes, the Mint of good jests, an Ordinary of fine discourse."[24] Even if these lexical innovations were only a small bonus added to the main value of the product, the competitive situation helps to explain several quirks in the so-called War of the Theatres (involving Jonson, Marston, and others), as well as the "inkhorn controversy," the publishing of the first English dictionaries and guides to the "canting" languages of London's criminal underclass, and the economic language persistently associated with the literary "coining" of new English words.

Costard's folly in mistaking "remuneration" and "guerdon" for units of money in *Love's Labour's Lost* (3.1.131–73) contains an element of insight.[25] In the alchemy of the Shakespearean stage, words could be turned to gold – could be coined.[26] Calling Don Armado's neologisms "fire-new words" (1.1.178) suggests a minting of metal.[27] Mocking pretentious verbal mannerisms to the paying audience at such a verbally mannered play as *Love's Labour's Lost* was an audacious act of brinkmanship on Shakespeare's part, calculated to let him have his fancy Euphuistic layer-cake and – through Berowne's renunciation of Russian performances and French courtesies in favour of "russet yeas and honest kersey noes" (5.2.402 ff.) – forswear it too. In fact, many of the words that characterize Armado's excess turn up elsewhere in Shakespeare's works in all earnestness.[28] *Love's Labour's Lost* provides the interest of both high Latinate neologism (through the schoolmaster Holofernes) and the more free-wheeling Continental variety (through Armado), while at the same time taking a dismissive commonsensical position against the vanity of such literary innovations when balanced against domestic common sense and the biological facts of life. It does the accused Costard no good to change the wench to a damsel, virgin, or maid: the sentence is the same (1.1.287–99). The linguistic show-offs can't stop re-naming naming itself: Nathaniel's "intitulated, nominated, or called" is framed by "Armado hight" in the opening scene and Holofernes's "ycleped" in the final one, encompassing some twenty other uses of "name" itself. When Holofernes and Armado use affected neologisms to attack each other's affected neologisms, they replicate a contradiction that pervaded the Elizabethan "inkhorn controversy." If many of the OED's first-use citations from this play, but few from *Hamlet*, can be antedated by electronic database searches (as Charlotte Brewer has provisionally noted), it may reflect the difference between a comedy that was mocking some recent ways of talking, and a tragedy that struggled to articulate some nascent ways of thinking.

Like many new businesses, the buying and selling of verbal riches involved risks as well as opportunities. The final scene of *Love's Labour's Lost* attacks, as mere regurgitators, those who seek socio-economic advantage by pilfering witty speech. Berowne thus belittles, yet also envies, Boyet, and puns on "utters" as both "saying" and "selling":[29]

This fellow pecks up wit as pigeons pease,
And utters it again when God doth please.
He is wit's pedlar, and retails his wares

At wakes and wassails, meetings, markets, fairs:
And we that sell by gross, the Lord doth know,
Have not the grace to grace it with such show. (5.2.315–20)

For every such Boyet, there must have been many boys who lacked the suavity to succeed in this maneuver; amorous plagiarists abound but do not thrive in Renaissance drama. For every Henry V, who wins Katherine's favour by deflating the grand rhetoric of formulaic courtship and mocking his own efforts to reach from English into French, there must have been dozens of Navarres who earned only the mocking laughter, not the submissive hands and disputed lands, of the princesses they courted in a high literary style. Although he is not one of the fools in plays from this period who acknowledge learning their overblown verbiage at the theatre – such as Thomas Tomkis's Trinculo, who woos "with compliments drawn from the plays I see at the Fortune and Red Bull, where I learn all the words I speak and understand not"[30] – Andrew Aguecheek offers a memorable cautionary example, vowing to master "'Odors,' 'pregnant,' and 'vouchsafed'; I'll get 'em all three all ready," but unable to handle "accost" or (despite his vaunted linguistic skills) "*pourquoi*" (*Twelfth Night*, 3.1.90–1, 1.3.49–59, 90–1). Shakespeare and his colleagues were already making the basic joke of Cole Porter's song "Brush Up Your Shakespeare": no classy dame is really going to fall for a street tough just because he can quote (in an incongruous accent) a few exalted words from Elizabethan drama.

At the risk of complicity in a professorial tendency to underrate the sheer playfulness of plays and to overrate their pedagogical intent, I want to emphasize Shakespeare's diligence and ingenuity as a teacher of vocabulary in a one-large-room schoolhouse. Through Holofernes, he could make fun of the sixteenth-century humanist method that taught language by corny *copia*: "The deer ... hangeth like a jewel in the ear of *caelo*, the sky, the welkin, the heaven, and anon falleth like a crab on the face of *terra*, the soil, the land, the earth" (4.2.3–7). But Shakespeare recognized the sanity in this method, and put it to his own uses, regularly finding ways to make the innovations both memorable and thematically important. In this as in other areas, he deftly combined *dolce* with *utile*, Ariel with Caliban, the delights of his art with the practical business of his theatre. As Edmund Gayton observed, "men come not to study at a Play-house, but love such expressions and passages, which with ease insinuate themselves into their capacities."[31] In Elizabethan London, the mastery of new language was pleasure and profit conjoined.

Clearly Shakespeare's original audiences enjoyed his language, not because (as modern readers tend to assume) they knew all those strange locutions, but partly because they didn't yet. Ralph Alan Cohen has written that "Shakespeare's audience went to the playhouse not in possession of the language they would hear there but in search of it ... The only advantage the Elizabethan audience had over today's audience was a delight in new words."[32] Even if one doubts the "only," the implications for teaching and editing are immense, and support the already compelling case against modernized-diction texts of Shakespeare. This is especially true for younger students, who are generally the ones most avidly protected from Elizabethan diction, but also the ones best equipped mentally, developmentally, to learn unfamiliar words and constructions, as they must do every day by seeing them in context and, ideally, surrounded by memorable explanatory actions, as they would be in the materialized memory-palace of the theatre.

3 ·

However small his Latin and less his Greek,[33] Shakespeare proved a daunting competitor for the scholar-neologists of his time. His commercial success in his own time, like his influence on modern English, depended partly on a talent for finding the right degree of variation to make neologisms attractive – and offering contextual definitions that made them comprehensible. In an era of multicultural anxieties, remaking English from within (by exchanging parts of speech or adding prefixes and suffixes) proved at least as effective as high humanist importations, and Shakespeare was willing to attempt both, willing even to jumble them together.[34]

Though, to my unhappy surprise, I have not found any satisfactory list of the famous Shakespearean neologisms,[35] many instances can be located simply by noticing that seeming redundancies are often actually glossaries. The system was far from flawless, and about a third of Shakespeare's neologisms have not survived.[36] But he cares for his young conscientiously, surrounding them with their kin, and there are few *hapax legomena* – words strutted once on stage, and then heard no more – among his many creations. Regan's neologistic claim that she is "alone felicitate" in Lear's affection is prepared by her synonymous claim, two lines earlier, that she is "an enemy to all other joys" (1.1.73–5). When Goneril urges Lear "A little to disquantity your train" (1.4.249), Shakespeare accompanies the new verb with enough discussion about numerical reduction to make the meaning obvious: one hundred, fifty, twenty-five, ten, five, one, zero (this is a particularly bold example, because Latin would not permit "dis-" to be added to verbs; but Goneril is not much for rules, and often puts a thin veneer of sophistication over her transgressions). The definition of "decimation" – a word Shakespeare probably learned from North's translation of Plutarch, but otherwise unknown in this sense during the sixteenth century – becomes similarly mathematical: a Senator urges Alcibiades, "By decimation, and a tithed death, / ... take thou the destin'd tenth" (*Timon*, 5.4.31–3). Falstaff's "dwindle" was another novelty for the idea of diminution (here spatial rather than numerical), but Shakespeare offers plenty of help: "Bardolph, am I not fall'n away vilely since this last action? do I not bate? do I not dwindle? Why, my skin hangs about me like an old lady's loose gown; I am wither'd like an old apple-john" (*1 Henry IV*, 3.3.1–4). The only other recorded use before 1610 was also by Shakespeare (if the scene is), and again he nestles it amid synonyms: "dwindle, peak, and pine" (*Macbeth*, 1.3.23).

Consider the two uses of a more elaborate word, once in a new form and once in a still-rare one:

1 SIR TOBY: Am not I consanguineous? Am I not of her blood? (*Twelfth Night*, 2.3.77–8)
2 CRESSIDA: I have forgot my father,
I know no touch of consanguinity;
No kin, no love, no blood, no soul so near me
As the sweet Troilus. (*Troilus*, 4.2.96–9)

Earlier in *Troilus and Cressida* (1.3.106), Ulysses discusses "The primogenity and due of birth" (the Folio has the equally unprecedented "primogenitive" here); so we may sense Shakespeare repeatedly offering Latinate replacements for Teutonic roots (such as "blood" and "birth") as the classical story stands in satirically for Renaissance England – though Jonson would surely observe that Shakespeare ought here to be using Greek rather than Latin forms. In fact, the first scene set in the Greek camp is replete with doublets (within a single speech at 1.3.5–30, Shakespeare gives us "Tortive and errant," "Bias and thwart," "artist and unread," and a half-dozen others)[37] and with neologisms derived from both classical languages.[38] Presumably Shakespeare is signalling – along with a shortfall of language that matches the inefficacy of vows – the alien character of that world, in this weirdly alienating play. This is, and is not, English.

Like Marston, Shakespeare enjoyed playing with blunt, body-based Teutonics, as well as with grander classical constructions. "Dwarfish" was extremely rare elsewhere in the literary record – Marlowe's *Hero and Leander* provides a lonely but prominent precedent – but not in Shakespeare, who seems to have enjoyed its sound, made its meaning obvious every time,[39] and used its tone for contrast when Hermia complains that Helena

> hath urg'd her height,
> And with her personage, her tall personage,
> Her height, forsooth, she hath prevail'd with him.
> And are you grown so high in his esteem,
> Because I am so dwarfish and so low?
> How low am I, thou painted maypole? Speak!
> How low am I? I am not yet so low
> But that my nails can reach unto thine eyes. (*Dream*, 3.2.291–8)

Hermia mockingly replaces "height," based in Old English and German, with the Norman-French "personage," then corrects it back to "height," to deride Helena's implied assumption that stretching implies superiority. Aided by the courtly etymology, the length of "personage" implies *hauteur* based on height; and the assonant suggestion that Helena will cease to "prevail" when Hermia wields her "nails" performs the same kind of work, as the tough little monosyllables chase the lengthy speech to its close.

Antony offers an instant gloss when he complains that his former followers "discandy, melt their sweets" (*Antony*, 4.12.22). Lady Macbeth's rejection of "compunctious visitings of nature" (1.5.45) is escorted by multiple definitions of natural conscience, and Banquo's "exposure" arrives already defined as nakedness, in opposition to hiddenness: "when we have our naked frailties hid, / That suffer in exposure" (2.3.126–7). For an antonym to "exposure," *Macbeth* places a new adjectival form between two less novel versions:

"cabin'd, cribb'd, confin'd" (3.4.23). Isabella's reference to Angelo's "circummur'd" garden is attended by redundant, over-determined imagery of surrounding walls (*Measure*, 4.1.28–33).

Prospero's obsessive anxieties allow Shakespeare to offer redundant contexts for a nearly new word, "sanctimonious," and a brand-new word, "abstemious" (the Riverside edition chooses the Folio reading "abstenious," suggesting a derivation from "abstain"). Prospero admonishes Ferdinand that, until

All sanctimonious ceremonies may
With full and holy rite be minist'red, ...
Look thou be true; do not give dalliance
Too much the rein. The strongest oaths are straw
To th' fire i' th' blood. Be more abstenious,
Or else good night your vow! (*Tempest*, 4.1.16–17, 51–4)

Unlike a seemingly simpler neologism for the same concept – "unfix," which Shakespeare repeatedly accompanied with overlapping contextual definitions (2 *Henry IV*, 4.1.202–7; *Macbeth*, 4.1.94–8) – "deracinate" has survived, perhaps because Shakespeare aired its roots: Burgundy laments the leas that weeds "root upon, while that the coulter rusts / That should deracinate such savagery" (*Henry V*, 5.2.44–7). "Savagery" too was apparently a Shakespearean formulation, and when he first presented it, he did so with plenty of explanatory parallels:

SALISBURY: This is the bloodiest shame,
The wildest savagery, the vildest stroke,
That ever wall-ey'd wrath or staring rage
Presented to the tears of soft remorse. (*King John*, 4.3.47–50)

"Invulnerable/vulnerable" turns up four times, with due explanatory diligence performed in each instance:

1 KING PHILIP: Our cannons' malice vainly shall be spent
Against th' invulnerable clouds of heaven. (*King John*, 2.1.251–2)
2 ARIEL: The elements,
Of whom your swords are temper'd, may as well
Wound the loud winds, or with bemock'd-at stabs
Kill the still-closing waters, as diminish

One dowle that's in my plume. My fellow ministers
Are like invulnerable. If you could hurt,
Your swords are now too massy for your strengths,
And will not be uplifted. (*Tempest*, 3.3.61–8)

3 MACBETH: Thou losest labor.
As easy mayst thou the intrenchant air
With thy keen sword impress as make me bleed.
Let fall thy blade on vulnerable crests. (*Macbeth*, 5.8.8–11)

4 MARCELLUS: For it is as the air, invulnerable,
And our vain blows malicious mockery. (*Hamlet*, 1.1.145–6)

Hamlet – the dysfunctional home of "words, words, words" – abounds with instances. The tautology in "windy suspiration of forc'd breath" (1.2.79) is also a built-in glossary. When Claudius agrees with Laertes that "No place indeed should murther sanctuarize," Shakespeare has already established the vivid and specific image of murder in a church in the previous line, and then rephrases the meaning in the next one: "Revenge should have no bounds" (4.7.127–8). When the Ghost calls Claudius an "adulterate beast" (1.5.42), Shakespeare again packs the gift in more extensive and familiar definitions of the crime. We know that "malefactions" must be bad doings, even if we miss the etymology, by the example that follows (2.2.592–3). Nor would anyone have had much trouble understanding "survivor" or "condolement" – the latter also used and instantly glossed in *Pericles*, but with a different meaning[40] – thanks to the way Shakespeare has Claudius frame them:

'Tis sweet and commendable in your nature, Hamlet,
To give these mourning duties to your father.
But you must know your father lost a father,
That father lost, lost his, and the survivor bound
In filial obligation for some term
To do obsequious sorrow. But to persever
In obstinate condolement is a course
Of impious stubbornness, 'tis unmanly grief,
It shows a will most incorrect to heaven … (1.2.87–95)

To help "survivor" survive (it was seldom used outside of legal discussions), Shakespeare will revisit it in *Coriolanus* 5.6.17–18: "the fall of either / Makes the survivor heir of all." "Impious" is promptly defined here, and (we will see) receives extensive aid through "pious," which is itself repeatedly defined. An exception proves the rule: Shakespeare might have been able to save "cerements" – a rare term for burial wrappings – had his parallelism not misleadingly implied that it was merely a synonym for "sepulcher":

> HAMLET: Why thy canoniz'd bones, hearsed in death,
> Have burst their cerements; why the sepulchre,
> Wherein we saw thee quietly inurn'd,
> Hath op'd his ponderous and marble jaws
> To cast thee up again. (1.4.47–51)

Another technique emerges when Claudius (at 3.1.166) worries about "the hatch and the disclose" of whatever Hamlet is brooding over. Claudius uses two words unfamiliar as nouns to help us recognize not only what they mean, but also how he is redeploying them: the former one of the first such uses in English (along with Shakespeare's similar "the hatch and brood of time" in *2 Henry IV*, 3.1.86), the other only the second, according to the OED (indeed, even as I write this, Microsoft Word's grammar-checker is protesting the placement of "disclose" as a noun). This double verb-to-noun move is reversed when Hamlet warns Gertrude not to let rationalization "skin and film the ulcerous place" (3.4.147). When the Ghost worries about making Hamlet's "knotted and combined locks to part" (1.5.18), the familiar first term illuminates the second, which was apparently a neologism, though it has since become common. To support "pious," which was then extremely unusual (especially outside theological tracts), Polonius warns Ophelia against "unholy suits" proffered "like sanctified and pious bonds" (1.3.129–30); Claudius later laments that "with devotion's visage / And pious action we do sugar o'er / The devil himself" (3.1.46–8); and during the subsequent decade Shakespeare repeatedly offers "pious" conjoined with synonyms such as "holy" and "saint-like."[41]

So, in addition to the thematic function of this doubling of nouns (and sometimes verbs) as masterfully traced by William Empson, George T. Wright, Frank Kermode, and Patrick Cheney,[42] and the pairing of Germanic and Romance roots masterfully tracked by Jürgen Schäfer,[43] the rhetorical structure called *hendiadys* also allowed the definition of new words by edging toward *synonymia simplex*. Linguists who assume that synonyms exist to permit alliteration and prevent repetitiveness tend to neglect this pedagogical function.[44] Even Rosencrantz (half of a human hendiadys) joins in with "mortis'd and adjoin'd, / ... small annexment, petty consequence" (3.3.20–1).

Other plays employ the same tactic: for example, "Th' inaudible and noiseless foot of time" (*All's Well*, 5.3.41), "fertile and conceptious womb" (*Timon*, 4.3), or "Countless and infinite" kisses (*Titus Andronicus,* 5.3.159). "Critical" – though occasionally used in astrology and medicine – almost never carried the sense of "censorious" until Theseus rejects "some satire, keen and critical, / Not sorting with a nuptial ceremony" (*Dream*, 5.1.54–5). Sometimes, with a not-quite-new word, an escorting synonym is sufficient: "most courtly and fashionable" (*Timon*, 5.1.27), or "ceremonious and traditional" (*Richard III*, 3.1.45). "Affined" was almost unknown, so it generally travels with an assistant: "affin'd, or leagu'd"[45] (*Othello*, 2.3.218), and "affin'd and kin" (*Troilus*, 1.3.25).

The technique itself was hardly new. The juxtaposing of synonyms arguably derived from William Caxton's fifteenth-century translations, emerged as a tool for teaching Latin in Erasmus's *De Copia* (1512), and developed into a kind of thesaurus-function, and then into a stylistic quirk of sixteenth-century humanist rhetoric.[46] When he could not find an English synonym that would be familiar to ordinary readers of his 1550 translation of Peter Martyr Vermigli's Latin treatise, Nicholas Udall "added suche circumstaunce of other words, as might declare it and make it plain."[47] Sir Thomas Elyot's *Boke of the Governour* (1531) "sensibly followed the practice established from Middle English of pairing neologisms with established words and phrases to make the newcomers comprehensible,"[48] a practice continued in Puttenham's domestications of Latin rhetorical terms. Thomas Cooper's *Thesaurus Linguae Romanae et Britannicae* (1565) – a book which Shakespeare clearly knew, perhaps from the copy a schoolmaster bequeathed to the Stratford grammar school – could have suggested not only Shakespeare's thesaurus-like method of explaining new words, but also many of the specific instances cited here, including "abstemious," "condolence," "consanguinity," "adulterate" (Cooper offers the Hamlet-friendly example of "adultry with his brothers wife"), "affined," "compunctious," "audacious," "suspiration," and perhaps "relume," by glossing their Latin roots into English.

No one, however, seems to have taught by tautology as industriously as Shakespeare himself. Nor were others as ingenious in using interlingual hendiadys to establish the meaning of the plays as well as of the words: when, just before the first battle scene in *Henry V*, the Chorus says that every Englishman of "pith and puissance" has joined the invasion of France (3.0.21), the near-synonyms not only match the itinerary of the expedition they describe, and help define each other; they also capture in miniature exactly the difference between blunt Anglo-Saxon earthiness and Gallic vainglory that the play repeatedly suggests will enable the "bastard Normans, Norman bastards" (3.5.10) to conquer the French. This trick of sliding from the native term to its exotic near-synonym would become crucial to Shakespeare's characterization of the expatriate Othello just a few years later.[49] The device of delineating characters by their neologisms – as in *Love's Labour's Lost* and *Troilus and Cressida* – thus becomes a much subtler tool: a brush for tragic portraiture rather than broad comic caricature or satiric disorientation.

The production and elucidation of neologisms seems to drop off significantly in Shakespeare's late plays. Perhaps the boom of verbal innovation was tapering off in England; the tic of *copia* had certainly gone out of fashion. Perhaps the extended absence from London in 1607–10 posited by Jonathan Bate[50] withdrew Shakespeare from what was left of the neologistic ferment. Perhaps he was well enough established that he no longer needed to offer vocabulary as a supplement to the other pleasures of his plays. And perhaps his innovative energies went instead into the syntactical rigours of his late verse, which Russ McDonald has explored so masterfully;[51] in the building of the new English language, Shakespeare eventually moved from brick-making toward early-post-modern architecture.

4·

Shakespeare's neologisms – and this category inevitably includes words he did not absolutely originate, but helped to popularize – were certainly not merely items for display and sale. Like several of his younger contemporaries,[52] he waged protracted campaigns on behalf of some locutions that filled gaps in his expressive palette. The previous section briefly traced his development of several words ("compunctious," "abstemious," "exposure," "critical," and "pious") that articulate a boundary between the ethical, thoughtful, withheld or withholding inner self, and an external world consisting of that self's objects and obstacles. His half-dozen efforts to sustain the dying sense of "revolve" and "revolving" as pondering an idea at length – turning it over in the mind – suggest the same need. Twice "revolve" comes paired with "ruminate" (*1 Henry VI*, 5.5.101, *Troilus*, 2.3.188), as it does in Cooper's gloss on *ruminatio* – and "ruminate," while not new as a term for human meditation, was evidently returning from obscurity, since it appears in a series of fashionable new words that the foolish Juniper mishandles in Jonson's *The Case Is Altered* (published in 1609, but probably written in the late 1590s).[53] Shakespeare seems to have seized on this revived verb for the process of thoughtful, artful planning, and dutifully explained it: "Then she plots, then she ruminates, then she devises" (*Merry Wives*, 2.2.305–6); "ruminate strange plots" (*Titus Andronicus*, 5.2.6); "ruminated, plotted" (*1 Henry IV*, 1.3.274); "Sit patiently and inly ruminate" (*Henry V*, 4.0.24); "To ruminate on this so far, until / It forg'd him some design" (*Henry VIII*, 1.2.180–1); "a studied, not a present thought, / By duty ruminated" (*Antony*, 2.2.137–8); "speak to me as to thy thinkings, / As thou dost ruminate" (*Othello*, 3.3.131–3); and "the sundry contemplation of my travels, in which my often rumination wraps me in a most humorous sadness" (*As You Like It*, 4.1.17–20). These add up to more uses than the Literature Online database shows in all the plays of Shakespeare's competitors combined.

The boundary these words explore corresponds to a pervasive scholarly recognition of Shakespeare as a withdrawn figure (a Romantic biographical tradition developed by Dowden, and more recently, with an emphasis on philosophical skepticism, by several other fine scholars),[54] and as an inventor of human interiority and subjectivity (a more recent and high-theoretical view).[55] In other words, several of Shakespeare's most assiduous developments of vocabulary would seem to confirm, at a microscopic level, some of the largest speculations about his character and characterizing practices.

Shakespeare makes three further attempts (four, if we count "retirement") to invent and promote new words for the concept of pious retreat or isolation, of withdrawal from the world compelled by principle or psychology. "Lonely" is now so common that it is hard to believe that it once needed such direct definition, but it did: hence, "I go alone, / Like to a lonely dragon" (*Coriolanus*, 4.1.29–30), and later, "I keep it / Lonely, apart" (*Winter's Tale*, 5.3.17–18).[56] Observers of Prince Hal "never noted in him any study, / Any retirement, any sequestration / From open haunts and popularity"

(*Henry V*, 1.1.57–9). Othello invents another noun form to prescribe, for the dangerously social and passionate Desdemona, "A sequester from liberty: fasting and prayer, / Much castigation, exercise devout" (3.4.40–1).[57] "Reclusive" gets similar conceptual support:

> FRIAR FRANCIS: You may conceal her,
> As best befits her wounded reputation,
> In some reclusive and religious life,
> Out of all eyes, tongues, minds, and injuries.
> (*Much Ado*, 4.1.240–3)

Both the glossary function and the contemplative emphasis are stark when the Bishop of Winchester condemns Gloucester for coming "with deep premeditated lines, / With written pamphlets studiously devis'd" (*1 Henry VI*, 3.1.1–2). In a clearly Shakespearean section of *Two Noble Kinsmen* (1.1.134–7), the audience receives similar guidance with an otherwise-unknown form of the same word, followed by a rare one grown from the same root: "what you do quickly / Is not done rashly; your first thought is more / Than others' labored meditance; your premeditating / More than their actions."

Perhaps I am cherry-picking my instances – many of Shakespeare's new words lack this intellectual character – but he does seem to spend a remarkable amount of neologistic energy on expressing these mental states, or more tellingly, states of mental reservation: we may add "deceptious" (*Troilus*, 5.2.123), "denotement" (*Othello*, 2.3.317), "dishearten" (*Henry V*, 4.1.112, and *Macbeth*, 2.3.33–4), "the pauser, reason" (*Macbeth*, 2.3.111), "the tranquil mind" (*Othello*, 3.3.348), and "give preceptial med'cine to rage" (*Much Ado*, 5.1.24). Those who believe that Shakespeare was a recusant may be especially inclined to add "equivocator" (extensively defined in *Macbeth*, 2.3.8) and "equivocal" to this list; they may also be intrigued to learn that the only evident precedent for Shakespeare's use of "rumination" was in the works of the famous Jesuit Robert Parsons.[58]

Literature Online shows only two instances of the word "dejected" in plays prior to 1599, but four others appeared by 1600 – a good indication that it was a word coming into fashion (perhaps because melancholy was also). Shakespeare made sure it was always well defined, either by context or by counter-point:

> 1 HAMLET: No, nor the fruitful river in the eye,
> Nor the dejected havior of the visage,

Together with all forms, moods, shapes of grief,
That can denote me truly. (*Hamlet*, 1.2.80–3)

2 EDGAR: To be worst,
The lowest and most dejected thing of fortune,
Stands still in esperance ... (*Lear*, 4.1.2–4)

3 SCARUS: Antony
Is valiant, and dejected, and by starts
His fretted fortunes give him hope and fear (*Antony*, 4.12.6–8)

Shakespeare persistently teaches his audiences that "speculation" has to do with seeing, but also with the limitations and partiality of seeing[59] – an important topic for an endlessly questioning playwright in an era whose revival of classical skepticism emphasized visual differences and distortions. For what is kept unreliably unseen, Shakespeare launches "undivulged," and sends several paraphrases after it to make sure the meaning cannot be missed:

LEAR: Tremble, thou wretch
That hast within thee undivulged crimes
Unwhipt of justice! Hide thee, thou bloody hand ...
... Close pent-up guilts,
Rive your concealing continents. (*Lear*, 3.2.51–8)

Shakespeare also spends considerable effort, especially in the history plays, developing antonyms to mark the polar opposites on a spectrum running from rebellious boldness to humble yielding. "Audacious" was fairly scarce[60] until Shakespeare made it a project early in his career, always signalling a combination of daring and insubordination.[61] Duke Theseus prefers "the modesty of fearful duty" to "saucy and audacious eloquence" (*Midsummer*, 5.1.101–3). Somerset admonishes York, "Obey, audacious traitor, kneel for grace" (2 *Henry VI*, 5.1.108). *Love's Labour's Lost* offers "audacious without impudency" (5.1.4–5) and "fear not thou, but speak audaciously" (5.2.104). "Submissive" (essentially an antonym of "audacious") is another early but temporary favourite, nurtured through its infancy.[62]

Although the emphasis in the sixteenth century was more on words than on syntax,[63] the teaching of rhetoric (professed explicitly by Peacham and Puttenham, and indirectly by Shakespeare and his rivals) often involved larger units. What Shakespeare accomplished by combining words far outweighs what he accomplished by inventing them. But the study of neologisms offers a narrow aperture that brings an overlooked aspect of early modern theatre and Shakespearean technique into focus. This aperture may also bring into view, if not yet into focus, the question of what teachers of language and literature – of vocabulary and sensibility – may have to offer in the global marketplaces of the twenty-first century.

5 ·

Those capable of teaching the latest cool way of talking have probably never lacked customers: what I am noticing in the emergent popular medium of the 1590s surely happened again in the 1950s with the distribution of Rat-Pack and beatnik slang (including this sense of "cool"), and on through the hip-hop hits of recent decades.

The school of Bourdieu – and I note with meta-critical chagrin that I invoke that name in the scholarly marketplace much the way I see Elizabethans hopefully invoking a fashionable term, more confident of its prestige than of its exact meaning – argues that "the linguistic market operates according to 'the unequal distribution of linguistic capital' and the competitive struggle for social 'distinction' through language."[64] But greed in this market does not manifest itself only as a push toward the established norms of the dominant group's discourse, controlled by the official educational system, as Bourdieu sometimes appears to assume. In a period of unprecedented ferment in the development of the language – one scholar estimates that thirty percent of the neologisms created in English during the entire Renaissance emerged between 1588 and 1612, which is to say, within the quarter-century scope of Shakespeare's career as a playwright and England's greatest era of theatre[65] – the possibilities were almost unlimited, and the pitfalls many. In other words, it was a perfect market for verbal guides, and playwrights seized the opportunity and (like the canting cheats of Jonson's *The Alchemist*) bickered over the division of the profits.

The economy of words in England was changing because words were rapidly becoming easier to manufacture, thanks to the ferment of immigration and urbanization, and to the loss of inflections that had prevented the kind of zero-derivation neologisms favoured especially by Shakespeare, in which (for instance) an existing noun becomes a verb. At the same time, due to some of the same social changes, the business of teaching upwardly mobile behaviour thrived. These staged diction-lessons are a subset of that business: plays for the common man analogous to Castiglione's *Book of the Courtier*.[66] Even within dramatic language, the lessons went far beyond vocabulary, into flourishes of style and innovations of syntax. My hope is simply that neologisms offer a helpfully concrete instance of an overlooked function of Elizabethan and Jacobean theatre – a function that can be understood only by combining literary and materialist approaches to the production of culture.

The Elizabethan and Jacobean theatre offered verbal rungs for a social climb, even if there was always the danger of a humiliating fall. As Cathy Shrank observes, Renaissance reformers of English such as Thomas Wilson worried that "language overburdened with foreign neologisms threatens to drive apart, not bring together, the national community by hindering communication, particularly for the less educated, accentuating social difference."[67] Wilson's solution was to "banishe al suche affected Rhetorique," but a ban was unlikely to hold when the use of such rhetoric conferred status. Instead, we see a progression: "Where, in the 1540s, Andrew Borde used 'difficult' Latinate words to flatter an educated elite, and in the 1550s Wilson sought to remove them, the dictionary writers of the late sixteenth and early seventeenth centuries were concerned to explain and 'democratize' them."[68] We may trace a parallel evolution in the English drama of the same era, moving from the university wits to the public-theatre playwrights, and it may explain why the elaborate classicist neologisms of Marston – clearly designed to "flatter an educated elite" – were mocked by Jonson (who makes a Marston-figure vomit up such indigestible terms in *Poetaster*) and eventually superseded by Shakespeare's determination to offer a public audience the power of a rapidly expanding language. If Renaissance drama "retails elements of high culture to the middling sorts,"[69] one such element was surely lexical.

The theatre was also one of several genres that sold the culture of the underclass upwards. The street-slang lesson Prince Hal offers to Poins, Shakespeare offers to us at the same time: "They call drinking deep, dyeing scarlet" (*1 Henry IV*, 2.4.15; see also *2 Henry IV*, 4.4.68–71). A popular early Elizabethan tract also offered translations of a new criminal language "halfe myngled with Englishe when it is familiarly talked"[70] – a lowly version of Othello's mixed parlance. Tricksters lived on the boundaries of normal speech. A poem in dialogue form depicting a con-artist pretending not to know English – "me non spek englys by my fayt / My servaunt spek you what me sayt"[71] – may anticipate Princess Katherine's coy tactics in the final Act of *Henry V* distinctly enough to remind us that the niche of obscured language has always been a haven for disempowered people. Opening that niche to the ruling class through coney-catching guidebooks presumably limited the effectiveness of that sanctuary. Doubtless there was an element of salesmanship, even a kind of linguistic protection-racket in offering defenses against criminal language at least partly invented by the author. We need not take these tracts at face value, as purely objective revelations of real dangers, to recognize that they sold access to an emerging lexicon, and thereby control over a perceived threat from below.

Restoration England is the morning-after of the Elizabethan-Jacobean verbal binge, its symptoms aggravated by an overdose of imported French. A potentially destabilizing social practice (especially a social-climbing practice) is clearly in decline when high-cultural authorities can comfortably mock it to a popular audience; and John Dryden – whose Preface to his version of *Troilus and Cressida* complains that Shakespeare sometimes went "beyond the bounds of Judgment … in coyning of new words" – derides the use of unusual (and usually imported) words to imply superiority. In *Marriage à la Mode*, Philotis hires Melantha "for furnishing me with new words for my daily conversation," but because of Philotis's insufficiencies, her efforts to display her expanding French vocabulary "began at Sottises, and ended en Ridicule."[72] In this, she was evidently not alone.

Materialist readings of Shakespearean drama have become prominent, even dominant, in recent years. Yet no commercial analysis of what Dekker called "that light commodity of words" has emerged. Perhaps the fact that language is evanescent, almost *im*material, has discouraged analysis of how it was sold, and how that trade affected the class system. That the theatre was a marketplace (and vice versa) is hardly a new idea.[73] I am suggesting that we look more closely at what it had to sell. Something big was happening in the manufacture and distribution of this evolving lexical commodity in the Renaissance, as Mikhail Bakhtin suggests: our "world of free and democratized language" exists because the "hierarchy of discourses, forms, images, styles that used to permeate the entire system of official language and linguistic consciousness was swept away by the international linguistic revolutions of the Renaissance."[74] Where better than at the new, popular, socially fluid, legally marginal institution of London's public theatres?

Shakespeare's Sound Government: Sound Defects, Polyglot Sounds, and Sounding Out

PATRICIA PARKER

... a sound, but not in government.
A Midsummer Night's Dream

... it cannot be sounded; my affection hath an unknown bottom ...
As You Like It

In *A Midsummer Night's Dream*, Quince's mispunctuated Prologue (which comically turns a potential compliment into an insult) is described by Hippolyta as "like a child on a recorder – a sound, but not in government" (5.1.122–4).[1] The line calls attention to the government of sound itself, by the "stops" of a recorder or the punctuating "points" of proper discursive "partition" (5.1.167). Far from yielding a simple joke at the artisans' expense, however, Quince's mispointing echoes that of other subjects of Theseus who put "periods in the midst of sentences" (5.1.96), subtly suggesting a connection between the government of sound and sound government of other kinds. In a Shakespeare canon that elsewhere evokes a "jesting spirit ... govern'd by stops" (*Much Ado* 3.2.59–60), Hippolyta's "recorder" re-sounds in Hamlet's objection to attempts to "govern" his "stops" (3.2.357), in a tragedy whose potentially ungovernable instruments include players whose antic disposition Hamlet himself attempts to control or govern through a written script (3.2.38–45). "Sounding" in "you would seem to know my stops, you would pluck out the heart of my mystery, you would sound me from my lowest note to [the top of] my compass" (*Hamlet* 3.2.364–7) combines an instrument to be played upon ("a pipe for Fortune's finger / To sound what stop she please" [3.2.70–1]) with the sense of fathoming or sounding out, already exploited in Polonius's plan to "sound" out his son (2.1.42), in *Julius Caesar*'s "shall we sound him" (2.1.141), and in *As You Like It* in Rosalind's "that thou didst know how many fathom deep I am in love! But it cannot be sounded; my affection hath an unknown bottom" and Celia's "or rather, bottomless – that as fast as you pour affection in it, it runs out" (4.1.205–10).[2]

"Sound" in its multiple senses is repeatedly foregrounded in Shakespeare, including as the "whole," undiseased, or opposite of "unsound," as in the exchange on "diseases," syphilitic "French crowns," and "three thousand dolors" in *Measure for Measure* (1.2.53–6):

> [1. GENT:] Thou art always figuring diseases in me, but thou art full of error: I am sound.
> LUCIO: Nay, not (as one would say) healthy; but so sound as things that are hollow.

Resounding with the "dollars" in "dolors" as well as the "hollow," sound registers simultaneously here as unaffected by sexual disease,[3] a claim to wholeness or soundness that ironically resonates in Berowne's "my love to thee is sound, sans crack or flaw" (*Love's Labour's Lost* 5.2.415) together with the possibility of hollow or mere sound, not yet perhaps Macbeth's "sound and fury, signifying nothing" (5.5.27) but potentially only "Idle words … / Unprofitable sounds" (*The Rape of Lucrece*, 1017). In a period when "to fall into a sound" designated its own homophonic double *swoon(d)*, not even the semantic boundaries of sound itself could be wholly governed.[4]

> Here's no sound jest …
> *Titus Andronicus*

> … the eye of man hath not heard, the ear of man hath not seen …
> *A Midsummer Night's Dream*

Impossible as it is to fathom the bottom of sound, we might here at least foreground some sound jests that have escaped attention, perhaps because they are not easy for the eye to hear. In *Titus Andronicus*, a "written" message to Chiron and Demetrius, whose rape of Lavinia has been "deciphered" (4.2.8), involves verses from "Horace" familiar from Lyly's Latin grammar (4.2.20–1): "*Integer vitae, scelerisque purus, / Non eget Mauri jaculis, nec arcu*" ("The man with integrity of life, pure of crime, needs not the arrows or bow of the Moor"). But Aaron the Moor not only comprehends that Titus has sounded out or "found their guilt" and "sends them weapons wrapp'd about with lines / That wound beyond their feeling to the quick" (4.2.26–8), but re-sounds the aural (or sound) jest within "Horace" itself (4.2.24–6):

> Ay, just – a verse in Horace, right, you have it.
> [*Aside*] Now, what a thing it is to be an ass!
> Here's no sound jest!

The lines turn on "sound": not only because what Aaron calls "no sound jest" could "not be sounder,"[5] because the scroll's "written" message is not "sound," or because "no sound" suggests the unsound or unhealthy, but also because of the familiar "sound jest" on "ass" and "whore" within the august Roman "Horace," in a period when Aeneas, Midas, and other names ending in "ass" were routinely subjected to such conflations of high and low through their ungoverned sounds. In a play whose "sound" (or unsound) conflations include "goats" and "Goths" or "Jupiter" and "gibbet-maker," and a translingual context where Latin *integer* itself ironically means whole or sound, "no sound jest" thus manages to sound out an action or "gest" that is anything but healthy or "sound," through the coupling of "whore" and "ass" that appears nowhere to the eye within the "written" script, ferreting or sounding out as the other parties to this "crime" the Moor and Tamora, the "witty Empress" who would herself "applaud Andronicus's conceit" (4.2.30).

Shakespearean sound effects (or sound defects) depend not only on hearing with the eye (as in Sonnet 23) but also on seeing with the ear, including through the vivid reports of the *nuntius* or messenger who produces not "ocular proof" but what might be called a (potentially unsound) "evidence effect," turning the ear into a substitute *oculus* or eye.[6] In *Much Ado About Nothing*, where sound jests on "nothing" and "noting" are joined by the *nothus* or Latin for "bastard," representing "reportingly" (3.1.116) generates a potentially tragic substitute for ocular proof that in *Othello* makes the messenger who puts hearers in "false gaze" (1.3.19) a forerunner of Iago (or Iachimo in *Cymbeline*), a dependence on "auricular assurance" (*King Lear* 1.2.92) that is strikingly foregrounded in *The Winter's Tale*, in a Recognition Scene wholly dependent on seeing with the ear ("that which you hear you'll swear you see" 5.2.32).

In *A Midsummer Night's Dream*, which begins by invoking things momentary "as a sound" (1.1.143), seeing with the ear is part of the apparent nonsense of a Bottom whose "bottomless" dream cannot be sounded, including in "I see a voice! … / To spy and I can hear my Thisby's face" (5.1.192–3).[7] But soundings beyond the reach of the eye are underscored repeatedly in this as in other plays, including in Hermia's "Thou art not by mine eye, Lysander, found; / Mine ear, I thank it, brought me to thy sound" (3.2.181–2), in a scene where Lysander's defection realizes the earlier ungoverned sounds within his own name: "Lie further off yet; do not lie so near … / For lying so, Hermia, I do not lie … / Lysander lied" (2.2.44–57). In a play where the Indian boy who is pivotal to the plot may never actually be seen on stage,[8] his mother the Indian votaress is pure sound effect (2.1.123–35), like the vivid report of the death of Ophelia in *Hamlet* (4.7.166–83), whose "melodious lay" and "clothes spread wide" simultaneously resound with sounds not "in government," yielding the aural ghost-effect of "close spread wide" as well as a different kind of lying or "lay."[9]

… a non est woman …
Barnabe Riche

I haue seene a Ladies Nose
That ha's beene blew …
The Winter's Tale

The sound defects produced by omitting stops that prevent sounds from running together have their counterpart in what might be called elision's "soundeffects." The "all ways" and "always" that sound within Titania's "Faieries be gon, and be alwaies away"[10] confound on the ear what is differentiated in print. The "all swell" that sounds within *All's Well That Ends Well*, a play preoccupied with dilation or swelling,[11] evades ocular proof like the "strumpet" within "The Moor! I know his trumpet" (*Othello* 2.1.178), in a tragedy whose re-soundings range from the "O" in "Othello" or "demon" in "Desdemon" to the "hideous" in the "hid," or "whore" within the "pliant hour" of Othello's speech on his wooing of Brabantio's daughter, just after the evocation of her "greedy ear" (1.3.149–51), contributing to the forging of its "preposterous conclusions" (1.3.329).[12] In *Hamlet* – where poisoning through the ear and Claudius's abusing of the "ear" of Denmark with a "forged process" or report of Old Hamlet's death (1.5.37) anticipates Iago's plan to "abuse" the "ear" of the "Moor" (*Othello* 1.3.395) – such ungoverned sound effects include the "poison ingest" that sounds in "poison in jest" (3.2.234) or the "causeandefect" resounding ironically within the lines that culminate in Polonius's "effect defective comes by cause" (2.2.103), as he promises to ferret or sound out the "cause" of the madness of Denmark's son (or sun).

Such "soundeffects" as well as polyglot soundings were endemic in the period. A "non est" yields an "honest" open to suspicion in Barnabe Riche's "May not a non est woman lodge men and women all together in one chamber,"[13] while Middleton's *It's a Mad World, My Masters* depends for its bawdy not only on the familiar sounding of the low within the apparently high (including "de-*stink*-shuns" in "distinctions") but on the "hole and skirt" within the apparently innocent "Holland skirt."[14] Exploiting what Day's *Isle of Gulls* called the "baudry" of "an ell deepe, and a fathome broad,"[15] Shakespeare's *Comedy of Errors* (3.2) elides the "kitchen wench" Nell with "an ell" (or span of 45 inches), potentially sounding to the ear as a "Nell" broad. In relation to the ear's notoriously open porches (*Hamlet* 1.5.63), the problem of governance or stops posed by such "soundeffects" includes whether there is any stop to potentially infinite jests (quite apart from the unfathomable issue of whether they are intended). Should we tell a student, for example, not to hear (as one recently did) another "Athenian eunuch" in "You Nick Bottom" (1.2.20; 5.1.45), in Shakespeare's comedy of a potentially "bottomless" sounding, when the line immediately preceding it is "Name what part I am for" (2.1.18–19)?

Yet another problem of "sounding out" involves not only regional inflections but also the impossibility of knowing how words in Shakespeare actually sounded, though we know now that it was not like Received Pronunciation or particular constructions of the Bard as an icon of Englishness from earlier colonial periods (projecting the "government" of "sound" across more imperial dominions). Personal histories of intimidation with regard to how Shakespeare "should" sound might be recounted by many of us from different geographies and generations. I remember my embarrassment as a child when my Irish immigrant father taught me to pronounce "ache" the same way as the letter "H" and I was rebuked for my ignorance by a teacher, long before discovering that an entire exchange in *Antony and Cleopatra* (4.7.8) depends on the homophonic sounding of "ache" and "H."

Such divergent Early Modern soundings extend not only to homophones such as "one" and "own" or "sea" and "say" but also to sound effects obscured by differentiated spellings. The "eye," "ay," and "I" rendered in modern editions of *Richard II* as "Ay, no; no, ay; for I must nothing be" (4.1.200) appears in the Folio and other early texts as "I, no; no I,"[16] just as "eye" and "I" (as well as "ay") resound throughout *A Midsummer Night's Dream*, from the opening scene's "Ay me! for aught that I could ever read" (1.1.132) to Hermia's "Methinks I see these things with parted eye" (4.1.189), in a plot where eyes, consent (or "ays"), and the problem of differentiating "I's" play such a major part.[17] Even the letters whose "alphabetical position" Malvolio attempts to construe in the Folio text of *Twelfth Night* ("O shall end, I hope ... I, or Ile cudgell him, and make him cry O ... And then I comes behind ... I, and you had any eye behinde you") may resound with a Chaucerian "nether eye" in a play filled with arsy-versy inversions and "backtricks" of all kinds.[18]

In ways that differently underscore what may be obscured by editorial emendation or modernization, other sound jests that might be more visible even to the eye in the earliest texts are effaced by more modern standardizations of spelling and grammar. In *The Winter's Tale*, as Leontes's jealousy builds on conjectures that lack "sight only" (2.1.177), his newly suspected "boy," Mamillius, engages in an exchange that appears in modern editions as follows (2.1.13–15):

MAM: What color are your eyebrows?
[1.] LADY: Blue, my lord.
MAM: Nay, that's a mock. I have seen a lady's nose
That has beene blue, but not her eyebrows.

But what is here potentially obscured by the spelling of "blue" appears in the Folio as the double-meaning sound of "blew" (Folio: *TLN* 602–05):

MAM. ... What colour are your eye-browes?
LADY. Blew (my Lord.)

MAM. Nay, that's a mock: I haue seene a Ladies Nose
That ha's beene blew, but not her eye-browes.

Readers of modern editions may miss the "mock" (or confusion) entirely here, since it depends not only on the sound and Early Modern spelling of "blew" for the colour we know as "blue" but on a construction that modern grammar would render as a nose that has been "blown" (not "blew"). But as with so many Shakespearean sound jests, what might seem only a marginal quibble has much larger resonances within the play as a whole. In the same scene as this sounding of things that can (or cannot) be "blew," Leontes assumes the legitimacy of his own sounding out of what is lacking in "sight" or ocular proof, and Hermione tells Mamillius (of his "tale" best for "winter") to "giv't me in mine ear" (2.1.32), in a plot whose Recognition Scene will depend on what is seen by the ear and a play whose very title begs the question of the "credit" (5.1.179) or credibility to be given to reports or "tales."

Hermaphrodite phrases … halfe Latin and halfe English.
Nashe, *Strange newes*

Tailler. To cut, slit, slice, hew, hacke, slash, gash; nicke … also, to geld.
Cotgrave's *Dictionarie of the French and English Tongues*

As with the Latin lines from "Horace" in *Titus Andronicus* or the macaronic sounding of English "honest" in Barnabe Riche's "a non est woman," polyglot soundings resonate throughout the works of Shakespeare and his contemporaries in ways we need to hear for interpretive and not just more narrowly linguistic reasons. In *The Merchant of Venice*, for example, the Clown who abandons the "Jew" for the service of a "Christian" is named not Lancelot (the spelling in modern editions) but "Lancelet" or "Launcelet," identifying him with the knife that Rabelais called "le lancelet qu'utilisent les chirurgiens,"[19] or the surgeons' "lancelet" associated with the bloodletting, circumcision, and castration that are central within the entire play.[20] In *Othello*, the "Signior Angelo" on whom so much critical ink has been spilled in attempts to locate a precise historical referent for the messenger who puts the Venetians in "false gaze" (1.2.16) bears (like "Angelo" in *Measure for Measure*) a name that identifies him not only with the devil disguised as an "angel of light"

(2 Corinthians 11:14), but also with the familiar generic term for such a bearer of reports (from Greek *angelos* or messenger), exploited in Nashe's description of Harvey as "no Angell but ANGELOS, id est, Nuntius, a Fawneguest Messenger."[21]

In *Antony and Cleopatra*, whose transvestite staging is foregrounded when the Egyptian queen evokes the "boy" actor who plays her (5.2.220), "Salt Cleopatra" (2.1.21) resonates not only with Latin *sal* or "salt" but also with the *saltator* or dancer familiar from Plautus's and other descriptions of seductive transvestite dancers,[22] a term Shakespeare repeats (with a different inflection) in the "Saltiers" or dancers of *The Winter's Tale* (4.4.327). Antony's wearing of Cleopatra's "tires and mantles" (2.5.22) involves not just a gendered but a cultural cross-dressing, in a period where the "tyres of the head"[23] came (like the English *attire*) from "the Latine word *Tiara*, which is an ornament of the heads of the Persian Kings, Priests, and Women ... such as the Turkes weare at this day."[24] And in this play where the "captainship" of Antony is described as emasculated or "nicked" (3.13.8), "tailors of the earth," in a passage that includes "members" and "cut" (1.2.168–76), turns on the French sense of *tailleur* (cutter or gelder) as well as on the familiar sexual sense of "tail" exploited in *Romeo and Juliet* (1.2.40) or the Tailor scene of *The Taming of the Shrew*.

The Shakespeare who would later become an icon of "Englishness" but whose language reflects the more polyglot resonances of early modern London is thus frequently more easily heard by students or interpreters who may be less narrowly Anglocentric. My Spanish-speaking students in California can hear not only the market sounding in the "Mercatio" of *Two Gentlemen of Verona*, but, in contrast to my English-only students from San Diego, the Santiago or St. James in whose name the Moors were driven out of Spain, evoked by the name of Iago in *Othello*, in a period when Dekker in *The Whore of Babylon* could refer to St. James's in London itself as "St. Iago's" and a linguistic environment in which the related name of King James could be alternately sounded as Jacobus, Jacob, Jacques, or Jaques.[25]

Such polyglot soundings also made it possible for Shakespeare and his contemporaries to exploit the ear's ability to hear sounds simultaneously and macaronically in multiple linguistic registers. Nicholas Udall could play on the vernacular "rice pudding cake" sounding within the more august Latin *respublica*.[26] Thomas Nashe could hear Latin *moechus* (fornicator or adulterer) as well as the "Mecca" where "Mahomet was hung up" sounding within the English "mechanicall."[27] *Twelfth Night* and *Much Ado* depend on the sound of the French "cinquepace" (or "five steps" dance) as the "sink-a-pace" (or "sink-a-piss") of its vernacular resonance. A man's "good foot" in *Much Ado* (2.1.14) and the wordplay in *Love's Labour's Lost* on "Loves her by the foot ... He may not by the yard" (5.2.668–9) turn on the sounding of French *foutre* in English "foot," while French *fautre* compounds this sound (or unsound) nexus with the sense of female (or sexual) "faults" crucial to *Hamlet*, *Merry Wives*, and other Shakespeare plays. In *A Midsummer Night's Dream*, the comic rendering of "Ninus's tomb" as "Ninny's tomb" turns on yet another bilingual "sound jest" – since in the Ovidian Latin when Pyramus and Thisbe plan to meet "ad busta Nini," the genitive *Nini* for this Babylonian ruler already sounds like "ninny" or fool. In *The Merry Wives of Windsor* (Shakespeare's only "English" comedy), the genitive case itself famously sounds as "Jinny's case" to the vernacular ear of Mistress Quickly or Quick-lie, in a scene of translation where "vocative" is heard as "focative," Latin *horum* as English "whore'um," *qui*'s, *quae*'s, and *quod*'s as sexually doublemeaning "keys," "case," and "cods," *pulcher* as "polecats" or prostitutes, *caret* (or "lacks") as phallic "carrot," and Latin *lapis* as English "pebble" or the ungoverned sound of "peeble" or testicle (4.1).

In the linguistic borderland of Navarre that provides the setting for *Love's Labour's Lost*, the "feast of languages" repeatedly depends on such polyglot or translingual soundings, including not only the Latin *quis quis* heard as English "kiss kiss," *haud credo* as "old grey doe," and *ad unguem* as "ad dunghill" (already glossed by editors), but also polyglot sound jests that may be more difficult for us to hear, including the French "sign of she" (or *elle*) in the wordplay on "sorel" (4.2.58–60), or the *sorella* or sister that was the familiar *lingua franca* for a less than "honest" woman in the scene that also features a "pricket" (4.2.12–59).[28]

In *Henry V*, where the fiction of a defective Welsh sounding produces the comparison of the English king to "Alexander the Pig," and undermining faultlines, breaches, or "leaks" continue to sound even in ostensibly faithful (and successfully subordinated) Welsh "leeks," macaronic soundings that are themselves compounds or hybrids (like the "compound ... boy," half French, half English) undermine the very sense of secure boundaries or dominion that the play's rhetoric of mastery and containment labours to construct, simultaneously suggesting (in "Anglois" or "Anglish") the angles or breaches that threaten the England described as a "nook-shotten isle."[29] Even the ungovernable, uncontainable, or incontinent sound of "leek" (or "leak") may be echoed in the play's bilingual rendering of the Salic Law as the "Law Salique" (1.2.11), or "Sal-leek," generating the curious scene of "salt" and "leek" inserted between the triumphant Chorus of Act V and the final "Wooing" scene,[30] where (in a reminder of the past and future vulnerability of inheritance through a "female" line) Henry both marries the French king's daughter and insists that he be named son (or "fils") and heir or "Héritier de France" (5.2.339–40).

Together with the likelihood that Shakespeare read the narrative source for *Othello* in Italian,[31] the evidence of other sources accessed in French, and the echoes of Ovid's Latin (and not just Golding's Englishing) elsewhere in the canon, *Henry V* provides the most striking staging of a Shakespeare who was clearly not "English only." But not even this play's macaronic or polyglot soundings have been exhaustively sounded out. Deanne Williams has recently argued, for example, for even more interlingual connections within its famous Language Lesson, including its sounding in "arma" (for "arm") of the famous opening of the *Aeneid* (*Arma virumque cano*, "I sing of arms and the man"), appropriate for a play that repeatedly invokes the "Roman disciplines" of war (3.2.73) as well as the expansion of English empire or dominion.[32] At the same time, the language lesson of *Henry V* provides in its re-sounding of English "gown" as the sexually suggestive "count," a clue to its sounding elsewhere in Shakespeare, in the "loose-bodied gown" described as "quaint" (another homophone of "count") in *The Taming of the Shrew* (4.3), in the scene where Petruchio threatens to beat the tailor with his "yard" and Grumio concludes (of "Take up my mistress' gown to his master's use!") that "the conceit is deeper than you think" (4.3.86–162). In relation to the translingual soundings of French and English, *Henry V* may also provide a useful language lesson. The French-English scenes of *Henry V* include the English Pistol and his French prisoner, whose very name ("Monsieur Le Fer" or "Master Fer") not only occasions bawdy sound jesting on English "fer and ferret and firk" (4.4.26–31) but macaronically sounds the *ferre* at the root of the play's insistent harping on ferrying, translating, or conveying (including the sense of "convey" as "steal"), together with the French "iron" (or *fer*) that makes this scene a comic declension not only from any sense of a "golden" age but even from the "brass" sounding just before it in the King's claim that the English victory will "live in brass" (4.3.97), ironically re-sounded when Pistol hears the prisoner's French "bras" (or arm) as "brass" ("Offer'st me brass?") and, expecting gold, contemptuously rejects it (4.4.16–20). Even within an apparently English-only range, sounds are difficult enough to govern, as Quince's misstopped Prologue makes clear. But in a linguistic environment that exploited the translative sounding of French "Dieu" in Pistol's English "Dew" (4.4.6–7) or, in a much higher register, could sound an "adieu" in Hamlet's "a dew" (1.2.130), putting a stop to the macaronic effects of sound or sounding a bottom is even more uncertain.

In a canon where the Folio's "Fortinbras" (which we might at first think should be pronounced as in modern French "bras" or "-BRA") appears in the Second Quarto as "Fortinbrasse,"[33] the fact that not only English but French could sound differently from the way we have been trained to pronounce it may also affect other sound effects in Shakespeare and his contemporaries, as well as our ability to sound them out. Lines in *As You Like It* turn on a French-English pun on "boys" and "bois" (or woods) that is difficult to sound out because we do not hear "boys" in modern French "bois" (even though it is the sound still heard in the pronunciation, for example, of the name of the twentieth-century writer W.E.B. Du Bois). But the sounding of "boys" within "bois" may provide not only an instructive language lesson for *As You Like It* (a play that after all foregrounds both a "Ganymede" and the French-sounding "de Boys"), but also for the "boys" (or "damn boys") sounding within Chapman's *Bussy D'Ambois* (a name we are used to pronouncing instead as modern French "d'AmBWA"), a play whose "B" text exploits the "ambo" (or "both") within Bussy's last name "D'Amboys" and a plot that moves in both directions across the hetero-homo divide.[34] At the same time, far from being mere verbal "quibbles," such polyglot or homophonic soundings frequently forged larger cultural associations in the period. The pervasive discursive network that conflated Barbary and the "barbarous" with barbering or cutting of all kinds, including castration and circumcision, was compounded by translingual influences to which the best guides are the period's own polyglot dictionaries, though they are still not widely used by cultural historians or critics. Minsheu's *Guide unto the Tongues* (1617) observes that "Barbers shoppe" appears in other languages as "Barberie" or "Barberia," while Cotgrave's *Dictionarie of the French and English Tongues* (1611) notes that French "Barbarie" simultaneously designated a "barbarisme," "the trade of a Barber," and "a port, or Province, of Affrike." Florio's Italian–English *Worlde of Wordes* (1598) records that *Andar in barberia* meant "to go and be cured or laide of the pocks," while *Barbiera* was not only a "shee-barber" but a "common harlot" (1598) or "strumpet" (1611), an important contributor to contemporary associations of "Barbary" with the loss of hair through syphilis. When Ben Jonson treats of "A half-witted Barbarism! which no Barber's art, or his balls, will ever expunge out," Sir John Harington combines "barbarous" Latin with "Mydas Barber," or Joseph Swetnam compares a lascivious woman to "a Barbers chaire, that so soone as one knaue is out another is in" – a connection likewise evoked in the "barber's chair" of *All's Well That Ends Well* (2.2.17) – the nexus of associations is one that was enabled by such homophonic and macaronic crossings, in a period when "barbe" itself was used in English for the beard (as in Shakespeare's variant sounding of Roman Enobarbus as "Enobarbe"), even though "barbe" and "beard" do not come from the same root.[35]

The sound (or unsound) conflation of "barbarous" and "barberous" or Barbary with "Barbery," its contemporary variant spelling, may be heard not only in the "barberous" Moor of *Titus Andronicus* (5.1.97; 5.3.4; 1594 Quarto) who engineers Lavinia's barbaric cutting, or in Enobarbus's description of Antony as "barber'd ten times o'er" at his first meeting with the Egyptian Queen (*Antony and Cleopatra* 2.2.224), but also in the "barbers of Barbary" identified with castrating or gelding in Heywood's *Fair Maid of the West*;[36] in the "Barbor" named Nick in Beaumont's *Knight of the Burning Pestle* (3.2.78), who by calling himself "Barbarossa" (3.3.28) echoes the famous Barbary corsair and the barber (or *barbero*) Nicolas from Cervantes' *Don Quixote*, and in Dekker's *Gull's Hornbook*, which glosses its extended discussion of hair and the shaving of captives by the "Mahumetan cruelty" of the "Turks," in a new chapter that professes to be wearied by sailing along these "shores of *Barbaria*" (17). But the contemporary association also sounds within non-literary reports of the North African or Barbary coast, in descriptions of the shaving, circumcizing, or castrating of Christian captives by "barbarous" (or "barberous") others, including the description in Hakluyt of the voyage in which Englishmen were forcibly "circumcised" as well as "most violently shaven, head and beard" by "infidels" in "Barbarie."[37]

Such polyglot soundings traverse even the most famous Shakespearean tragedy, *Hamlet*, whose early texts bear the traces of a much less "English" production than its subsequent edited version might suggest. Spanish-sounding terms include the *malhecho* of the Folio's "Miching Malicho" (140–1);[38] "student" is spelled "studient" in both Q1 and Q2 (34–5), influenced by what we render into modern French as *étudiant*; the variations between the Folio's "wee coated them on the way," Q2's "we coted them on the way," and Q1's "We boorded them a the way" (100–1) depend on the French *aborder* and *à côté* that likewise sound within the passage of *Twelfth Night* on "Mistress Accost" ("'Accost' is front her, board her, woo her, assail her," 1.3.52–9). The French-sounding "car(r)iage(s)" of all three texts of the speech of the figure known in conflated modernized editions as "Osric" (252–3) may take us back to the first scene's "carriage of the article desseigne" (Q2; "Article designe" in F), a phrase that may bear the trace of French *desseigné* (18–19) in the lines (on a "Moity" or "moitie competent" and other French-inflected terms) whose spellings of "Fortinbras" (F), "Fortinbrasse" (Q2), and "Fortenbrasse" (Q1) summon the complex that Pistol had already evoked in his iteration of French *bras* as English "brass."

Similarly, toward the end of *Hamlet*, the "gentleman of Normandy" who is himself seen only through the ear is called in the Second Quarto "Lamord," a French (or Norman) name that combines the sounds of both "amor" and "la mort" – anticipating the multiple corpses of the Graveyard and final duelling scenes. Q2's "Vpon my life *Lamord*," with the description of this figure in both Q2 and F as "incorps't" in the compound senses of "embodied" and "corpse," makes the sound jest even more pointed. At the same time, in a play that is filled with reminders of blackness, including the "Moor" that sounds within the Closet Scene's contrast of the Queen's two husbands, in Hamlet's condemnation of his mother for battening on "this moor" (3.4.67; Q2, Folio "Moore"), "Lamord" resonates with the familiar contemporary homophones of "Moors" and Latin "death" or *mors*, foregrounded in the description of death itself as a "black word" in *Romeo and Juliet* (3.3.27), in the death's head of the casket chosen by "Morocco" in *The Merchant of Venice*

(2.7.63), in the visualization of Black Death as a Moor, and in the skulls that appeared on maps of Africa in the period.[39]

Within the wider Shakespeare canon, the polyglot sounds of *amor* and *à mort* resonate not only in the "grove of sycamore" (Folio "Sycamour") identified with the love-sick Romeo in *Romeo and Juliet* (1.1.121), but also in the "sycamore" (Folio "Sicamour") of *Othello* (4.3.40–5), as part of a rich network of multilingual soundings that forged connections in the period between *amor*, the "more" or "Moor" tree, *Mors* or "black" death, and *Moria* or folly,[40] resounding in this tragedy in which a Moor who describes himself as having "loved not wisely but too well" (5.2.344) is also, by the end, abjectly identified by Emilia with the moronic or "Dull Moor" (5.2.224) and the "coxcomb" of the fool (5.2.233). In the culture beyond the plays, the sound (or unsound) conflation of *amor* and "Moor" that can be heard as well in the overtones of "T'amo" and of *mora* or 'dark woman' in the name of "Tamora," paramour of the Moor in *Titus Andronicus*, influenced the representation of Moors in visual as well as in verbal contexts, from the demonizing description of "the great seducer Mahomet" as "a lustfull *Amoroso*"[41] to the decorative artistry of the Gresley Jewel, where a "Mora" or female Moor is surrounded by "Amoretti" or figures of Amor that were originally coloured black.[42]

In resonances that were so culturally charged – including the sounding of "wrath" as well as of "Amor" and "Moor" in the contemporary rendering of the Ottoman Amurath as "Amourath," or the conflating of "Muly" with "mules" in multiple texts of the period, including Middleton's *Spanish Gypsy* ("is it a mule? send him to Muly Crag-a-whee in Barbary") – sound forged connections beyond logic or even etymologic, producing conflations that resounded both within and beyond the literary or fictional.[43] Such soundeffects – far too pervasive and numerous to sound out here – likewise conflated "Moorian" with the "murren," "murrain," or "murrian" (the plague or pestilence associated with the biblical Egypt as the Land of Ham), assimilating blackness itself (described as an "infection") to a contagion identified with Ham's Moorish or black descendants. The threatened infection of "white" by such "murrion" contagion is evoked in a scene of Heywood's *Fair Maid of the West*, for example, when a Moroccan ruler attempts to kiss a virginal English Bess: "Must your black face be smooching my mistress's white lips with a Moorian?"[44] But it was, at the same time, part of a culturally much more pervasive nexus, conflating the blackness of "Moors" not only with the sound of a miscegenating or "murrian" contagion but with the polyglot overtones with which it was further compounded, reflected in Florio's 1598 Italian "*Moria*, an infection, a pestilence, a murrian, a rot or mortalitie that comes among sheepe. Also used for follie and taken from the Greeke." In such cases, unless we, as textual critics and editors or as historians of early modern culture, endeavour to hear the multiple soundings that contributed to such culturally overdetermined connections, we may not be able to see (with the eye or the ear) elisions of other kinds that were crucially important in the period.

Continental Sexuality and the Auditory Construction of Early Modern Englishness

LAUREN COKER

Ferdinand: You are a good horseman, Antonio. You have excellent riders in France. What do you think of good horsemanship?
The Duchess of Malfi 1.1.141–3[1]

Ferdinand's characterization of Antonio as a "good horseman" in Webster's *The Duchess of Malfi* reflects Antonio's occupation. But "good horseman" is also a nuanced characterization that speaks to Antonio's time in France and to Antonio's relationship to Ferdinand's widowed sister, the Duchess. It is therefore crucial to remember that an early modern English audience would hear (not read) the jealous Ferdinand's dialogue. What looks to a reader like "horseman" can be processed by listeners as horseman and "whores-man" – a lascivious insult that attempts to make Antonio a panderer and the Duchess a prostitute. Yet sexually charged puns on "horse" or "horseman" are not restricted to *The Duchess of Malfi*. The auditory construction of Italian or French characters as hyper-sexualized stereotypes – by way of horse puns – appears in various early modern English texts and dramas. These *double entendres* elicit a community of insiders: in this case, an English-speaking audience who "gets" the pun on Continental outsiders. Indeed, puns on horses and horsemanship in early modern English texts such as Sidney's *An Apology for Poetry*, as well as in dramas such as Webster's *The*

Duchess of Malfi and Shakespeare's *Henry V*, construct Continental sexuality as lascivious and other.[2] The puns also allow for rhetorical constructions of English identities within an exclusively English discursive framework. The word "horse" lacks any obvious linguistic trace of Continental influence (particularly Latin, French, or Italian).[3] Puns, defined by Jonathan Culler as a presentation of "the disquieting spectacle of a functioning of language where boundaries – between sounds, between a sound and letter, between meanings – count for less than one might imagine," create a community of insiders and outsiders. In this case, the insiders are early modern English audiences who hear and process the *double entendres*.[4]

These puns not only resound with what audiences hear but also more generally with early modern notions of methods of horsemanship – and even types of horses – as representative of one's national identity. As Karen Raber and Treva Tucker stress, the "English approach [to horsemanship] was juxtaposed to the continental one in ways that made it clear that the English method was not merely different from but also far better than that practiced by the (detested) French and those who followed their ideas." Raber and Tucker emphasize that "the specifically English" type "thus can be seen as one expression of a burgeoning national identity, in which horsemanship served to create a sense of both cultural differentiation and cultural superiority."[5] Because national identities were linked to types of horses and horsemanship, I explore the resonances of "horse," "horseman," and "horsemanship" alongside Walter J. Ong's conception of the residually oral nature of early modern English textuality and, by extension, "Englishness."[6] Though Renaissance humanist education and composition are rooted in Continental intertexuality through the emphasis on the Classics and Latin-language learning,[7] the English pun on "horse" bridges an assortment of social classes of English speakers and listeners.[8] In the cases of Sidney, Webster, and Shakespeare, representations of cultural inferiority via Continental horses/whores are amplified through their relationship to sexual deviance. The portrayal of Continental horsemanship, though accompanied by often humorous *double entendres*, alludes to bestiality, prostitution, and incest – common taboos of sexual and social otherness.[9] By hearing the puns on horses as whores venture into socially restricted sexual taboos, English-speaking listeners are encouraged to identify with non-deviance and to align themselves with a "healthy" English body politic – and distance themselves from a sexually aberrant French or Italian national body.

THE "FERTILENESS OF ITALIAN WIT": BREEDING ENGLISH RHETORIC IN *AN APOLOGY FOR POETRY*

Although it was not performed on stage for an audience, *An Apology for Poetry* contains residually oral elements that can be processed not only through visual engagement but also through auditory interaction. As Ong has argued, Renaissance authors composed texts as though they had a listening audience, and Early Modern English texts such as Sidney's *Apology* were oral and written hybrids often meant to be read aloud.[10] Similarly, Patricia Parker aptly explains that audiences of these texts were intended to be "seeing with the ear" and "hearing with the eye,"[11] while Paul Saenger emphasizes that although "[m]odern reading is a silent, solitary, and rapid activity," reading in earlier periods "was usually oral, either aloud, in groups, or individually, in a muffled voice."[12] In Sidney's opening to *An Apology for Poetry*, the puns on Italian horsemanship allow rhetoric and national identity to come together. The oration begins with a narrator praising the "horsemanship of John Pietro Pugliano," an Italian soldier who "had the place of an esquire in his stable." Sidney's narrator continues, "And he, according to the fertileness of the Italian wit, did not only afford us the demonstration of his practice, but sought to enrich our minds with the contemplations therein which he thought most precious." The narrator then recalls one of Pugliano's most memorable speeches, saying, "But none I remember mine ears were at any time more loaden than when … he exercised his speech in praise of his faculty." The narrator adds that Pugliano has attempted to argue that "soldiers were the noblest state of mankind, and horsemen the noblest of soldiers." The narrator then points out that Pugliano has claimed that "no earthly thing bred such wonder … as to be a good horseman." The narrator concludes: "[I]f I had not been a piece of a logician before I came to him, I think he would have persuaded me to have wished myself a horse. But thus much at least with his no few words he drave into me, that self-love is better than any gilding to make that seem gorgeous wherein ourselves are parties."[13] Sidney's opening operates as a meta-rhetorical commentary on the construction of language and argument as well as its occasional ineffectiveness. The opening is also laden with references to breeding: the Italian horseman has a certain "fertileness" of wit that has "bred ... wonder." Sidney's references to fertility and breeding are, of course, bound up with sexuality. A subtly erotic relationship also surfaces between Pugliano's voice and the narrator's ear. Pugliano's paean on horsemanship has aurally penetrated – or, as Sidney writes, "loaden" and "drave into" – the narrator as the horseman speaks (even to the point where the narrator almost wishes himself a horse).

The opening's imagery entangles with constructions of Continental sexuality as excessive and – in its flirtation with bestiality – socially taboo. The sexuality stands out when considering early modern conceptions of horsemen. In fact, one of the earliest denotations of "horseman" (1400) refers to "one skilled in riding and managing a horse,"[14] reflecting a sense of agency and control – stereotypically masculine qualities. Another early modern denotation of "horsemanship" (1566) reads, "[T]he breeding, rearing, and management of horses."[15] Breeding and riding are terms that can easily transfer to the carnal body and copulation. Because Sidney's narrator posits the visual of nearly wishing himself a horse for the horseman who "drave" words into him, animal breeding parallels human homoeroticism – with the horse-turned-narrator, on the surface, becoming a product of domination and feminization. The narrator's invocation of breeding also conjures images of bestiality. Furthermore, given the conflation of the early modern woman with an uncontrollable mare,[16] the narrator's ultimate evasion of wishing himself a horse to a sexually and rhetorically uncontrollable Italian horseman also becomes an assertion of English – and stereotypically masculine – discursive autonomy. The description brims with eroticism while positioning Pugliano as a figure of hyper-sexuality. But since Sidney's narrator chooses not to be persuaded by Pugliano's speech, and because he ultimately claims the speech is a product of "self-love," the Italian horseman's praise for soldiers of the same occupation ultimately becomes an autoerotic and useless endeavour, which, ironically, lacks any "fertileness."[17] Sidney's mockery of Pugliano as Italian horseman and rhetorician, moreover, is historically in line with the general attitude towards Italian horsemanship in late sixteenth-century England. According to Nicholas Russell, the Italian horseman, horse, and breeder were initially idealized; however, "[t]he direct influence of Italian horsemen in England seems to have ceased in the early 1580s."[18] By suggesting that Italian horsemanship and Italianate rhetoric are lacking, Sidney opens up his argument for an "English" approach to discourse.

In addition to the visual descriptions Sidney uses to characterize the Italian horseman (and his going out of favour among English riders), the residually oral nature of Sidney's opening cannot be ignored. English-speaking listeners would arguably process the *double entendre* of "horsemanship," and this is a unifying experience for those who hear the term's dual meaning. Walter Redfern, in his 1984 study on puns, engages with the history and criticism of wordplay, citing the pun's ability to "'[transcend] class distinctions.'"[19] In the case of Sidney's *Apology*, Redfern's claim rings true, as the words would have a discursive resonance to English audiences – allowing already lewd constructions of the Italian wit to become even more comical puns. These puns play not only with a stereotype of the nation's sexuality but also with the nation's excessive and self-praising use of rhetoric. In addition, although Patricia Parker has suggested that some audiences of non-English nationalities can often detect Early Modern puns with greater ease,[20] English audiences (particularly those who knew Italian) could imagine that the puns on horsemanship in *An Apology for Poetry* would be less obvious or possibly even inaccessible to the Italian-speaking soldier or other Italian-speaking audiences in question. None of the Italian words for "whores" visually or orally resemble the English word "horse."[21] In essence, Sidney creates a community of English insiders and a cast-out group of Italian outsiders by discursive and rhetorical mockery aimed at Pugliano.

Sidney thus separates English audiences and English rhetoric from their Italian equivalents, and carves a space for his upcoming oration that devotes itself to an English discursive identity. Sidney's push for an English discursive identity is significant in the context of the English Renaissance: "English" as we know it was in a nascent stage of formation during the early modern era. In fact, Paula Blank points out that Early Modern "English" was essentially a foreign language – even to native speakers.[22] But Blank maintains that, at the time, "language ... stood in relation to other languages."[23] By distinguishing "English" rhetoric from "Italian" rhetoric, while concurrently playing with the stereotype of Italian sexuality through horse/whores imagery and puns (a technique which is, essentially, low and grotesque humour hidden within an eloquent and traditional model of oration), Sidney creates a group of English insiders who understand and laugh at the wordplay on horsemanship. In this "insider" group formation, a separate and unique English national identity surfaces. This English identity works, as Blank might claim, to make "the British empire as a single 'body,' naturalizing the disparate peoples it contains as one people."[24]

Although Sidney later claims drama is inferior to poetry, the ability of both genres to shape a discursive national body by way of puns allows for continuity between Sidney's opening to the oration and the dramatic works of his contemporaries. Unlike an *Apology for Poetry*, dramas such as *The Duchess of Malfi* and *Henry V* were explicity intended for a listening audience. As Ong has contended, "When a speaker is addressing an audience, the members of the audience normally become a unity, with themselves and the speaker."[25] The early modern English theatrical audience, as we know, was composed of attendees from a variety of social spheres, but the sense of unity prompted through audience and speaker is applicable to the "us" (British) versus "them" (French and Italian) puns in *Henry V* and *The Duchess of Malfi*. Yet the discursive construction of an early modern English linguistic identity becomes even more complex when considering representations of horsemanship on the Renaissance stage. Portraying these dramas on the Continent (in Webster's case, Italy, and in Shakespeare's case, France) or staging Continental characters within an English setting – all the while performing them in England for an English audience – creates a distinct auditory opportunity for English audiences of various social strata to unite as a national discursive body. Shakespeare, for example, employs several puns on horses and horsemanship throughout *Henry V*, brought to the stage in 1599 (only five years after the posthumous publication of Sidney's *Apology*). *The Duchess of Malfi* also uses horse puns to construct Continental characters as sexually other.

"MY HORSE IS MY MISTRESS": BESTIALITY AND THE FRENCH CAMP IN *HENRY V*

A majority of Shakespeare's *Henry V* takes place in France, and the Prologue indicates the upcoming setting from the drama's outset. He teasingly asks, "Can this cock-pit hold / The vasty fields of France?" (11–12)[26] The Prologue's rhetorical question seems, on first blush, to point to theatrical underpinnings: of course, the audience only sees the "pit" of the stage and must rely on imagination and the actors' discourse to conceptualize other locales as the drama's action unfolds. Yet the term "vasty fields" also evokes the feminine. It connects with a grassy and overgrown feminized French landscape.[27] Thus, while the Prologue's question is playful, the aural and visual images within it establish a pattern for the drama's development. The feminized French fields are contained (or, as the Prologue puts it, held) within the "cok-pit" of the English theatre and, by extension, England. While transporting the "vasty fields of France" to the English stage, Shakespeare devotes significant attention to framing the audience as English-speaking. He highlights the varied turns of phrase and colloquialisms that English speakers from varied social backgrounds may use. Several English dialects are represented, ranging from Henry's to those of the socially lower-tier English speakers in the London slum of Cheapside, to the slightly inferior Scottish and Irish dialects of Jamy and Macmorris. In Cheapside, several characters (in particular the Hostess) use truncated words and informal colloquialisms (2.3.9–23). Likewise, Macmorris, the Irishman, often uses "tish" to articulate "it is" in ways that reflect on his on discursive and national identity. He asks, "Of my nation? What ish my nation? Ish a villain and a bastard and a knave and a rascall? What ish my nation?" (2.3.61–2) Jamy, a Scot, swaps "gud" for "good," saying, "It sall be vary gud, gud faith" (3.3.43–5). Linguistically, the *meaning* of their speech remains accessible to the English-speaking audiences of *Henry V*. Even though these dialects are varied, and although they do reflect (and, at times, satirize) speakers of numerous social and geographical backgrounds, they all *share* the English language.

The audience is directly addressed by the Chorus, who acts as a guide for the spectators as they metaphysically transport themselves from England to the new French setting for the latter portion of the drama. The Chorus tells audience to "leave *your England* … For who is he … that will not follow / The culled and choice-drawn cavaliers to France?" (3.0.19–24, emphasis added). The Chorus's use of the plural "your" to address "England" demonstrates a collectivity among the spectators – regardless of social standing. In other words, the discursive hierarchy mirrors the lack of a social hierarchy among the English-speaking characters on stage. Because the Chorus addresses the English-speaking audience communally, the hierarchy becomes less apparent – even subverted – upon the play's relocation to France. Instead, a group mentality surfaces by way of audience-specific dialectic turns. The implied audience, a community of English speakers from varied social and geographical positions, is allowed to unify and laugh at Shakespeare's construction of the French, particularly through the dialogue at camp. The sexuality bound up with the horsemen at the French camp in Shakespeare's *Henry V* correlates with homoeroticism and bestiality. For instance, the Constable claims Orléans has "the best horse of Europe" (3.7.5). Bourbon then interjects himself into the dialogue by characterizing the mythic status of his horse:

> What a long night this is! I will not change my horse with any treads but on four pasterns. Ah ha! He bounds from the earth as if his entrails were hares – *le cheval volant*, the Pegasus, *qui a les narines de feu*! When I bestride him, I soar, I am a hawk; he trots the air, the earth sings when he touches it, the basest horn of his hoof is more musical than the pipe of Hermes. (3.7.11–17)

The resonance of "horse" to the (English-speaking) audience would resemble "whores" once more. In this instance, Bourbon's description of his horse comes across as a sexual celebration. Although the men are preparing for battle, Bourbon turns a lengthy night of dread into a night of excitement spent with an animal. Bourbon says "long night" in an exclamatory phrase. He then exclaims "Ah ha" in ways that reverberate as a breathy echo of erotic exuberance when recalling his interactions with the horse as he soars while riding him. While Bourbon defamiliarizes riding his horse into a mythological experience, the *double entendre* on horse as whore crafts a different message for the audience. The message is, for English-speaking listeners, a comical representation of Continental bestiality – and, because Bourbon's horse is male, homoeroticism.[28] The insertion of homoeroticism alongside bestiality thus undercuts any potential for praising the French horseman's sexual prowess, particularly because (at least initially) Bourbon stumbles on to the bestial relationship with his horse as whore; he is unaware that his boasts are laden with erotic and sexually taboo undertones.[29]

As Bourbon and Orléans continue their discussion, the dialogue shifts from an image of mythical bestiality between Frenchman and (male) horse to a more rhetorically based reflection:

> BOURBON: Turn the sands into eloquent tongues, and my horse is argument for them all. 'Tis a subject for a sovereign to reason

> on, and for a sovereign's sovereign to ride on, and for the world, familiar to us and unknown, to lay apart their particular functions, and wonder at him. I once writ a sonnet in his praise, and began thus: 'Wonder of nature!–'
> ORLÉANS: I have heard a sonnet begin so to one's mistress.
> BOURBON: Then they did imitate that which I composed to my courser, for my horse is my mistress. (3.7.31–40)

Even though "mistress" generally refers to a female, Bourbon continues to refer to his animal as male. Bourbon also turns his whore/horse into a muse for both sovereign and poet – offering a biting commentary on the French body politic as well as French arts. The French sovereign is "to ride on" the horse/whore for political inspiration, and the French poet is (when considering the near-homophones "write" and "ride") also to "write on" the horse/whore for artistic motivation. The rhetorical and governmental activities are carnivalesque inversions of sexual and political inspiration, which draw from a bestial take on whores and horsemanship. These humorous rhetorical inversions therefore distance the English body politic from the French body politic.

Bruce Boehrer also reads the French characters' dialogue on horses in *Henry V* as an "association of horses with foreignness." He suggests that it is horse*play* that acquires prominence in such passages; the Dauphin and Orléans discuss horsemanship as if it were an end unto itself, and this fact exposes the degeneracy of their fondness for equitation, which no longer exists in the context of military training but has devolved instead into a form of pastime and social display. The Dauphin's horse, coupled with his mistress as an object of sonnetry, emerges from this exchange more as an accessory of courtly love than as a weapon.[30]

Outwardly, Boehrer's reading of the horse-turned-mistress in *Henry V* suggests that Shakespeare constructs the French as masculine – but their masculinity is more dependent on sexual conquest than on achievement in battle. Boehrer, however, overlooks the bestiality and occasional homoeroticism that Shakespeare weaves into the dialogue. The French preference for "courtly love" over battle and weaponry in this dialogue at camp – via the male horse as an "object of sonnetry" – offers an invitation to reread French poetry in a different light. Shakespeare not only distances the French body politic from the English by using puns on whores and horses. Shakespeare also distances French poetry from English, as he has rendered the poet's muse and subject a male horse.

Although the earlier portion of the conversation speaks to the French arts and body politic, the latter portion of the dialogue builds on the mistress-as-horse connection in order to combine the act of horseback riding with the act of intercourse. The Constable suggests that Bourbon's mistress "shrewdly shook your back." Bourbon retorts, "So perhaps did yours" (3.7.44–6). The pair continues to throw out a series of sexual derisions that rely on the horse/whore correlation:

> CONSTABLE: Mine was not bridled.
> BOURBON: O then belike she was old and gentle, and you rode like a kern of Ireland, your French hose off, and in your strait tossers.
> CONSTABLE: You have good judgment in horsemanship. (3.7.47–51)

On the surface, this dialogue between Bourbon and the Constable merely comes across as a bawdy attempt to mock one another's sexual conquests. But in the context of how Shakespeare uses the horse-as-whore *double entendre* to construct the French, there is a further attempt to characterize the French as lacking awareness of social and sexual boundaries. The horse/whore is unbridled and beyond the Constable's control. Moreover, the Constable's horse (unlike Bourbon's) is female. Female horses have, throughout history, been viewed as uncontrollable. As Lynda Birke and Keri Brandt point out, "there remains considerable prejudice against mares within many parts of the horse world: mares are widely thought to be fickle and unpredictable, while males are thought to be more reliable."[31] In essence, these *double entendres* on horses, whores, and mistresses in the dialogue are ineffective for both parties: Bourbon's engagement with his horse is homoerotic, and the Constable's engagement with his horse is emasculating in that "the maleness of the horse … reflects the masculinity of the rider."[32]

Shakespeare also uses this scene to insert biting commentary on origins of sexually transmitted disease. Bourbon later claims the horse is a safer option to the mistress, for the horse will not lead him to "foul bogs" – or lead to hair loss as a result of venereal disease. Bourbon's commentary on venereal disease would strike a chord with the audience, as early modern English people generally referred to venereal disease resulting in hair loss (i.e., the pox) as the "French disease":[33]

> BOURBON: Be warned by me then: they that ride so, and ride not warily, fall into foul bogs. I had rather have my horse to my mistress.
> CONSTABLE: I had as lief have my mistress a jade.
> BOURBON: I tell thee Constable, my mistress wears his own hair. (3.7.52–7)

The Constable concludes, "Yet I do not use my horse for my mistress ... Even as your horse bears your praises, who would trot as well were some of your brags dismounted" (3.7.62–3). Although the references to syphilis in this passage are significant, the French violation of social-sexual boundaries most prominently persists through the overt connections to bestiality. Because "jade" can denote "horse" or "whore," the Constable continues to interchange the horse, whore, and mistress. Bourbon continues to voice his sexual preference for a male horse over a female mistress.

Overall, *Henry V* offers a positive construction of the English body politic – chiefly through its representation of the English defeat of the French. But in the camp scene in particular, Shakespeare frames the French as metaphorical "whores-men" by marrying puns on horsemanship with references to the taboo sexual practice of bestiality. Shakespeare's construction of French sexuality through imagery and puns on horsemanship is not unique. Michael Drayton and Nicholas Morgan similarly rely on sexual imagery and puns to reflect national identity and horsemanship. Drayton's "The Ballad of Agincourt," for example, uses references to horses in order to generate English/French binaries related to English masculinity, French femininity, and Henry V's conquest. Drayton writes, "Like a storme, sodainely, / The English archery / Stuck the French horses."[34] Although many early modern English references to horses reflect a hyper-sexualization of the French, Drayton's diction uses puns on horses/whores in a sexually effeminizing way. The phallic and masculine English archery violently penetrates the French whore/horse. Drayton's ballad concludes with further nods to English masculinity and sexuality: "O! when shall Englishmen / With such acts fill a pen, / England breed agen / Such a King Harry?"[35] Drayton's conclusion of the poem bolsters the English body politic and English authorship by suggesting phallic, masculine penmanship is inspired by the English creation (or breeding) of King Henry V.

Morgan equally reflects a tiered attitude towards nationalities and literary constructions of the "horse" in his 1620 work *The horsemans honour, or The beautie of horsemanship*. In a similar vein to Shakespeare's satirical constructions of Jamy and Macmorris as inferior to the English but far superior to the French, Morgan considers English horses to be of "strong and great stature, stout courage and good shape." He claims "there is none [that] can exceede them." Morgan continues, "[t]he horses of Scotland ... are much lesse then those in England, yet not inferiour in goodnesse."[36] Morgan also describes French horses: "Now for the French horse, or horse of France, though he be the worst ... he a good plane ordinary Souldiers horse."[37] Morgan's catalogue of horses deals directly with animals as representative of the body politic, and it reveals a comparable stance to the one put forth in *Henry V*. Morgan suggests the English national identity is superior to the Scottish, and the British national identity is superior to all national identities – particularly the French. Morgan was also known to attack the Italian horse and Italian approach to riding.[38] In this context, although his commentary on horses of varied nationalities lacks sexual undertones, Morgan takes an animal-turned-commodity and renders it a representation of the English nation.[39]

Shakespeare's *Henry V* begins in England and transfers its setting to France, but Webster's *Duchess of Malfi* (though performed in England) has an Italian setting throughout. The Italian location serves as a backdrop for puns on French and Italian sexuality – especially through representations of horsemanship and the commodification of women.[40] However, the sexually driven horse/whore puns and imagery throughout Webster's drama move beyond comical jabs at Continental masculinity. The laughter elicited by horse puns in Sidney and Shakespeare is replaced by a dark critique of Continental (specifically Italian) systems of gender and patriarchy. The representations of gender and patriarchy in Webster's drama provide a tragic mirror to the puns that authors such as Shakespeare and Sidney put forth through representations of the horse as whore. There is, in *The Duchess of Malfi*, a lack of audience unification through laughter at the (often rhetorical) buffoonery of the Continental other on stage, as is the case in *Henry V*. Instead the English audience unifies in its horror at Ferdinand's incestuous relationship to his sister, which is reflected in his construction of the Duchess as a whore/horse figure. Horsemanship *double entendre* and imagery in Webster's drama thus allow the English audience to become an "us," but only in its juxtaposition with the sexually corrupt Continental "them."

THE "SHAMEFUL ACT OF SIN": ITALIAN INCEST IN *THE DUCHESS OF MALFI*

The Duchess of Malfi opens with Delio commenting on Antonio's physical transformation after having spent time in the French court, telling him, "You have long been in France, and you return / A very formal Frenchman in your habit" (1.1.2–3). From the outset, Antonio is framed as an Italian who has taken on French characteristics. In terms of Englishness, Antonio's position deserves acknowledgment; Paula Blank has asserted that "the idea of a 'natural' English was … often associated, rhetorically, with the preservation of an original – and threatened – national identity."[41] By metatheatrically reminding audiences of Antonio's costuming, Webster renders Antonio's fluid national identity a product of his time away from his home. It is also in this scene that Ferdinand establishes Antonio as a "good horseman" (1.1.141). Thus, again, while "horse," "horseman," and "horsemanship" *read* like references to an occupation and an animal, the terms *sound* like different variants of the word "whore" and "whores-man" to English theatre-goers. But it is worth mention that Antonio is often made into a horse/whores-man by the Italian characters on stage: Ferdinand manipulates language in order to deflect his own lascivious behaviour onto Antonio (and later the Duchess). Therefore, while Antonio's time in France does feed into how Italian characters within the play perceive him, the drama's true criticism is situated on Italianate sexuality – which Webster represents through Ferdinand's reliance on incestuous systems of patriarchy and the commodification of women.

Ferdinand, struggling with the Duchess's status as widow, renders his sister an "unbridled" horse/whore figure. After the Duchess compares herself to a diamond of "most value" that has "passed through most jewelers' hands," Ferdinand retorts, "Whores, by that rule, are precious." Immediately after, he tells her, "[y]ou live in a rank pasture" (1.1.302–8). Through the invocation of whore – and through his equation of the Duchess with the term – while characterizing her living situation as a "rank pasture," Ferdinand visually conjures the image of her home as a place for horses. Given the phonetic interchangeability of "whores" and "horse," it is quite feasible that Ferdinand views – and constructs – his sister as mountable and animalistic property: she, like a prostitute and a horse, is rendered a commodity. Hence, while Ferdinand has aurally constructed Antonio as whores/horseman, Ferdinand's actions suggest that he plays an even larger role in the commodification of his sister. As the Duchess selects Antonio as her husband, she expresses her intent to go "into a wilderness" where she believes she "shall find nor path nor friendly clew / to be [her] guide" (1.1.360–2). At this point, the Duchess apparently believes that independence exists in her new marriage to Antonio. However, by taking an animalistic path into "wilderness," the Duchess continues to follow Ferdinand's construction of her as the stereotypical whore / unbridled horse. It is thus worth noting that Mark Breitenberg addresses the English conception of female sexuality as "unbridled," contending that it is sometimes figuratively symbolized by an "uncontrollable horse."[42] While the Duchess leaves the metaphorical "pasture," she still exists in the unbridled whore/horse form that Ferdinand creates for her.

To confirm the assertion that the Duchess adheres to Ferdinand's lewd construction of her as whore / unbridled horse, the Duchess says, "I hope in time 'twill grow into a custom / That noblemen shall come with cap and knee *to purchase* a night's lodging of their wives" (3.2.4–7, emphasis added). In effect, the Duchess expresses her desire to serve as a prostitute for her husband. The Duchess attempts to assert a form of autonomy by marrying Antonio, and thus ultimately adheres to stereotypes of female horses (and, by extension, whores) as "fickle and unpredictable."[43] Indeed, the Duchess opts not to take a fixed path and instead chooses to go into an uncharted, feminized landscape – a "wilderness."[44] Yet the Duchess's accidental complicity in becoming a horse/whore figure is, arguably, one of the less disturbing constructions of Continental sexuality stemming from the "horse" in Webster's drama. Ferdinand's sexually taboo desire – incest – is a subtle but more unsettling feature. In rendering his sister a horse/whore commodity, Ferdinand exhibits an increasing preoccupation with the Duchess's property as well as her physical body. Ferdinand's preoccupation generally comes across through sexual symbolism and undertones. Early on, Ferdinand says to his sister, "Pray let me entreat for / The provisorship of your horse" (1.1.215–16), suggesting he wants to control her (sexual) commodities by proxy as well as to "gain / Access to [her] private lodgings" (1.1.282–3). Later his obsession with her property and "private lodgings" explicitly extends to sexual realms: Ferdinand imagines the Duchess "in the shameful act of sin" with "some strong-thighed bargeman" or "some lovely squire" (2.5.41–5). He then, in a jealous rage, claims that he will burn the bodies of anyone he catches with his sister, and that he will never sleep until he knows who "leaps" the Duchess (2.5.78). He eventually enacts a figurative rape; Ferdinand gains a "false key" to "her bed-chamber" (3.1.80–1) and gives her a phallic poniard so that she can, in the literal and orgasmic sense, "[d]ie, then, quickly!" (3.2.73). Ultimately, in his rendering of the Duchess as sexual property – figured symbolically as a whore or unbridled horse – Ferdinand factors incest into what also could be an out-of-control obsession with his sister-turned-fetish object.

Ferdinand also metaphorically toys with another sexual taboo: necrophilia. He gives the Duchess a dead man's hand, with a ring on it, to kiss (4.1.43–6). The Duchess even acknowledges her brother's incestuous desire for her while again pointing to necrophilia prior to her execution: "Come, violent death ... Go tell my brothers, when I am laid out, then they may feed in quiet" (4.2.231–4). Finally, although Ferdinand relies on the horse-as-whore *double entendre* and imagery to grapple with his sister's widowed status, the sexual taboos of necrophilia and incest are emblematized in Ferdinand himself. These taboos compel English audiences to distance themselves from him, as he is the lascivious other in his disregard for sexual boundaries. Ferdinand's position as a duke in Italy is thus significant: he, too, is a representative of the Italian body politic. This body politic figures into the construction of Italian sexuality as emblematic of sexual corruption. The early modern English textual practice of constructing French and Italian sexuality as corrupt is common. Yet what stands out in Webster's drama – as well as in Shakespeare's *Henry V* and Sidney's *Apology* – is that the construction is not only visually enacted but aurally felt through the audience's processing of the "horse" puns and *double entendres*.

CONCLUSION

Shakespeare's *Henry V* and Sidney's *Apology* play with the resonance of "horse" to unite English-speaking audiences in laughter aimed at a Continental target. But *The Duchess of Malfi* more directly weaves both image and orality to construct Continental characters. The *double entendre* is ominously enacted by Ferdinand and the Duchess – rather than reflected in mere fantasy as when characters such as Bourbon describe their "horse." However, in terms of the English language and identity formation, each text uses *double entendres* related to horses and horsemen to characterize a Continental drive towards early modern sexual taboos such as incest, necrophilia, and bestiality. The use of puns to portray Continental characters as sexually corrupt fosters a sense that the borders and boundaries of English language and identity are caught up not only with linguistics but also with behaviours. These early modern English texts ultimately construct the Continental as a debased other – both sexually and discursively. Overall, this sexual and discursive othering of the Continental attempts to frame English linguistic and national identity as collectively superior.

Introducing "Intrelinguistics": Shakespeare and Early/Modern English

PAULA BLANK

Are Shakespeare's poems and plays written in English?

This is either a very silly question or a very serious question – depending on whom one asks. For linguists, no doubt, the answer is an unqualified "yes," since what we call Early Modern English is phonologically, lexically, and syntactically continuous enough with our own Modern English that scholars cannot and do not draw formal language boundaries between them. Yet as teachers of Shakespeare's texts, and as purveyors of film and theatre adaptations of the plays, we know very well that Shakespeare's language can seem alien to many contemporary readers and audiences, even if our two "Englishes" fail a strictly linguistic criterion of mutual unintelligibility. Technically it is the same vernacular, but experientially Shakespeare may be a foreign language.

This experience has led to recent calls to translate Shakespeare into Modern English, not only from desperate students, but from seasoned Shakespeare scholars as well. The notion that Shakespeare's Early Modern English needs "translation" suggests the extent to which we have started to treat his works seriously as foreign texts. Over a decade ago Susan Bassnett wrote a piece that appeared in the British daily, the *Independent*, titled "Shakespeare's in Danger. We Have to Act Now to Avoid a Great Tragedy." For Bassnett, the "great tragedy" we face isn't *Hamlet* or *Lear* per se but their superannuated language: "The problem with Shakespeare today is linguistic. The language has become obsolete; Shakespeare's jokes are meaningless; actors and audiences alike struggle to make sense of a language that might as well be Tibetan." As a result, "boredom and

Shakespeare increasingly go hand in hand," she writes, citing the apocryphal story about a foreign director who pities us as native English speakers, because we have to read Shakespeare in the original. Bassnett argued that only Modern English translations can avert the tragedy of Shakespeare's otherwise inevitable extinction.

Although her jeremiad caused a stir, it did not inspire a reckoning, since most scholars still appear convinced of Shakespeare's continued accessibility and proceed as if it is just a matter of providing enough context on sixteenth-century English for contemporary readers to grasp and appreciate his particular uses of it. Most, in fact, still insist that Shakespeare's Early Modern English is necessary and indispensible to our experience of his works, despite the consensus that other modern, foreign-language translations, into "almost every imaginable national or regional tongue, as well as … a range of such unlikely languages as Neo-Latin," are successfully "Shakespearean."[1] Russ McDonald contends that "Shakespeare in other words is not Shakespeare,"[2] while perhaps the best-known scholar of and popular guide to Shakespeare's language, David Crystal, titles an essay on the topic "To Modernize or Not to Modernize: There Is No Question" (i.e., there is no question that we *shouldn't*).[3]

My own best guess is that eventually, *will we*, *nill we*, Shakespeare's Early Modern English works will go the way of Old English poetry, and Middle English poetry now, too. That is, some day in the not-so-distant future Shakespeare will be available in Modern English editions, and ones that (we can only hope) surpass our current offerings, the feeble and often unintentionally farcical "No Sweat Shakespeares" and "No Fear Shakespeares." In any event, my point in this essay is not to weigh in on the pros and cons of translating Shakespeare. Instead, I would like to destabilize the debate altogether by suggesting a new approach to Shakespeare's language, designed specifically for native speakers of Modern English. We may be missing an opportunity when we imagine we must either choose Shakespeare's original language (albeit with glosses and other scholarly apparatus to explain particularly hard words and usages) or exchange it for ours. What follows falls between a manifesto and a method for what we can learn from the very friction between the two.

As it appears in titles of earlier books on the subject, the phrase "Shakespeare's language" refers to the resources of Early Modern English, the formal properties and potentialities of the English vernacular spoken and written in the sixteenth and early seventeenth centuries, and the uses Shakespeare put them to. This has always been and remains a reasonable way to approach the topic. After all, besides the prosaic but absolutely necessary task of seeking to understand what Shakespeare's words actually meant back then, how else could we possibly understand the effects of Shakespeare's language, except in relation to what was linguistically and rhetorically possible at the time? There is just one problem with this commonsensical approach: Readers and auditors of the poems and plays experience all manner of such effects even if they know nothing at all about Early Modern English, and perhaps even in spite of what they do know. Whether we are bored or moved, delighted or confused, excited or disturbed, put off or uplifted, we can't entirely help hearing Shakespeare's language through or against or alongside ours, although if we are historicists, we will consciously work against anachronism in our accounts of what we hear and feel when we read his works. And yet rather than juxtaposing Shakespeare's language to ours inadvertently, begrudgingly, or even with some shame, we might deliberately put on an anachronistic disposition towards Shakespeare and compare his idiom to our own. We might focus on what we *think* we hear, what we *think* we understand about his language, even when our impressions are erroneous from a strictly historical perspective. Such an approach, while it may seem anachronistic, would be rather more fully historical, in that it aims to resituate Shakespeare's language in a "story of English" that includes us.

I call this way of reading Shakespeare "intrelinguistic." The term is an adaptation of and an addition to Roman Jakobson's seminal taxonomy of the varieties of translation. Jakobson distinguished between "intralingual" translation (the process of replacing verbal signs belonging to a particular language with others belonging to the same language) and "interlingual" translation (replacing a set from one language with a set from another).[4] Jakobson's taxonomy is still productive within more current translation theories. But which term is appropriate for describing the ways we move between two different historical phases of the same language? By "*intre*lingual," I mean to provide an intermediary term, one that acknowledges that in many or even most ways Shakespeare speaks our language ("*intre*lingual" is pronounced the same way as "*intra*lingual"), yet also acknowledges a bilingual difference. An "intrelingual" reading considers both the proximities and the divergences of one version of a language to another as the basis for interpretation. Its use need not be restricted to our apprehension of Shakespeare's Early Modern English, but might apply to any attempt to make sense of "Englishes" that are within reach but yet alien to us, whether because the language has changed so much over time, as with Chaucer's Middle English, or has been consciously altered by an individual author, as with the English of James Joyce. Shakespeare's language is a version of what we might call a "proximate Other English"; if we "fear" it or "sweat" it, it is because it is too familiar and too unfamiliar to us at once.

I've come to an intrelinguistic perspective on Shakespeare, in part, because of hitting a wall in my own, earlier work. With many others, I always implicitly disavowed my impressions of Shakespeare's language as irrelevant, distracting, and/or potentially misleading. David Crystal acknowledges that our interest often begins when we notice a linguistic feature, "something which strikes us as particularly interesting, effective, unusual, or problematic (*often because it differs from what we would expect in Modern English*)."[5] Next, "we ... have to describe the feature," and finally "we have to explain why the feature is there." One of the key objectives of Crystal's three-step process is to learn how to "avoid superimposing [linguistic] norms/rules from later periods onto Shakespeare."[6] Crystal thus concurs with Hilda Hulme, who decades ago asserted that "we must disregard knowledge as well as acquire it," when we study Shakespeare's language because, after all, when "we learn a foreign language we hear sound-distinctions which to a native speaker are non-meaningful, while at the same time our ear fails to record significant distinctions which, in our own tongue, would mean nothing."[7] The scholarly consensus seems to be that understanding Shakespeare means refuting many of our first, uninformed judgments, pleasures, and displeasures. As I will demonstrate later with examples, intrelinguistic reading still relies on historicizing Shakespeare's language as a primary method of investigation. But I also hope to show that when we seek answers about our experience of Shakespeare's language, our *exclusive* insistence on historicist explanations sometimes occludes or even "explains away" some of what we most enjoy about it, what moved us to seek explanations in the first place.

This approach to reading Shakespeare derives from three existing methodologies from three different fields of literary and linguistic study, though none of them has as yet been applied to Shakespeare's English. The first, not incidentally, involves theories of translation. Stephen Booth has suggested that the apparatus of glosses to Shakespeare's text turns readers into translators; I want to expand this insight to reading Shakespeare generally, as we unconsciously gloss Shakespeare with our own linguistic competencies and judgments. Gayatri Chakravorty Spivak has said that "[t]ranslation is the most intimate act of reading";[8] I would add the converse, that reading Shakespeare, today, is the most (or at least, a most) intimate act of translation. Most germane are theories of translation that conceptualize the process as a creative interplay *between* two languages, as one language reinterpreted by and through another.

Walter Benjamin's seminal essay, "The Task of the Translator" (1923), is a famous example. Benjamin argued that "[t]ranslation ... ultimately serves the purpose of expressing the central reciprocal relationship between languages."[9] He believed the goal of translation was not an exchange of one for the other, but the discovery and emancipation of what he called a "pure language," which is delivered by the co-existence of both the translation and original. This pure language can be achieved, crucially, because "[l]anguages are not strangers to one another."[10] "It is the task of the translator," Benjamin writes, "to release in his own language that pure language which is under the spell of another, to liberate the language imprisoned in a work in his re-creation of that work."[11] Translations, however, can only be provisional because "in [its] afterlife ... the original undergoes a change. Even words with fixed meaning can undergo a maturing process" and "what sounded fresh once may sound hackneyed later; what was once current may someday sound quaint."[12] In the meantime "the mother tongue of the translator is transformed as well": "Translation is so far removed from being the sterile equation of two dead languages that of all literary forms it is the one charged with the special mission of watching over the maturing process of the original language and the birth pangs of its own."[13] Benjamin's ideas about linguistic collaboration, proceeding not only despite time but in time and because of time, are essential here. Reading Shakespeare intrelinguistically lets one participate in what Benjamin describes as the "perpetual renewal of language"[14] that results from translation – in this case, the perpetual renewal of the English language.

George Steiner's notion of the "hermeneutic motion" of the translator, in his masterwork *After Babel*, is also based on notions of linguistic collaboration. *After Babel* begins, not incidentally, with a chapter called "Understanding as Translation" and a discussion of Shakespeare's *Cymbeline*; Steiner unravels what might go into translating even a single one of the play's passages. In his chapter on the history of translation theory in the West, Steiner focuses on "[t]he perennial question whether translation is, in fact, possible," which he claims has persisted "over some two thousand years of argument and precept."[15] The "postulate of untranslatability"[16] essentially rests on the notion that form and content are so closely connected in a text "that no dissociation is admissible,"[17] and thus "no language can be translated without fundamental loss."[18] The many incarnations of this philosophical position, he notes, ultimately go back to religious notions of God's Word. But "[t]he case for translation has its religious, mystical antecedents as well," especially in the story of the Tower of Babel.[19] Steiner cites Benjamin as among those who "[conjure] up by virtue of unplanned echo a language nearer to the primal unity of speech than is either the original text or the tongue into which he is translating."[20] The debate over translating Shakespeare into Modern English, it seems, is particularly prone to polarization along the theoretical extremes that Steiner describes. On the one hand, Shakespeare's language is our "Word," necessary and inviolable; on the other hand, it conveys universal ideas best served by greater linguistic accessibility.

Steiner, however, proposes a third way. For Steiner, the "crux of the metier and morals of translation" is the "enactment of reciprocity."[21] Steiner's theory of reciprocity, however, emphasizes the translator's cognitive and affective processes. The translator's hermeneutic motion thus begins with an "initiative trust" that there is something in the source text that may be understood.[22] That trust is followed by aggression towards the source text and a fear that the translator may be mastered and consumed by it. The translator resists the difference of the foreign text by "elective affinity,"[23] in a "dialectic of embodiment" that finally proceeds towards "incorporation" – or the diffusion of two languages into one another.[24] But crucially, once again, "incorporation" refers not only to the new, translated text, but to something that transpires within the mind of the individual translator. As Steiner writes, "[T]o experience difference, to feel the characteristic resistance and 'materiality' of that which differs, [is] to re-experience identity";[25] and, conversely, the "insinuation of self into otherness is the final secret of the translator's craft."[26] Only then does translation result in a fully integrated, interlinear text, a work he describes, in one of his more provocative iterations, as "close to the poet's dream of an absolute idiolect."[27]

The notion of translation as a unique consummation of two languages – or two particular writers' particular versions of two languages – persists in more recent theoretical works. Lawrence

Venuti writes of translation as an "intercultural collaboration,"[28] Antoine Berman describes it as "a mode of interpersonal dialogue,"[29] while Jacques Derrida imagines that in translated texts "one language licks another, like a flame or a caress."[30] Such theories validate what I argue comes naturally as we, as Modern English speakers, approach Shakespeare's language – sometimes with resistance to his "foreign" text, and sometimes with desire for that same difference, as Derrida's implicit pun on erotic, "interlingual" relations suggests. To the extent that we imagine that Shakespeare speaks "our" language, that he speaks the way we feel inside, we, too, engage in a kind of "elective affinity" with his texts. And we, too, consummate our relationship by integrating our words with his.

Of course, insofar as our ordinary experiences of reading Shakespeare are not directed to the production of a second text, translation can never be an entirely apt model for intrelinguistics. In its sustained emphasis on the cognitive experiences involved in reading a foreign language, and more specifically, on the process of reading a "strange" language from the perspective of a more familiar one, second language acquisition studies provide a promising intervention. In the late 1950s, applied linguist Robert Lado introduced a new way to study the obstacles learners face in trying to attain a second language, a methodology that he called "contrastive analysis." Contrastive analysis involves a systematic, bilingual comparison of phonology, morphology, and syntax. Lado, considering the persistence of habits we form after years of speaking a native tongue, hypothesized that "those elements which are similar to the learner's native language will be simple for him, and those elements that are different will be difficult."[31] Although this hypothesis has been disproven (degree of difference isn't predictive of the ease or difficulty of learning a second language), the field has maintained its focus on "interference" and "language transfer" as key processes of acquisition; both concepts pertain to the conscious or unconscious projection of elements of one's native language onto another. Language transfer goes a long way towards explaining the nature of what is known as a learner's "interlanguage."

An "interlanguage," in the disciplinary context of second language acquisition studies, refers to "the product of a psycholinguistic process of interaction between two linguistic systems, those of the mother tongue and the target language."[32] The partly idiosyncratic, partly predictable linguistic admixtures we jokingly call "Spanglish" or "Franglais" are examples of interlanguages. Interlanguages have also been compared to dialects, somewhere between idiolects (unique to every individual learner) and social dialects (belonging to a group): "While these dialects are not 'langues' [i.e., in Saussure's sense of the totalized linguistic competence of a community of speakers], in the sense that they are not shared by any social group identifiable according to the criteria of the sociologist, nevertheless the idiosyncratic rules are not unique to an individual but shared by others having similar cultural background, aims or linguistic history."[33] The discovery and elucidation of a learner's interlanguage proceeds by way of what is known as "error analysis." Distinguished in principle from "mistakes," which may be quirky or random, "errors" are understood to be systemic, shared among speakers of the same tongue. Once again, there are limits to the applicability of second language acquisition theory, since most Shakespeare readers are not seeking to "learn" Shakespeare's Early Modern English in order to produce it themselves. Still, the idea of "interlanguage" is productive for intrelinguistics, as it suggests ways of understanding the errors we make when we read Shakespeare not as signs of failure, but as evidence of a revealing and valid psycholinguistic experience.

A third theoretical framework comes from a body of work that falls within Shakespeare scholarship, although its relevance to the study of Shakespeare's language has not yet been explored. Although many literary scholars disavow such knowledge, most books written for and/or by actors concern themselves, directly, with how a modern speaker (that is, a modern actor) can best deliver the demands and the difficulties of Shakespeare's language to today's audiences, and thus how today's audiences might receive them. Performance-oriented Shakespeareans, not coincidentally, tend to be the most amenable to the idea of Modern English translations, as Ton Hoenselaars has noted: "After all, it is in performance that the failure of Early Modern English to communicate it is most apparent."[34] Susan Bassnett complained about the gimmicks that contemporary actors resort to, from slapstick physical comedy to the use of technical effects on stage, because "[they] can't understand the words and compensate with silly antics." Her appraisal is probably not very fair. However deep their understanding of Shakespeare's language may be, theatre people still have to contend with general expectations of naturalism – detailed, "everyday," contemporary reality – in their performances. For actors who subscribe to the "Method" or any of its variants, especially, Shakespeare's language is a real challenge for achieving and projecting emotional and psychological authenticity, of actually "living on the stage," as Lee Strasberg put it.[35] But classically trained actors, too, have struggled with the gap between modern feeling and premodern forms. As Michael Gwilym, of the Royal Shakespeare Company, once described the problem: "[The actor], especially in emotional scenes … thinks, 'I know exactly how this character feels, I know the depth of his passion, and I know about what his brain is doing, but why have I got these flipping words in the way?'"[36]

Yet many actors also feel that Shakespeare's words are the only way, and sometimes the truth and the light as well, when it comes to access to the "real" impact of the plays. Acting coach Patsy Rodenburg, in her book *Speaking Shakespeare*, imagines actors ultimately discovering Shakespeare's language "flowing in their bloodstreams, a familiar part of them rather than something baffling, strange or difficult."[37] Actor Simon Callow believes that its difficulties today are only apparent: "We don't need an interpreter – we speak the same language: or at least we used to."[38] In *Freeing Shakespeare's Voice*, Kristin Linklater goes further, rhapsodizing on Shakespeare's language as the key to unlocking all English-speaking minds and hearts, if not minds and hearts everywhere:

> It comes from the soul of the English language, and once the soul of the language has been discovered by the speaker, the soul and voice of the speaker is liberated to tell her or his own story … Speaking Shakespeare leads us to the sources of our own power because we find a language which expresses the depth of our experience more fully, more richly, more completely than our own words can.[39]

This kind of talk is frankly embarrassing to most literary scholars, who often express admiration for Shakespeare's language, but avoid the question of their own, or their readers', personal experiences of it. Seth Lerer's dodge is typical. In his recent book *Inventing English: A Portable History of the Language*, Lerer asserts Shakespeare's "greatness" as a commonplace, rather than declaring it himself: "Shakespeare: The very name evokes the acme of the English language."[40] Beyond a longstanding discomfort with affective criticism, scholars today are also likely to treat expressions of Shakespeare's timelessness or universality as political anathema. Thus Jean Howard and Marion F. O'Connor have repudiated the idea that Shakespeare is "a kind of cultural Esperanto, a medium through which the differences of material existence – differences of race, gender, class, history, and culture – are supposedly cancelled."[41] W.B. Worthen has unmasked what it means for actors to see Shakespeare as part of their own natures, to "embody" his words:

> While Shakespeare – that remote, verbally dense, intellectually imposing figure of cultural authority – might be expected to represent the otherness of texts, their irreducible distance from the discursive "naturalness" of the body, actor training works to close or occlude that gap. The complicity of actor training in ideological formation is nowhere more visible than at this point: 'Shakespeare' becomes a naturalizing metaphor on the order of the body itself, representing the universal, transcendent, and natural in ways that both legitimate and render questionable the dominant discourse of the stage.[42]

These scholars remind us that constructing Shakespeare as a lingua franca, among bodies or among peoples, is a projection of a false consciousness, in which a historically remote and elite language is naturalized as a universal one. From this perspective, what Linklater describes as "freeing" Shakespeare's language looks a lot more like a form of cultural oppression.

It may be true that actors and directors, who are generally (and appropriately) credited with progressively expanding the bounds of what Shakespeare is and might yet mean, are sometimes simultaneously the most old-fashioned in their faith that Shakespeare's language is the voice of the human heart. Yet their approach, too, is ultimately based on notions of a reciprocal interaction with Shakespeare's words, albeit of a more physiological and emotional kind. It would be good to find a way to incorporate actors' willingness to talk about "how we feel" about Shakespeare's words into intrelinguistic theory. The challenge is finding a way to do so without recourse to global assertions of their timelessness, or their synchronicity with human nature, a method that straddles the divide between too much particularity and too much overgeneralization. If we try to articulate how Shakespeare's language makes us feel, how do we go beyond describing what is only our own, private response, or, alternatively, speaking as if his language were a universal tongue?

There are currently two main types of books on Shakespeare's language. First, there are linguistically oriented studies, which proceed with chapters on Shakespeare's phonology, lexicon, and grammar. Second, there are rhetorically oriented ones, which play out in separate chapters on Shakespeare's verse (i.e., his meters), his prose, his uses of tropes and schemes, and his wordplay (often with an emphasis on puns). There are also a few books such as Frank Kermode's *Shakespeare's Language* which proceed more holistically; Kermode's study traces the development of Shakespeare's dramatic language from the more formal rhetorical exercises of the early plays to the rich, dense, obscure forms and formulations of the late plays. And there are of course also plenty of specialized studies that take up just one of the subtopics I mention above (for example, Shakespeare's grammar, Shakespeare's meters, or Shakespeare's puns). But none of these foreground our cognitive and affective impressions of Shakespeare's language.

Of course focusing on effects will always raise some serious objections. To begin with, "effects" are a matter of subjective response, rather than objective analysis and so perhaps unavailable for critical examination. But it is essential to remember that the purpose of rhetoric itself is the creation of effects – emotional, psychological, intellectual – via language. As David Crystal reminds us, "[O]ne should never examine a linguistic nut or bolt without asking 'what does it do?' And 'what does it do' means ... how does it help us appreciate the dramatic or poetic effect of what is said?"[43] As readers and interpreters, we should go beyond identifying a writer's use of certain syntactic variations, or tropes and schemes; our goal is always to ask *why* they are used, i.e., to what *effect*. Whatever the intrinsic interest of ascertaining the etiology and constitution of linguistic forms themselves, sooner or later we have to take the leap from forms to what those forms provoke us to think or feel. The study of Shakespeare's language must always progress, in the end, to its impact on our own sensibilities; perhaps it's time to bring that end to the fore.

Then there's the problem of projecting a subjective impression of Shakespeare's effects – in the examples below, my own "feelings" about them – as a general one. How can I presume a "we" of "me," a world of modern readers who might respond with any measure of consistency and predictability? This is a problem that can't be fully resolved. Yet it must be said that traditional books on the topic don't fully resolve it, either. Historicist studies of Shakespeare's language also presume a "we," or rather, given that their purview is the past, a "they" – an interpretive community of Renaissance readers who can be counted on to have shared a similar if not identical linguistic experience. Yet surely Renaissance people were no more unanimous in their apprehension of Shakespeare's language than we are. Historicist studies implicitly construct a "normal" Renaissance response by way of the norms of Early Modern English, against which Shakespeare's language would have been construed. I am suggesting, in turn, that we use the norms of Modern English as a touchstone for interpretation. If my "we" is in part a critical convenience, it is designed, as linguists say, for "capturing the generalization" of contemporary intuitions about Shakespeare. It is unlikely that the examples below will speak to everyone whose native tongue is English, let alone universally or transcendently. But if we can agree that "Modern English" constitutes a site of some kind of shared consciousness, albeit a variable and mutable one in its own right, our own language may provide at least a rough standard by which we can speak of a collective response to Shakespeare's.

Of all the studies currently available on the topic of Shakespeare's language, John Barton's *Playing Shakespeare* comes closest to theorizing intrelinguistics, the ways we unconsciously collaborate in Shakespeare's words and their effects on us. In his master's workshop on performing Shakespeare, the eminent Royal Shakespeare Company director notes how important it is for actors to distinguish between "naturalistic" and "heightened" language in the plays. He says that the "simplest way of defining [heightened language] would be to say that it refers to … any bit of text where there are images and metaphors and similes or rich, surprising language."[44] One participant in the workshop, the actress Cicely Berry, added that heightened language "has to do with a feeling that poetic writing is in some way less than real – for one thing there are an awful lot of words!"[45] Barton and his actors thus maintain that the difference between "naturalistic" or "real" speech and "heightened" or stylized speech inheres in Shakespeare's language itself. Yet they also discuss the possibility that what we call "naturalistic" may not have anything to do with essential properties of language at all. Perhaps,

Barton writes, it is rather the "jargon for a particular style": "We mean by it a style which deliberately gives an impression of ordinary everyday speech and behavior. We don't mean it in the more general sense of 'being true to nature.'"[46] The actor Ian McKellan, a fellow participant, adds, "I suspect that actors from Richard Burbage, the man who first acted Shakespeare's heroes, have all been concerned with truth, reality, and nature. It's just that we've all had different perceptions of it."[47] As contemporary readers, too, we may find some of Shakespeare's language more "natural" to us, and some of it more "heightened," "poetic," or simply strange. Crucially (and to expand upon McKellan's insight), actors need to distinguish what might have been "heightened" in the sixteenth century from what no longer, still, or only now seems heightened because of our own contingent, historically conditioned expectations for English. But while Barton and his actors concern themselves with "playing" to the rhetorical biases of contemporary audiences, they stop short of acknowledging such biases as a potential source of, rather than merely an obstacle to, dramatic interpretation and performance.

I will turn now to some examples of an intrelinguistic, Early/Modern English Shakespeare. At the start of *The Merchant of Venice*, the character Antonio says: "In sooth I know not why I am so sad" (1.1.1). Barton calls these words beautiful, and I think they are, too. Barton also says it is impossible to talk about why, precisely because the line is "quite naturalistic." That makes it "easy to overlook and quite different from the overt poetry we find in rich and heightened language."[48] Nevertheless, he ascribes to it "a poetic ring, uneasy, haunting."[49] For Barton, the line is an example of Shakespeare's "hidden poetry": "There's a resonance which can't be defined or pinned down."[50] I believe that the resonance Barton is talking about (I hear it, too) is Shakespeare's language resounding against ours, "hidden" because it is not actually "there," except in the relation between them.

If we listen to the words, "In sooth I know not why I am so sad," it isn't hard to discern a few "poetic" things about them, in the strictly objective sense of that term. The line is liltingly iambic and contains alliteration (*sooth ... so ... sad*). But it is also a very simple line, written as it is in simple, monosyllabic words. The overall effect of the line was and remains naturalistic, as Barton describes it. Yet these ten simple words also include two phrases that are quite unusual to us, if easy enough to understand. Both the phrase "in sooth" and the syntactic structure "I know not" are archaic in Modern English, if not out of use entirely. We may recognize "sooth" as an older word for "truth," perhaps because it survives in the obscure but not-quite-dead-yet word "soothsayer." In the context of the line as a whole, in which Antonio confesses that he does not know why he is sad, the old sound of "in sooth" is expressive, in and of itself, of a "truth" that is half-forgotten, nearly lost to us. I must emphasize, once again, "to *us*." "In sooth" is a very common, perfectly ordinary, current phrase in Early Modern English. Shakespeare himself uses it forty-two times in his plays. If the line sounds "haunting" to *us*, it is partly because the phrase *itself* haunts us from the past.

The phrase "I know not" contributes even more powerfully to this effect. Our modern form, "I do not know," was already in use in Early Modern English, but the older form, subject+verb+negator, is the general pattern of negation in Shakespeare's works. "I know not" is "naturalistic" for Shakespeare (the phrase occurs no fewer than 216 times in the plays) but peculiarly "heightened" for us. We no longer use it now, except in a few surviving archaisms: "He loves me, he loves me not." Like "in sooth," "I know not" sounds old to us, but there is more to it than that. Whereas "I do not know" or "I don't know" can come across as a mere statement of fact (as for example, in the Boy's "I do not know the French for fer, and ferret, and firk" [*Henry V* 4.4.28]), "I know not" sounds more jarring, even contradictory. (Compare the way absolute contradiction may be expressed in contemporary American slang: "I know. Not.") In the context of Antonio's line as a whole, the strangeness of the construction "I know not," for us, makes his "simple" statement skew towards one that bespeaks a more profound alienation, an epistemological crisis. I hear the phrase this way whenever I come across it in the plays, such as in the new King Henry V's "I know thee not, old man" (5.5.45); or in Hermia's "I am amazed, and know not what to say" (*Midsummer* 3.2.345); or in Hamlet's "dread of something after death" that makes us "rather bear those ills we have / Than to fly to others we know not of" (3.1.80; 83–4). I hear it, for that matter, in the Early Modern English of the King James Bible: "Father, forgive them; for they know not what they do" (Luke 23:34). We might call what we hear or think we hear in such phrases "post-syntactic effects," a key component of our Early/Modern interlanguage. Post-syntactic effects do not exist in Shakespeare's language, but in the space between his language and our own.

Here is a second, very different kind of example. In 2 *Henry IV*, Warwick explains why Prince Hal chooses to hang out with low-lifes and thieves: "[T]o gain the language," Warwick says, "'Tis needful that the most immodest word / Be look't upon and learnt" (4.3.68–71). Warwick is speaking metaphorically about Hal's slumming. Even so, he puts forward an interesting theory about "gaining" a foreign language: to become fully fluent, one must learn the "dirty" words, too. Considering how many modern Shakespeare glossaries focus on the playwright's sexual vocabulary, it seems we concur. Like many specialized dictionaries (for example, ones that deal in Shakespeare's musical, legal, or military diction, among other "terms of art"), modern sexual glossaries of the poems and plays define the meanings of words that are obscure or extinct in Modern English, i.e., that are "foreign" to us now. We learn from Eric Partridge's seminal *Shakespeare's Bawdy* (1947) and Gordon Williams's *A Glossary of Shakespeare's Sexual Language* (1997)[51] that the words *callet*, *drab*, *punk*, *stale*, *trull*, and *quean* all meant "whore" in the sixteenth century. But there is something different about our dictionaries of Shakespeare's *sex* talk. Along with their focus on his sixteenth-century sexual vocabulary, these works elucidate the *hidden sexual meanings* of words that have literal, non-sexual denotations, what we sometimes call Shakespeare's *double entendres*. What makes Shakespeare's sexual language seem so "needful" to us is how coded, cryptic, or closeted his language seems to be. We tend to think we are in on the joke, but perhaps we still don't quite get it.

We should consider, for example, Shakespeare's sexual "euphemisms," words and phrases we think the playwright uses to avoid speaking of sex directly. Scholars have identified a lot of these in Shakespeare; as Partridge puts it, "[t]o cite every [sexual] euphemism [in the plays] were as tedious as unnecessary."[52] Most scholars seem to think there are even more than we realize. Russ McDonald notes that "[l]inguistic changes over the past four centuries may prevent us from apprehending many slang terms and euphemisms common in the early modern period," and gives us, as examples, "the word *will* for sexual organ ... *yard* for penis; *ring* for vagina; and *aunt* for prostitute."[53]

As a historical matter, however, euphemism turns out to be an unusually difficult rhetorical device to identify. Knowing what is euphemistic, in any given text or given culture, requires tracking semantic conditions that are very short-lived. Steven Pinker has described what he calls the "euphemism treadmill": originally borrowed or created to avoid using taboo words, euphemisms tend to evolve into taboo words themselves.[54] A well-known example is the word *pudendum*. In its original Latin *pudendum* meant "that of which one ought to be ashamed," but by the fourteenth century it had come to denote the "thing itself," that is, the "external genitals." Shakespearean euphemisms for the female genitals have been said to include *lap*, along with *belly*, *nothing*, *ring*, *case*, and *wound*. Since "lap" is innocent of sexual meaning in Modern English, we might imagine that Hamlet is being deliberately euphemistic, as well as equivocal, when he asks Ophelia, "Lady, shall I lie in your lap?" (*Hamlet* 3.2.101). Yet the word "lap" referred directly, not metaphorically, to the "female pudendum" in Early Modern English. Pompey isn't beating around any bush when he speaks of plucking "the ne'er lust-wearied Antony … from the lap of Egypt's widow" (*Antony and Cleopatra* 2.1.38–9). Nor is Gloucester when he determines to "make [his] heaven in a lady's lap" (*Richard Duke of York* 3.2.148). Nor is Romeo, when he complains that Rosaline refuses to "ope her lap to saint-seducing gold" (*Romeo and Juliet* 1.1.207). These characters are not being evasive here, nor trying to avoid some offense. On the contrary, each is speaking as salaciously as possible.

But the point of this intrelinguistic intervention, once again, is not simply to identify a possible mistake in our understanding, but rather a productive "error." We think of euphemisms as verbal substitutions, whose aim is obfuscation. As Quentin Crisp notoriously quipped, "Euphemisms are unpleasant truths wearing diplomatic cologne." So what unpleasant truth is "lap," for example, "covering up" for? We may implicitly assume that it must be the word "vagina," since that is our most basic and direct word for it, and because "vagina" remains taboo in many contexts despite being a so-called "clinical" term, as the continued success of Eve Ensler's *The Vagina Monologues* has made clear. But Shakespeare probably had no thought of a "vagina," since the word did not come into use in English for another century. He might have been thinking of "pudendum," but it is impossible to say, precisely because he never uses the word in any of his works. The truth is that we do not know what specific words (if any) Shakespeare was trying to hide when he wrote "lap," – or "belly," or "ring," or "nothing," or "wound." When it comes to the female genitals, at least, we seem to think there must be some awful truth lurking behind Shakespeare's language. Or rather, some awful word – maybe even a Modern English word we have thrust into a linguistic breach. Reading Shakespeare euphemistically, we may be shocking ourselves with the secret of our *own* language, in an erotic, intrelinguistic "transfer" of terms.

A final, and again very different, example: In Act 2 of 2 *Henry IV*, a saucy Page rails against Mistress Quickly, who wants to have his master Sir John Falstaff arrested for theft: "Away, you scullion! You rampallian! You fustilarian! / I'll tickle your catastrophe!" (2.1.52–3). This is hilarious, although the chances are that we don't understand a word of what the Page is saying to the Hostess, or barely a word. There is a popular consensus about how funny such insults are, as the dozens of books on the subject now available on the topic from Amazon.com attest, not to mention mugs, refrigerator magnets, and online Shakespearean insult-generators. It appears that the more illegible, inscrutable, and opaque Shakespeare's insults are, the funnier they seem to us now, *no matter their relative difficulty back then*. Thus, in the case of the Page's verbal assault on Mistress Quickly, we may be in sync to some extent with Shakespeare's audiences, for whom *rampallian* (ruffian) and *fustilarian* (frowsy slut) were neologisms or, as they were known in the sixteenth century, "hard words," too. *Scullion*, once a common word for kitchen menial, isn't common any longer, so the Page's insult is "harder" than ever. But today, insults based on ordinary Early Modern English words, such as Doll Tearsheet's "You basket-hilt stale juggler, you" (2 *Henry IV* 2.4.110) or Prince Hal's "[T]hou knotty-pated fool, thou … greasy tallow-catch" (1 *Henry IV* 2.5.210–11) or Kent's "You whoreson cullionly barber-monger" (*King Lear* 2.2.28–9) are just as funny as the Page's taunt. From the vantage point of Modern English, they are all comparable examples, no less than the most highfalutin figures of speech in the poems and plays, of Shakespeare's "heightened" language. And from the perspective of intrelinguistics, this is another case in point for why the difficulties of Shakespeare's language are not necessarily best translated away, and how Modern English has, in effect, invented some of the pleasure we take in Shakespeare's Early Modern vernacular.

As David Crystal has shown us, Shakespeare's English is formally continuous in most ways with our own. He calculates that only about ten percent of English grammar has changed since the sixteenth century, and only five percent of Shakespeare's lexicon has shifted in meaning.[55] The numbers seem to prove that there is no need to "translate" Shakespeare into Modern English, or to change course in the way we study his words. Yet despite this, many of us still have the sense that "Shakespeare's language" is something unique and singular, and that for all our knowledge we still haven't quite grasped why. We could seek to know more, and better, by existing methods, but my guess is we would still be missing something. Something is coming between us and Shakespeare's words, "interfering" in our reading – our *relationship* with Shakespeare, understood in its own right.

Above all, intrelinguistics is a response to a field of study that has become somewhat stagnant over the years, bound to fixed ideas of what a "language" is, or what the "arts of language" consist of. However useful and important it is to do so, dividing Shakespeare's language into phonology, morphology, and syntax, or into prosody, diction, and figurative language, is treating his strange, beautiful, comic, dark, obscure, prosaic, lyrical, powerful, frustrating, comforting, wise, absurdist, wearying, challenging words as if they were something we already know how to process, how to control. I know that reading Shakespeare's Early Modern English through and against Modern English must inevitably seem a very subjective or idiosyncratic method, even as the goal is to ring as many bells for as many readers as possible. Yet in sharing some of our own intuitions as native speakers of Modern English, some of what yet remains hidden about our experience of reading Shakespeare may come to light. Or, better yet, it may "modestly discover to yourself, / That of yourself which you yet know not of."

PART THREE

Shakespeare and Cultural Voice

Monument, Mountain, Root: Figures of Translation, from Romeo to Julia

BRIAN GINGRICH

Romeo and Juliet is, more than any Shakespearean drama, an enigma of translation. It doesn't feature any exceptional interlingual punning, and it doesn't do much to reference the language of its Italian and French precursors. But the local conflict it portrays is so determined by linguistic-cultural barriers – barriers successively broken and bolstered by the characters' speeches – that the entire drama takes the form of a dialectic of translatability.[1]

That dialectic extends far beyond the internal order of Shakespeare's play. It extends, most obviously, to the countless other representations of the Romeo and Juliet myth – to folkloric fragments and sixteenth-century Italian novellas, to Arthur Brooke's *Romeus and Juliet*, and to the centuries of retellings and restagings, transformations and translations, that follow the Shakespearean text.[2] To trace a line between any of those instances is to sense the pulsing of a history as dynamic as that between *The Odyssey* and *Ulysses*, between *King Lear* and *Ran*, or between all manner of Fausts.

Here I trace one translation in particular. In the early 1850s Gottfried Keller, a Swiss author and one of German literature's finest storytellers,[3] wrote a novella: *Romeo und Julia auf dem Dorfe* [*A Village Romeo and Juliet*]. Keller's story is a masterpiece in modest clothing. It transforms *Romeo and Juliet* into an apparently simple tale of a rural family feud; but in its simplicity there is a quaintness that suggests its own cunning. Retelling the lovers' legend, Keller takes up the enigma of translation prefigured in Shakespeare's drama, and his work takes on an intricate form – usually called 'realist,' but only for lack of a better term – that seems to naturalize its act of literary transformation. Whereas Shakespeare's work brings the artifice of linguistic signs to the surface, Keller's uses that artifice to bury those signs in the natural world. The naturalizing touch has, in all art, a smoothness that invites suspicion – a smoothness that suggests itself the product of some equally rough abrasive force, of culture or of history. That, in fact, is the case here. Romeo and Julia are much more than a forlorn country couple in an imaginary Swiss landscape. Ultimately, they are part of the most aggressive cultural appropriation of Shakespeare in history.

Throughout literary studies, the claim that a work's lyrical, naturalistic, or ahistorical qualities contain an expression of its link to society, ideology, or history has become so implicit as to risk losing its meaning. For that view to retain its insight, it should arise less out of an arbitrary obligation to a theoretical ideal and more out of a willingness to delve into the immanent structure of a text, to use the formal features of that structure as guideposts to worlds outside it. In moving between *Romeo and Juliet* and *Romeo und Julia auf dem Dorfe*, I'm guided by two features in particular: first, the remarkable consciousness with which these two works regard translation within their structures, and, second, the artful mastery through which they represent that regard figuratively.

The figures of translation in these works take a fantastical range of forms. They appear as pagan idols, pastoral fields, sublime peaks, city walls, and, ultimately, sheer words; they span centuries and support whole nations. Yet when the two texts appear alongside each other, their forms interact; they merge and morph, arranging themselves into a single structure, and in this new structure three figures stand out above all: monuments, mountains, and roots. More than mere figures of translation, these are figures of translatability; they represent the potential for translation in and between Shakespeare's play and Keller's story. More than mere metaphors, they are practical models of translation – models proposed in the texts' own terms and based on the context of their mutual interaction. To trace such figures, to test them as models, to lift them out of their texts and set them against each other, is to develop a theory of translation both born out of the internal order of each text and imitative of the play of difference that occurs in broad historical-linguistic contexts. In this essay, the development of that theory is above all a development of a set of terms essential to the relations between the three major figures.

The most important of these terms – *monumentality*, *singularity*, *naturalization*, *rootedness*, *idolatrousness*, *legitimacy* – are among the most powerful, most unstable concepts in the theory of representation and translation. Defining them here, I try to stabilize them slightly, and I offer them as tools for determining cultural meaning elsewhere, in the other figures of translation that abound where literary craft meets the process of its own linguistic transformation.

> CAPULET: O brother Montague, give me thy hand.
> This is my daughter's jointure, for no more
> Can I demand.
> MONTAGUE: But I can give thee more,
> For I will raise her statue in pure gold,
> That whiles Verona by that name is known,
> There shall no figure at such rate be set
> As that of true and faithful Juliet.
> CAPULET: As rich shall Romeo's by his lady's lie,
> Poor sacrifices of our enmity![4]

I'll limit our focus on *Romeo and Juliet* to one aspect in particular: Shakespeare's work aims to construct a monument.

In the most literal sense, this monument is a pair of statues, of a pair of children, of a pair of households alike in dignity. (Pairings pervade the text.) But the monument is itself all too literal: Montague and Capulet each give their word, and that is all. A theatre audience watching these final speeches sees beside the lords not a conjuring of statues but only the still-present corpses of their children. And what the audience hears – a kind of rushed grandiloquence, culminating in rhymed couplets – may resonate far too well with the rhetoric the lords have inhabited all along. Capulet, offering his daughter's jointure, again usurps her marital will. Montague, outdoing Capulet's offer, reassumes the competitive posture of the feud. As Capulet matches Montague's vow to build a statue, the two return to a relation of mimetic rivalry. And, as the rivalry restructures itself on superlative terms of value – richness, pure gold, highest rates – the subjects whose value is to be represented lose a meaning that might have proved transformative.

The conjunction of these results is key: a monument is proposed, its value is inflated, and the meaning proper to its human referents is *de*flated. Bracketing the question of what that proper meaning is, for now it's enough to note that the monument, by consisting of these words of the fathers, pronounces not a resolution of the feud but a re-establishment of the rhetorical order that structured it all along. I'll call this order – casually, and with only vague reference to some greater symbolic order – the monumental order. Even in an exchange as brief as that between the lords, all the monumental order's primary characteristics are apparent: *patriarchal misrepresentation* (of another's particular will); the *claim to singularity* (in the presence of a similar and symmetrical opponent); and, most importantly, an *overvaluation of signifiers*. It is predicated on a linguistic bias that compels a group to represent its singularity through signs – names, statues, houses, tombs – that transfer emphasis, excessively, from signified to signifier. The signs are made to function as exaggerated monuments: they inspire awe and claim to memorialize some past referent, but their content is so fully concentrated in the signifier that memory is blocked – the referent lost, the origins of the feud made immemorial – and the signifier is all.

This amounts to a rejection of translation.[5] A translation, after all, is only possible if one signifier can be exchanged for another whose signified best matches that of the first. But when the worth of the sign is so fully invested in the signifier, no other signifier will do. All other signifiers are counterfeit, invalid, unexchangeable. The sign cannot be translated. And when that sign-become-pure-signifier is the emblem or monument of an entire cultural group, that group withdraws into its signifier – and defends it violently. The monument defines itself against translation; it becomes a figure of translation negatively.

But that's all at the end. Moving back to the beginning of *Romeo and Juliet*, it's possible to trace the legacy that ultimately condemns those final statues to purposeful untranslatability. In fact, one could discover that an overvaluation of the signifier – from "rose" to "banishèd" to the letter "R" – infects every word of the drama. (This, above all, is what distinguishes Shakespeare's work from other versions of the Romeo and Juliet legend.) For practical purposes, though, I'll limit our focus to the monuments that, more than any others, determine the fate of the play's protagonists. For Juliet, these are proper names; for Romeo, walled spaces.

Alongside the legend of Romeo and Juliet, another myth lies uniquely within Shakespeare's drama, a myth that can be reconstructed, in a playful manner, from the structure of the speeches and the action. If this myth is the expression of a law, as myths generally are, then that law is to respect the status of the signifier; and if that law has an authority, it is an authority represented by the monumental order. From the perspective of that order, the drama's beginning represents an ideal state: two groups, seemingly equivalent and uncannily symmetrical, regard their relationship as one of absolute asymmetry and difference.[6] Each group, in order to assert its distinction from the other, identifies itself through exaggerated signifiers professing a singularity that isn't really there. – Not that the signs or emblems *mean* more than they should. The opposite is more the case. They signify little other than themselves, their particular form of signification. They refuse to denote, and the reason why seems obvious: their meanings, on either side of the feud, are basically the same. The Prince represents the drama's beginning state precisely when he describes the feud's violence as "bred of an airy word" – a volatile signifier, void of any meaningful or signified content.[7] But again, from the perspective of the monumental order, and in the framework of its cautionary myth, this state is not the problem; it's the ideal. The problem arises when the state is challenged and order has to be restored. In fact, the unfolding of the mythical conflict can be traced as corresponding distinctly to the act-structure of Shakespeare's work. Juliet's plotline is concerned with names and lies within the acts, while Romeo's, related to spatial boundaries, occurs mainly in the breaks.

Act I (CAPULET: "But Montague is bound as well as I")[8] Ideal State.
Break: Romeo jumps a wall and crosses into an orchard signifying Capulet space.

Act II ("Oh be some other name!/What's in a name?")[9] Disruption. Juliet challenges the monumental order by questioning the status of names – and the status of patriarchal signifiers in general.
Break: Romeo completes his symbolic transgression by marrying Juliet.

Act III ("Ah, my poor lord, what tongue shall smooth thy name,/When I, thy three-hours wife, have mangled it?")[10] Retaliation. The monumental order forces the lovers to recognize their error and honour the status of names; punishment is ordered.
Break: Romeo is banished from the walls of Verona and the lovers are separated once again.

Act IV ("As in a vault, an ancient receptacle,/Where for this many hundred years the bones/Of all my buried ancestors are packed")[11] Attempted Retribution. Juliet embarks on a symbolic journey, entering the primal seat of the monumental order for the Capulets – their tomb site – in final hope of rejoining Romeo.
Break: Romeo crosses back into Verona, imitating Juliet's pilgrimage.

Act V (MONTAGUE: "I will raise her statue in pure gold …") Sacrifice and Restoration. Romeo and Juliet are granted their wish to be rejoined, but at a cost: they are sacrificed so as to re-establish the monumental order, represented by the statues their fathers plan to build.

Sketching the work's structure this way allows the lovers' transgression to take definite form – as an act of translation. Romeo translates spatially, trespassing significant physical boundaries (lots of walls) and dissolving the aura of difference they sustain. Juliet, meanwhile, attempts a subtler, linguistic translation. She pleads with Romeo that they change their names, referring, in her reasoning, to something like the arbitrariness of the sign: "That which we call a rose / By any other name would smell as sweet."[12]

But Juliet's rose may just as well suggest something not so arbitrary in the signs that fill the text. It may suggest, by the very sound of it, an inherent connection with the name of Romeo's initial object of affection – "Rosaline." Jonathan Goldberg, for one, has taken up this suggestion. In a particularly ingenious reading of the play, he suggests that Romeo sees both Rosaline and Juliet as roses, as easily substitutable objects of the same desire; Juliet, for Romeo, is just a rose by another name – and hence, we might say, a simple translation of Rosaline.[13] But I wonder if this isn't just half the story. Rosaline, as the generic and unseen subject of Romeo's early Petrarchan gushiness, certainly does seem to stand for some fluid, infinitely translatable idea circulated throughout the sonnet tradition; she is, no doubt, very "rosy." And Romeo, in his early meetings with Juliet, certainly does try to match her to that idea and that tradition. But it doesn't work. Something hinders it. Juliet's name rejects the translation – ultimately, it seems, because she represents her name more than her name represents her. Juliet represents "Juliet," and "Juliet" only. She represents untranslatability.

Over and over again, the language of the drama insists on just how tragically Juliet's attempts at translation are mistaken. The language sabotages the lovers' claims to be beyond the signifier; it splits them into ambivalent proclamations of love and violence.[14] A plea as simple as "be some other name!" founders on the fact that its verb already makes Romeo equivalent to his name, and so condemns its (his) translation to failure. Plenty of critics have touched upon the signs of such a failure. James Calderwood points out how Juliet, in the brief moment that she retreats from the balcony in the orchard scene, is forced to realize the necessity of names: she returns and, not finding Romeo, immediately begins to call for him frantically, vowing that she would make Echo hoarse "with repetition of my Romeo's name"; from there, Romeo and Juliet's love "becomes a great name-singing celebration."[15] Jacques Derrida presents a Romeo "radically separated from his name," only to insist that "the separation, the aphorism of the name remains impossible."[16] Catherine Belsey, above all, recognizes the play's intransigent signifiers, for example in her commentary on Juliet's "wherefore" speech:

> Identity, the speech acknowledges, exists in the symbolic as the Name of the Father ... [T]he signifier, however arbitrary, is not at the disposal of the subject. Romeo's name precedes him, makes him a subject, locates him in the community of Verona. It is not optional. Later Romeo will offer to excise his murderous name, but he cannot do so without killing himself ... [Belsey then cites Romeo's threat, in Act 3, Scene 3, to "sack" the part of his anatomy where his name "doth ... lodge."][17]

As Romeo and Juliet bow under the acknowledgment that they are subjects to their names, they acknowledge, as well, that they are subjects to signifying space. The exaggerated impact of the word "banishèd" in the drama shows this clearly: when Romeo is sent to Mantua, translated physically out of Verona, the lovers suffer the inverse of the translation they sought with names. Their separation, it seems, can only be overcome by repentance – an act of surrender and a rite of atonement: a symbolic return to the space of the monumental order. And so the lovers find their way to the vault of the Capulets, that "ancient receptacle" which appears as the very seat of the monumental order in the play. In its ostentation and its emptiness, its purported meaning and its inner absence, the space of the vault reflects the essential truth of the identities professed by either family: it is a potent yet vacant signifier, fatal but itself dead, a hollow core for a grand idea. Its ultimate expression is its inner desolation. As Juliet delivers herself to the vault, a "poor living corse, closed in a dead man's tomb," she submits exactly to the conditions of the order: suffocating encapsulation within a patriarchal signifier.[18] When, at the scene of death, the Captain of the Watch declares, "We see the ground whereon these woes do lie, / But the true ground of all these piteous woes / We cannot without circumstance descry," he's wrong, but in a very precise way.[19] We can, in fact, descry the truth, and it's suggested in his very signifiers: "the ground" of the woes *is* "the ground" whereon they lie. The floor of the vault is the base of the order that brought the lovers to their death.

The drama, which began as comedy, ends in tragedy. Most critics who remark on this unusual generic transition describe it on the level of plot and character, citing, for example, the death of Mercutio as a cause of the play's eventual shift away from comedy.[20] But the transition occurs just as forcefully at the level of the signifier-monument. The early, comic instances of punning jest and wordplay – of free translation in dialogue – disappear amidst a tragic rigidity of words once Juliet, Eve-like, dares to defy the dominant linguistic order. From this view Mercutio's death is just as much an effect as it is a cause of the play's tragic turn. In an atmosphere where signifiers are so locked into place, so resistant to playful manipulation, he couldn't have had much to survive on anyway.

In the last lines of *Romeo and Juliet*, the Prince responds to Montague and Capulet's monumental plan:

> A glooming peace this morning with it brings,
> The sun for sorrow will not show his head.
> Go hence to have more talk of these sad things;
> Some shall be pardoned, and some punishèd:
> For never was a story of more woe
> Than this of Juliet and her Romeo.[21]

William C. Carroll has noted that critical responses to this ending tend to fall under one of two categories: either they find something positive in the resolution, some sign that the tragedy will not continue as a tragic cycle, or they are too overcome by the loss and the fathers' lack of understanding to see anything but irony in the scene.[22] I don't think I conceal that my own reading belongs more to the latter type. Many critics, including Carroll, justify a positive reading by acknowledging the tragedy and the farcical aspect of the fathers' reconciliation but accepting the story itself as a kind of positive takeaway. In such a view the Prince saves the play with his final lines, in which he ignores the statues but monumentalizes the lovers' story. Yet given what we have considered so far, these lines seem less like a positive gesture and more like the final and most crushing blow dealt to the lovers by the monumental order. The Prince, asserting an authority that goes beyond the petty patriarchy of feuding lords to unite with an entire state apparatus, seems to commandeer the long and messy summary of events just given by the Friar in order to cap the story off neatly – in the form of a singular monument ("never was ... more ... than this"). Even more, he publicizes that singularity by labelling it with the very signifiers the two lovers, in life, most sought to deny. He elevates Juliet and Romeo to "Juliet" and "Romeo," and ultimately to *Romeo and Juliet*: in one line, he resecures the monumental status of their names and extends them beyond fictional space so that they loop back, in a way, to the very title of the work, leaving Romeo and Juliet closed off in a totality, trapped in their wretched signifiers forever.

But all hope is not lost for a positive reading. For, in transforming Romeo and Juliet into *Romeo and Juliet*, in taking the two lovers' corpses and transfiguring them into inheritable icons, Shakespeare's drama detaches them from its internal structures, banishes them (for their own good) from the walls of its Verona, and delivers them back to the flux of adaptation and translation out of which they were first drawn. Four hundred years of Romeo and Juliet's reconfiguration – as "Romeus" or as "Julia," in all variety of places, contexts, and permutations – have proven that translation can indeed overcome the monumental order. Even if in doing so it continues to build its own monuments.

> Wenn man [Shakespeare], sagte ich, aus der englischen Literatur gewissermaßen herausreißt und als einen Einzelnen nach Deutschland versetzt und betrachtet, so kann man nicht umhin seine riesenhafte Größe als ein Wunder anzustaunen. Sucht man ihn aber in seiner Heimat auf, versetzt man sich auf den Boden seines Landes und in die Atmosphäre des Jahrhunderts in dem

> er lebte, … atmet man die Kraft die uns aus Ben Jonson, Massinger, Marlowe und Beaumont und Fletcher anweht, so bleibt zwar Shakespeare immer noch eine gewaltig hervorragende Größe, aber man kommt doch zu der Überzeugung, daß viele Wunder seines Geistes einigermaßen zugänglich werden …
>
> "Sie haben vollkommen recht," erwiderte Goethe. "Es ist mit Shakespeare wie mit den Gebirgen der Schweiz. Verpflanzen Sie den Montblanc unmittelbar in die große Ebene der Lüneburger Heide und Sie werden vor Erstaunen über seine Größe keine Worte finden. Besuchen Sie ihn aber in seiner riesigen Heimat, kommen Sie zu ihm über seine großen Nachbarn: die Jungfrau, das Finsteraarhorn, den Eiger, das Wetterhorn, den Gotthard und Monte Rosa, so wird zwar der Montblanc immer ein Riese bleiben, allein er wird uns nicht mehr in ein solches Erstaunen setzen."[23]
>
> I said: if one, as it were, tears [Shakespeare] out of English literature and transports him individually to Germany and regards him there, one cannot help but marvel at his colossal greatness. But if one visits him in his homeland, transports oneself onto the soil of his country and into the atmosphere of the century in which he lived, … if one feels the energy that emanates from Ben Jonson, Massinger, Marlowe and Beaumont and Fletcher, then Shakespeare remains a great and towering presence, but one gets the impression that many wonders of his mind become more or less accessible …
>
> "You are absolutely right," replied Goethe. "With Shakespeare it is as with the mountains of Switzerland. Transplant Mont Blanc to the middle of the Lüneburg Heath, and you will be left speechless in sheer wonderment at its greatness. But visit it in its own colossal surroundings, come to it through its great neighbors, the Jungfrau, the Finsteraarhorn, the Eiger, the Gotthardt, and Monte Rosa, then Mont Blanc will of course always remain a giant, but it simply will no longer move us to such awe."

Here, another figure: a mountain. Johann Peter Eckermann recounts an 1824 conversation in which Goethe makes Shakespeare into Mont Blanc and places him among the Alps. For our purposes, Goethe's figure acts as a bridge between *Romeo and Juliet* and *Romeo und Julia auf dem Dorfe*. It straddles the artificial monuments of the one text and the root-structures of the other. It moves us out of the internal order of Shakespeare's drama and into the open range of nineteenth-century German literature. It introduces us to another type of figure, in another setting, so as to imagine another version of translation.

On a basic level the two men are talking about the anxiety of influence. Goethe, attributing the freedom of his development as a writer to the absence of any formidable cultural predecessor, has just expressed how fortunate he was not to have confronted Shakespeare fully in his early years. Eckermann then supposes that Germans must be doubly intimidated now that they have general access to Shakespeare's works: they feel the full impact of his individual greatness, and they lack the cushion of knowing him in his context. Goethe seems to agree.

But the discussion is also a struggle to give form to certain problems of translation. *Übersetzen*, the typical word for *translate*, doesn't appear in the passage; instead, the idea of translation is expressed in broader and more spatial terms – terms consistent with those in which we've viewed it so far – through the more common verb *versetzen*, which means *move*, *shift*, *transport*, *relocate*, or *displace*. Eckermann uses *versetzen* first to describe transporting Shakespeare to Germany and then again to describe transporting oneself to Shakespeare's *Heimat*. When Goethe responds, however, he exchanges *versetzen* for a verb that suits his analogy to the natural world: *verpflanzen*, or *transplant*.

What is translation here? To start with, it's free, unfettered by the kind of monumental order that determined *Romeo and Juliet*. Though Shakespeare certainly is monumental, he's also translatable – and that's the issue: knowing how to contain the impact of the movable monument. Translation, in the terms of the discussion, is both psychological and physical, spatial. This is partly an effect of the broad and hence readily metaphorical valence of *versetzen*, but it's also consistent with a tendency among German thinkers of that time to emphasize a physical aspect in the etymology of *übersetzen*: the word also describes the ferrying of something across a body of water (the English Channel, maybe). J.G. Herder, one of the most influential proponents of Shakespeare in Germany, made much of this spatial definition, imagining translation as an act of "bringing the reader to the alien work of art."[24] He eventually passed the idea, along with an interest in Shakespeare, on to Goethe, but Goethe was careful to amend it. Whereas Herder saw translation as an act of ferrying the reader to a foreign shore, Goethe saw it as bringing the work over to the reader, adapting the foreign author to one's native setting.[25] In other words, Goethe believed in sparing his fellow Germans any metaphorical pilgrimage to Shakespeare's *Heimat*. But, judging from his conversation with Eckermann, he didn't want Shakespeare transplanted directly into German soil either. Where, then, should Shakespeare be transported, translated?

Actually, Goethe's answer to this question is already present in his exchange with Eckermann. To decipher it one need only consider his words there as a performance of the translation they claim to address. In a simple way this means that Goethe's statement acts as a translation of Eckermann's: Goethe repeats Eckermann's idea in different words; he retains the sense and, in certain ways, the structure of what Eckermann says while transforming his terms paradigmatically. But we might see something particularly sly in this performance. Goethe doesn't just translate Eckermann's words; he translates their referent – Shakespeare himself, his very origins. In constructing his analogy, he relies on a logic of representation that excludes England completely. If Shakespeare is to Germany as Mont Blanc is to the Lüneburger Heide, then the Lüneburger Heide stands for Germany and Mont Blanc stands for Shakespeare. The first of these representations is based on concrete relations of contiguity, synecdoche: the Lüneburger Heide is a central marker of German geographic identity. But the second representation has no such grounding, no rootedness. That Mont Blanc stand for Shakespeare, that Shakespeare's *Heimat* be represented by a set of mountains far beyond England's borders, is mere associative whimsy, a remarkably free translation. In the act of considering Shakespeare's translation to Germany – Mont Blanc's transplantation to the North German plains – Goethe's analogy allows one to ignore the fact that the figure is already once displaced. Struck with wonder by the moving of a mountain, we may forget to wonder how it was raised there in the first place.

Still, if the logic of translating Shakespeare to the Alps may be suspected for its lack of grounding, the form of the translation might serve well in making up for it. That's because Goethe's translation is, partially, a naturalization. It makes men into mountains and countries into natural landscapes. It creates the sense of a natural order – an order defined by necessity, essences, and roots, beyond temporal and human boundaries, signifying, above all, venerable constancy. Even the work of translation is naturalized, shedding its artificial character, to become a gentle act of *Verpflanzung*.

Very natural, then, that this should all find setting in *die Schweiz*. Switzerland, in the middle of the nineteenth century, lay curiously at the threshold of German culture. Its eastern, mostly German-speaking cantons were surrounded by the southwestern states of the German Confederation (*Deutscher Bund*), but its identity remained separate. Throughout the rest of this essay, it lingers as an odd kind of signifier. Switzerland appears more distinctly natural than political. Or, otherwise, it appears as politically romantic. It represents an ambiguity or an indeterminateness of national signification, not quite neutral, not quite international, not quite German (or French or Italian), but partly all. Such Swiss-ness is comparable to the Dutch-ness that Gary K. Waite portrays in his study of religious polemic throughout the Low Countries (in this volume): it is an identity that refuses to enforce itself as a rigid unity, an expression of tolerance in which the very idea of intolerance is exiled to other lands. In this particular case Goethe seems merely to have intended that Switzerland stand for a locus of simultaneous naturalization and internationalization. His list of mountains represents at least three different political entities of the time – France, regional Italy, and Switzerland "proper" – and in that sense it functions as a deferral of any specific representation. The *Gerbirge* could simply be seen as the setting for Goethe's notion of *Weltliteratur*: a space – somewhat foreign, but equally accessible to a variety of cultures – dedicated to the preservation of a set of literary figures whose greatness supposedly places them beyond national and epochal boundaries. Though figuring Shakespeare as Mont Blanc certainly does remove him from England, it does so in order to offer him up wholly to the rest of the (Eurocentric) world. Yet, as we will see, the figure still stands linked to the Germans who imagine it, and it remains open to less benevolent uses.

The constitution of this figure, ambiguity included, is very much in line with the general character of Shakespeare reception in Germany up to that point in history. Goethe and Eckermann's conversation comes at the end of what were later recognized – more, idealized – as the formative years of Shakespeare's introduction to German culture. This was the so-called classical-romantic period of Shakespeare reception, which began around 1760, when

G.E. Lessing recommended the style of the English dramatist as an alternative to that of French neoclassicism, and gained momentum as more and more prized literary and philosophical figures – C.M. Wieland, Herder, Goethe, Schiller, August Wilhelm Schlegel, Ludwig Tieck – discovered in Shakespeare's works something that corresponded to what they thought literature, and particularly the nascent German national literature, should be. Many of these figures were happy to point out what Roger Paulin calls a certain "affinity of Shakespeare's art with German taste and German *Geist*," and some of them even sought to subsume Shakespeare under a broad notion of Germanic or Nordic tradition: Herder saw Germany as sharing a loose "Anglo-Saxon" heritage with the likes of Shakespeare, and Tieck famously boasted, "Shakespeare und seine bessern Zeitgenossen sind auch deutsch."[26]

In general, though, Shakespeare wasn't forcefully incorporated into German culture at this time. The movement was more in the other direction: German literary trends consciously shifted themselves toward "Shakespearscher Stil," which itself tended more toward universality than cultural particularity.[27] In Shakespeare the Germans saw "an openness to a variety of traditions and a casting wide of the net"; his work stood for "all humanity, *Ganzes*, the full range of the senses and their extreme demonstrations."[28] As Paulin explains it, in the classical-romantic era "the Germans did not annex Shakespeare, as they were later to do in the nineteenth century, in the name of the German nation, but on behalf of the 'Universe', invoking still notions of a god-like genius, a Promethean creation, not confined by cultural borders."[29] This, again, is a Shakespeare of the Alps – a figure situated both at nature's most sublime limit and at its very core; extraordinarily singular, yet universal, and universally translatable.

From here the story could be told of how the spread of German nationalism in the nineteenth and early twentieth centuries brought about the full annexation and appropriation of Shakespeare; how the achievements of the classical-romantic era in comprehending and translating Shakespeare were mythologized and wielded as evidence of Germans' superior appreciation of his works; how Shakespeare's name was further removed from time and tradition to become an open cypher for German cultural purposes; how German scholarship and criticism proudly dominated Shakespeare studies around the world; how Shakespeare's dramas became widely popularized in German theatres, institutionalized in German schools, and standardized in the Schlegel-Tieck translation; how defenders of Shakespeare's greatness were pressed to frame him in increasingly nationalistic terms in order to avoid accusations that they preferred a foreigner to the likes of Goethe and Schiller – in short, how Shakespeare "zum festen Besitz der Deutschen geworden war."[30]

This story is more or less true, and it includes its fair share of monument-building: the great scholarly works on Shakespeare by scholars such as Hermann Ulrici and G.G. Gervinus; the founding of the world-famous *Deutsche Shakespeare-Gesellschaft*, as Germany's first literary society, in 1864; and the 1904 construction of the *Shakespeare-Denkmal* in Weimar, the first monument to Shakespeare on the European continent, which confirmed Shakespeare's place alongside Goethe and Schiller as the "dritter deutscher Klassiker." But for the most part monuments such as the *Gesellschaft* and the *Denkmal* were fairly belated.[31] The primary monuments had already been established during the classical-romantic era, in the more modest form of documented discussions, critical exchanges, and, most importantly, thoughtful translations of Shakespeare's works. These were the monuments that Shakespeare's later supporters continually referred back to as they defined their own terms of praise. The later nineteenth century was not so much a transformation as a reinterpretation of the figures that had already been set forth – figures such as Goethe's vision of Shakespeare among the Alps.

It seems worthwhile, then, to return to that vision once again and test the range of its interpretability. In fact, Goethe's figure, considered as a synchronic image, as a coherent symbolic structure, allows as many interpretations as correspond to the whole line of critical viewpoints on translation that arose out of nineteenth-century Germany. Such is an advantage of dealing with figures of translation. A single metaphor – posed historically at the very moment of transition between the classical-romantic era and the trends of the later nineteenth century – allows us to consider the multiple views of its surrounding time periods without having to subordinate them to a single historical delineation.

The ambiguity of Goethe's mountain-figure comes from something monumental in its character – the fact that it's both singular and universal. This monumentality has two sides to it. On the one hand, it corresponds to the altruistic mission of *Weltliteratur*: to find a common ground on which to place literary figures whose talents themselves combine the singular and the universal, in order to make them accessible everywhere. That common ground, figured through the seeming naturalness and neutrality of the Swiss Alps, serves as a place of preservation, a pure refuge from the apparent stains and superfluities of historical particularity and, theoretically, from the Babel of tongues that confound it. One may call this aspect Goethe's literary cosmopolitanism, though given the nature of the figure I prefer another 'cosmo-' term, which I'll introduce shortly.

On the other hand, it's not hard to see how a claim to joint singularity and universality could also serve another type of monumentality, this one more like the order that rules *Romeo and Juliet*: the monumentality of nations; nationalism. Lawrence Venuti has shown such a pattern in his studies of translation and national identity.[32] Venuti starts from Derrida's belief that "nationalism does not present itself as a retrenchment onto an empirical particularity, but as the assigning to a nation of universalistic, essentialist representation," and he points to instances of such representation even in Germany's classical-romantic era.[33] Instances like these suggest that the Germans, in their mountain-building, weren't just rescuing Shakespeare from a particular context and delivering him to universality; they were also claiming, themselves, to represent that universality.

Venuti focuses not on Goethe but on a pair of his more romantically inclined contemporaries, Friedrich Schleiermacher and A.W. Schlegel. These two differed from Goethe in that they saw translation more as the act of "bringing the reader to the alien work of art" that Herder had first outlined. While Goethe sought to make foreign authors accessible by presenting them to German readers in a more familiar form, Schlegel and Schleiermacher were determined to preserve the alien structure and feel of foreign texts. (Goethe advocated for prose translations of Shakespeare; Schlegel tried to approximate the form of Shakespeare's verse.) Yet alongside this apparent respect for the foreign there was also a distinct tone of national pride. For example, Schleiermacher:

> Our nation may be destined, because of its respect for what is foreign and its mediating nature, to carry all the treasures of foreign arts and scholarship, together with its own, in its language, to unite them into a great historical whole, so to speak, which would be preserved in the center and heart of Europe, so that with the help of our language, whatever beauty the most

> different times have brought forth can be enjoyed by all people, as purely and perfectly as is possible for a foreigner.[34]

Goethe's space of translation was, at least theoretically, a middle ground, separate from both the sending and the receiving nation. But for Schleiermacher that space is Germany itself, into which the outside work is readily carried and united, but somehow still left foreign. Schleiermacher's vision amounts to a full annexation of Goethe's symbolic Alpine realm. The Mont Blanc of that realm becomes part of Germany, as does Shakespeare. The idea of Switzerland – naturalness, purity, neutrality – spills over and dissolves into the expanse of the German nation (which itself was, at this time, an indistinct idea for a loose set of provinces and kingdoms). That nation, assuming its place at the "center and heart of Europe," is left free to select, translate, transport, and preserve that which it deems universal. Historically, of course, this custodial role was asserted with varying degrees of force. Oftentimes it was voiced passively, peacefully, or altruistically. But, as the nineteenth century moved forward, it revealed more and more an underlying aggressivity. One might take this, in fact, as greater evidence that Goethe's metaphor was well chosen. For, despite all the Romantic beauty his generation had come to see in the Alps, it was not forgotten that, traditionally, those mountains had always been viewed as dangerous, and menacing.

Between mountains and monuments, there is always some hint of mysticism. That religions have seen mountains as integral to their respective traditions – that they have built pyramids and temples in their likenesses – is either an echo or an origin of an impulse that leads cultures in general to see great skyward forms as monumental, as colossal markers of a symbolic order. In any case, the form of worship that these forms encourage, the act of their monumentalization, always borders on the religious. Looking behind Goethe's Alpine allegory, one finds the structure of a familiar proverb about bringing Mohammed to the mountain, whose German version is also very common: "Wenn der Berg nicht zum Propheten kommen will, muß der Prophet zum Berge gehen."[35] In fact, that proverb, and its perpetuation in instances such as Goethe's allegory, reveals all too clearly the fate that religious tradition often meets in monuments. The proverb is, significantly, a false representation. It doesn't belong to Mohammed, and it's by no means holy word. It comes from a set of satirical anecdotes by the thirteenth-century sage Khoja Nasreddin, and its central figure was originally a palm tree; the mountain was substituted once the proverb reached Europe, presumably as a reference to the Christian notion of faith moving mountains.[36] Misattribution, misrepresentation, and substitution: this, as we have seen, is the simple stuff of monumental translation. But it's also the stuff of idolatry.

The idea of idolatry comes up often in characterizations of the strange devotion that German culture has at times exhibited toward Shakespeare, as a falsely made foreign figure.[37] From our view the idea might seem to lead back to the order that structured *Romeo and Juliet* – its mode of excessive worship, its intense devotion to statues and icons. But idolatry also suggests infidelity to that order. The monumental order is – excessively, belligerently – monotheistic: it establishes absolute distinctions that separate a group from all that lies outside it, compelling that group to proclaim its singularity through a sacred signifying authority that it views as exclusively its own.[38] Idolatry, however, is a pagan activity. It violates the order by constructing a monument or worshipping an image that originates outside the singular group. When Juliet calls Romeo's self "the god of my idolatry" she is all too truthful: her love is idolatrous; it clings to an object outside her group's signifying order.[39]

Idolatrousness has its own place in the practice of translation. If the monumental order is, in its strict form of monotheism, a system that insists on the pre-eminence of its own signifiers and thus forbids any translation across its boundaries, then idolatry is a practice of building translatable monuments within that order – of translating false gods. But this activity is only called idolatrous when it occurs within, or is seen from the perspective of, the monumental order. If it happens outside such a domain, it's done freely. It resembles the open practice by which polytheistic groups translate the gods of their neighbours and transform them into their own holy monuments. Jan Assmann refers to this as "cosmotheism," a practice of "render[ing] different cultures mutually transparent and compatible."[40] In cosmotheism, one translates in order to "make more transparent the borders that were erected by cultural distinctions."[41]

Goethe can be seen as placing his mountain-monument in a cosmotheistic setting of his own. He offers the harmonious atmosphere of *Weltliteratur* as a positive alternative to the fundamental intolerance of monumental orders. By proposing it as a space in which translation may be carried out freely, he envisions a literary universe that will no longer foster accusations of idolatry or of false monumentalization, a universe in which Shakespeare can be both English *and* German (though Goethe may prefer he be neither). Yet those accusations will continue nevertheless. As the German nation becomes unified and begins to voice its identity all the more aggressively, its own monumental order will begin to harden and constrict. Monumental translation will be carried out as full appropriation – Shakespeare will become German, and only German – or else it will face the charge of idolatry.

> Diese Geschichte zu erzählen würde eine müßige Nachahmung sein, wenn sie nicht auf einem wirklichen Vorfall beruhte, zum Beweise, wie tief im Menschenleben jede jener Fabeln wurzelt, auf welche die großen alten Werke gebaut sind. Die Zahl solcher Fabeln ist mäßig; aber stets treten sie in neuem Gewande wieder in die Erscheinung und zwingen alsdann die Hand, sie festzuhalten.[42]

> To tell this story would be an idle imitation, were it not based on an actual event, as evidence of how deeply rooted in human life are those tales upon which the great works of the past are built. The number of such tales is modest; but they appear ever and again in new clothing, compelling the hand to arrest and preserve them.

This, the opening passage to *Romeo und Julia auf dem Dorfe*, introduces a third and final figure of translation: roots (*Wurzeln*). Keller, like Shakespeare and Goethe, builds a monument that functions as a model of translation. His story is a structure dedicated to the great works of the past and the fabular myths (*Fabeln*[43]) that underlie them. Yet it's also an attempt to dissolve the artificial substance of monuments. He takes Shakespeare's golden statues and Goethe's colossal mountains and embeds them in a state of natural moderation, rooting them deeply in the common soil of humanity. He completes the act of transplanting that Goethe only imagined with Mont Blanc. He naturalizes the entire process of translation.

But Keller's model is, like the rest of the seemingly effortless portrayals of nature in the story, a product of complex linguistic artifice. It's much more complex than the figures we've seen so far. In suggesting that his *Geschichte* acts as evidence that great works of fiction are rooted in human life, he relies on a dizzying strand of analogies. The link between his story and its corresponding event is compared both to the *Wurzeln* that link plant and soil and to the *Fabeln* that link literary work and human life (not to mention the figure of *Gewand*, or clothing). If one follows through with these analogies, an elaborate narrative unfolds. In the beginning, mythic tales grow out of the soil of human existence. They're nourished by it. As they develop, they extend their roots ever deeper into that soil and strengthen their hold on the reality from which they sprouted. Once established, a single set of roots – a single mythic tradition – can support countless instances of fictional regeneration and re-presentation. But by then its hold upon the soil – upon the reality of human existence – has become so fixed that the soil is, in a way, contaminated: it begins to resemble the fictions it nourishes. The fictions themselves gain an ever-stronger stake in real events. What once was a fiction-bearing reality now blends into a relativistic cycle of story-telling and story-living.

Within that cycle three processes perform, to some degree, the work of translation. First, and most obvious, is the translation that takes place from one literary work to another – in this case, from the great *Werk* of *Romeo and Juliet* to the *Geschichte* of *Romeo und Julia auf dem Dorfe*. The title of the novella already specifies its translation as (at least) linguistic and local. Keller characterizes it as *Nachahmung* (imitation) – or, more precisely, he suggests it *would* be a mere *Nachahmung* if it weren't combined with a second type of translation: the translation from reality to fiction, or from an actual *Vorfall* (event) to the fictional *Geschichte*. Keller's term for this relationship, far from any active notion of translation or transformation, is the verb *beruhen* (to rest upon; to be based on). It holds an especially authoritative status (hence its function as evidence) in that it claims to transmit a sense of reality into the text, however vague the means of that transmission may be. The third type of translation isn't exactly active within Keller's text. It is the curious translation from fiction to reality, from *Fabel* to *Menschenleben*, that occurs when humans transform and repeat the substance of fiction in their own lives. It is present in Keller's story only indirectly, due to his having taken such a translation (the *Vorfall* itself) as one of his sources, but it can be imagined nevertheless as having a latent influence upon its form.

First published in 1855, *Romeo and Julia auf dem Dorfe* tells the story of two peasant families that live in the rural Swiss Alps, not far from the city of Seldwyla (the fictional centre of Keller's novelistic universe). Unlike *Romeo and Juliet*, *Romeo und Julia* begins with the origin of the feud it portrays. The fathers of the two families, one having a son and the other a daughter, are launched into a dispute over the rights to a strip of land that lies between the fields they farm – though it's suggested that the land actually belongs to a shadowy third person, a fiddler occasionally seen around the village. The ensuing conflict leads to the demise of both families. Years pass, until one day the now-impoverished fathers – one with his son, now nineteen, the other with his seventeen-year-old daughter – come across each other while fishing. The fathers start to fight. As the two children struggle to pull them apart, their love for each other becomes present. The boy goes secretly to meet the girl, but her father happens upon them and, in a scuffle, is seriously injured by the boy. The lovers, convinced of the cursedness of their fate, run off together for what they plan as a last night of dancing, during which they encounter the fiddler mentioned above. The fiddler, strange and vaguely sinister, invites the lovers to join him and his friends to go live in the mountains, but they decline. Instead, they go to a nearby river, in whose icy waters they are found floating the next morning, having taken their own lives.

From the beginning of the story, one can't help but be struck by the lyrical smoothness of Keller's prose. It has an air of quiet reflection and idyllic calm. Consider the first lines that follow the opening passage from above:

> An dem schönen Flusse, der eine halbe Stunde entfernt an Seldwyl vorüberzieht, erhebt sich eine weitgedehnte Erdwelle und verliert sich, selber wohlbebaut, in der fruchtbaren Ebene. Fern an ihrem Fuße liegt ein Dorf, welches manche große Bauernhöfe enthält, und über die sanfte Anhöhe lagen vor Jahren drei prächtige lange Äcker weithingestreckt gleich drei riesigen Bändern nebeneinander. An einem sonnigen Septembermorgen pflügten zwei Bauern auf zweien dieser Äcker, und zwar auf jedem der beiden äußersten; der mittlere schien seit langen Jahren brach und wüst zu liegen, denn er war mit Steinen und hohem Unkraut bedeckt und eine Welt von geflügelten Tierchen summte ungestört über ihm.[44]

> Near the lovely river that flows by a half-hour away from Seldwyla, a wide sweeping ridge, itself well cultivated, slopes upward and then recedes into a fertile plain. Far off at its foot lies a village, home to several large farmhouses, and over the gentle slope there lay years ago three elegant, long fields, spread out like three vast ribbons alongside each other. One sunny September morning two farmers were out plowing two of these fields – namely, the two outer ones. The middle field seemed to have been lying fallow and desolate for years, for it was covered with stones and high weeds, and a world of little winged creatures buzzed about it untroubled.

A gently natural touch is given to the description, which draws the reader across a great landscape and settles onto an elegantly symmetrical space. Yet already one sees how the seeming lightness or passivity of the prose is combined with a compulsive firmness in its construction. As if to smooth over the roughness of third terms, the narrative immediately reconfigures the three fields it portrays into a balanced binary system – two fields separated by a divider, with two farmers plowing across from each other as harmonious mirror images: "Langsam und mit einer gewissen natürlichen Zierlichkeit setzten sie einen Fuß um den andern vorwärts und keiner sprach ein Wort … So glichen sie einander volkommen in einiger Entfernung; denn sie stellten die ursprüngliche Art dieser Gegend dar …"[45]

This portrayal of the farmers reveals two of the story's most basic structuring principles. First is the movement toward origins. The story is invested in representing something *ursprünglich*, something that occurs almost outside of history, so that it approximates an event at history's primal beginnings. This includes a movement toward the origins of the Romeo and Juliet legend. Not only does the setting of the story inch close to the geographic origin of the myth, just on the other side of the Alps; the form of the story – a novella – also imitates the earliest Italian sources. Even the pastoral sweep of the opening seems to harken back to the first lines of Brooke's poem or the initial setting of Matteo Bandello's *Giulietta e Romeo*.[46] The other principle of the story revealed here is its focus on the identical nature of the two families. The two farmers' names – Marti and Manz – echo each other (somewhat comically) to the point that they effectively defy the purpose of singular labels. Compared with *Romeo and Juliet*, Keller's story treats names with casual indifference. No last name is ever attributed to either family. By the time the reader discovers that the two children are named Sali and Vrenchen, several pages (and several years) into the story, the two names of the title have already superseded them: for the story's purposes, "Sali" and "Vrenchen" mean the same thing as "Romeo" und "Juliet" "auf dem Dorfe" – they are merely particular translations of Romeo and Juliet.

The story's true markers of difference, then, are not names or words; they're spaces. Space here has a much wider significance than in Shakespeare's drama. In Shakespeare's work Romeo's spatial transgressions are very particular and localized; they relate to specific places and territories that were established long ago; and otherwise the tragedy unfolds as a result of temporal incongruities – what Derrida noted as its being *à contretemps*.[47] Keller's conflict could be called *à contre-espace*: the entire feud takes the form of a spatial arrangement at odds with itself. When one day the two farmers tacitly decide that they will begin to plow diagonally into the middle field from either side, with one pass each day, they reflect each other's motives and means of spatial transgression. They cut incrementally further into the field, tossing each stone they find into the middle, until the stones stack high in a line like a "straight spine" [*ordentlichen Grat*] down the centre.[48] Their mirrored action builds the wall that divides them. When Manz decides to purchase the middle field at an auction and demands the space back that Marti had plowed into, they belittle each other with like insults and turn violently opposed. Their arguments revolve solely around spatial demands – that a line be straightened, a triangle made even, symmetry imposed. The middle field takes on a meaning so overdetermined as to evoke an entire philosophical tradition of portraying difference, from Rousseau to René Girard. Whether as a third term, or a symbol of otherness, or an odd remainder, or a common object of mimetic desire, the simple plot of land confounds and eventually destroys the two families.

Yet, for the purposes of this essay, the middle field is most significantly a site where Keller's figure of translation takes root. It becomes a monument ancillary to the one that he dedicated to great rooted fictions. Or rather, it becomes the instantiation of that monument in the story's own natural world.

Monuments, in the story, are clearly primitive constructions. They represent cycles of violence, both latent and active. When Sali and

Vrenchen play together as young children, they end up tearing a doll to pieces and burying it under what the narrator calls "an imposing monument of field-stones" [*ein ansehnliches Denkmal von Feldsteinen*].[49] When, only a few pages later, Manz gathers up the stones that had formed a wall between the two fields and dumps them onto the triangular space that Marti had carved out, the stones form "an enormous pyramid," a "nice monument" [*gewaltige Pyramide ... schöne[s] Denkmal*].[50] And, when Sali attacks and injures Marti – wielding a field-stone – Marti collapses onto this very pyramid-monument. Yet even as these monuments represent violence, they also remember a prior state of peace – or rather, they remember a state in which acts of violence like the children's doll-play were somehow benign. The stones and the transformation of the field, symbolic markers of difference between the two families, create a division across which translation – whether communicative or conjugal – is forbidden. But they also reveal that division as crude and arbitrary. Unlike the monuments of *Romeo and Juliet* – which, having been in place for generations, have had time to shed their link to any origin – these monuments cannot hide their relation to an earlier state that signified fluidity and sameness. They were created out of the identical nature of the farmers' activity and out of the common substance of the natural world. Above all, the monument of the middle field points back to the common source of nature that belies the separating tendencies of appropriative force. Like Keller's figure of translation, it points back to shared roots.

But why point back to roots? There's something more to this gesture than Keller's desire to allude to an oceanic unity at the origin of all difference and language – though that sense certainly lies within *Romeo und Julia auf dem Dorfe*, and it's powerful. The question might be restated: why did Keller bother to make the allusion to *Romeo and Juliet* in his title at all? The story clearly owes essential parts of its structure to the Romeo and Juliet legend, and numerous themes and events within it parallel those of the Shakespearean drama: from its first pages *Romeo und Julia...* incorporates cosmological imagery that plays off the notion of "star-cross'd lovers"; the fiddler, strangely enough, appears as a hybridization of Mercutio and the Friar; and Sali's visit to Vrenchen echoes Romeo's trespass into the Capulet orchard (his departure from her is marked by the singing of larks, and his violence against her father is equivalent to the slaying of Tybalt).[51] Keller had always had a strong interest in Shakespeare, though he was particularly dissatisfied with the way the dramatist had been treated by the German Romantics and later nineteenth-century scholars, who he claimed were unable to see Shakespeare for what he was: a wonderful inventor of situations and developments, "stripped of any clothing of time" [*entblößt von jedem Zeitgewande*], competing with other literary giants in an Olympian setting.[52] Such a portrayal surely resonates with Goethe's vision of Shakespeare in the Alps, and it fits generally with the universal natural realm in which Keller places his own monument to literature (note his use, once again, of *Gewand*). Keller even involves Shakespeare explicitly in the first story of the novella collection that includes *Romeo und Julia* (itself the second story). In *Pankraz, der Schmoller*, a young man begins to read Shakespeare's dramas but despairs that, though people like Shakespeare's characters do indeed exist in the real world, they never appear so "neatly together" as in his works – so that real life "can never fully turn out as a proper tragedy or as a good comedy."[53] Pankraz's concern is in fact instrumental in setting the tone for Keller's stories, which are a careful blend of tragedy and comedy, sincerity and irony. It also suggests why *Romeo and Juliet* – itself a strange mixture of tragedy and comedy, originally lauded by A.W. Schlegel but since overshadowed by the German obsession with *Hamlet* – was the (only) Shakespearean work that Keller chose to adapt.

Still, at least one of Keller's friends questioned his decision to make the reference to his Shakespearean source so explicit. Berthold Auerbach wrote to Keller with concerns that the story's title reminded him of literature for connoisseurs – the kind of literature that doesn't take life as its starting point, but rather the world of the printed word.[54] Keller responded in defense:

> First, what we ourselves write is also printed on paper and belongs as such to the world of paper, and second, Shakespeare, though also printed, is indeed nothing other than life itself, and not some lifeless reminiscence. Had I made no comment about the actual occurrence of the anecdote and about the similarity of the Shakespearean material, I would have been accused of a clumsy repetition, while by offering that short notice up front the story gains a touch of legitimacy; for to those who had not

> thought of *Romeo and Juliet* – and they are many, since these days reading is done so thoughtlessly – the whole thing would have been far too rank and fantastic.[55]

Keller begins this defense by offering himself up to the realm of paper – of printed words and, potentially, of fiction – while giving evidence, in the form of Shakespeare, that life itself can indeed appear within the paper realm. This is, in fact, almost an exact recapitulation of his root-model, which offers up the printed story with reference to the rootedness of Shakespeare's works in human life. But the rest of Keller's protestations seem unreasonable. Would audiences really have thought the story clumsy, rank, or fantastic if he hadn't prefaced it with those words? His concern with being accused of repetition seems just as unnecessary as his original defense against imitation. The main issue, apparently, is Keller's need for some touch of legitimacy [*eine berechtigte Pointe*]. But why is this need so strong?

The answer, it seems, is in the non-Shakespearean source of *Romeo und Julia auf dem Dorfe*. The full write-up of the incident on which Keller based his story appeared in the *Züricher Freitagszeitung* on 3 September 1847:

> In the village of Alsterhausen, near Leipzig, there fell in love a 19-year-old boy and a 17-year-old girl, both children of poor families, who however lived in mortal enmity and would not consent to a union of the pair. On August 15 they betook to an inn where poor folk were seeking their pleasures, danced in said location until 1 in the morning, and thereafter departed. In the morning the corpses of both lovers were found lying in a field; they had shot themselves in the head.[56]

The objective differences between the actual event and Keller's story are obvious (the setting, the form of the suicide) but the article nevertheless shows how more or less faithfully Keller translated something that occurred in reality, and it also shows how justified he was in comparing it to the Romeo and Juliet legend. Still, by noting the role of the article one is obliged to further specify the nature of Keller's translation. It should be clarified that the article itself was the source of Keller's idea for *Romeo und Julia*, not some firsthand experience of the event. The article was the primary material behind the translation. I make this distinction not to suggest that there was something fraudulent in Keller's drawing upon a source, nor to affirm that the form of the article has a particular influence on the style of the resulting translation (though it does – one can sense elements of its harsh and moralizing air in Keller's eventual portrayal of Seldwyla's bourgeois society, as well as in the touches of irony that penetrate the lyrical prose from time to time). I make the distinction to emphasize that the article, through its inclusion in the translation process, introduces the nineteenth-century newspaper into the structure of Keller's model as an integral mediator. The newspaper takes on an intervening role between *Menschenleben* and *Werk* – between life and literary work – and in doing so it claims a function equivalent to that of the *Fabel*. It taps into the soil of human life and produces stories that large communities read and interpret as real, so that the stories are gradually incorporated into the structures of human existence, and human existence, in turn, begins to repeat those same stories. ("How often do we see newspaper headlines like 'Romeo and Juliet in Belfast', 'Romeo and Juliet in Bosnia', 'Romeo and Juliet double teenage suicide'?" R.S. White asks in an introduction to a collection of essays on Shakespeare's play.[57]) The newspaper becomes the modern-day *Fabel*.

The newspaper-as-*Fabel* is the key to the historical specificity of Keller's translation. Just as the Romeo and Juliet legend established a set of roots in reality strong enough to support centuries of offshoots into the world of fictional *Werke*, so the newspaper of the nineteenth century plants itself firmly enough in reality to support another set of imagined works: national communities. "The newspaper reader ... is continually reassured that the imaginary world is visibly rooted in everyday life. As with [novels], fiction seeps quietly and continuously into reality, creating that remarkable confidence of community in anonymity which is the hallmark of modern nations."[58] This is how Benedict Anderson describes the "mass ceremony" of newspaper reading in his study of nations as "imagined communities."[59] Clearly, his portrayal isn't far from Keller's root-model. (The title of his first chapter, which includes the quote above, is "Cultural Roots.") But Anderson traces roots further than Keller does, or at least with more skepticism. He recognizes them as essentially fabricated, and he searches for the need that that fabrication satisfies. The need that he finds is, in fact, that confessed by Keller in his letter to his friend: legitimacy.

Plenty of factors explain a pervasive longing for legitimacy in developed eighteenth- and nineteenth-century communities. Population growth, expanded political territories, communication at a distance, greater movement: all of these circumstances had resulted in a social atmosphere of increased anonymity and unfamiliarity between countrymen, a lessened sense of belonging to a distinct space with a clear identity. Relationships were based more and more on imaginary and less on physical interactions. Secularizing tendencies had weakened reliance on concrete religious foundations. Laws and states no longer seemed absolute. Humans no longer felt anchored in their natural place. Institutions and words were suspected of illegitimacy. This summary of the situation is a set of generalizations, even platitudes, but it's confirmed, at least, in the efforts that were made at the time to counteract it – efforts to root the resultant imaginariness of communities in something real. The solutions were, in many ways, just as imaginary as the problem, but they were no less effective for being so. We've seen a few of them here: newspaper communities, artificial naturalizations, originary myths, and metaphorical roots. Figures of legitimacy.

But figures of translation as well. For, if we broaden our scope, we can see that these figures, at that moment, fit into a whole line of views on translation for which legitimacy is the determining factor. To trace that line we only have to retrace the narrative of this essay, as a sequence of figures and moments. We start at the monumental order – absolute, singular, grounded by signs firmly rooted in their places. This order presents its legitimacy as self-evident, and it insists that translation across its borders is impossible. But a subsequent force opposes it: Romeo and Juliet blaspheme, uproot, trespass, and translate; they reject the legitimacy of the monumental order and struggle to escape it. Over time, their idolatrousness becomes common. Later communities largely ignore the issue of linguistic or cultural legitimacy. By Goethe's moment, the issue is simply dissolved into an atmosphere of cosmotheism, or a cosmopolitan *Weltliteratur*: the translatability of everything. It is in the wake of this dissolution that we find Keller and his metaphorical roots. Keller read about the Leipzig lovers while living in Zurich in 1847. Months later he left for Germany, where he remained for seven years, all the while developing *Romeo und Julia auf dem Dorfe*. This was a meaningful political period, particularly for Keller, who had grown fairly radical in his liberalism. But it was characterized by an absurd contradiction:

the year 1848 had brought about the formation of a Swiss constitution and a federal state, a self-legitimizing political order; but it had also provided the stage for revolutions across Europe that, though mostly deemed failures, seemed to disrobe the legitimacy of the political orders they challenged. Keller was left in a state of sober disenchantment. He bemoaned the pathetic distance from which he and his Swiss countrymen had watched the political spectacle of that year, and he did so in a manner that's telling for our topic: it was, he said, as if they had looked down on it all from the mountains ("wahrhaft vom Gebirge herab").[60] We can imagine what he saw. The structures around him had been unmasked for their illegitimacy, but still they were left standing, in mock monumentality. Nothing was truly left with legitimacy or roots. Stories no longer seemed to cling naturally to their origins, nor did mere words; they floated freely, all too translatably, and authors were left the task of pinning them down, forging legitimacy in fiction as communities forged it in the daily news.

If we linger with the figure of Keller in the Alps just as we lingered with Goethe's figure of Shakespeare there, we're again faced with two ways of viewing a salient image. In one way, Keller can be seen as guilty of cultivating an illusion whose general acceptance would end in the reinstatement of a monumental order. This is partly to implicate him in a guilt that no great writer of his period seemed to escape fully: that of fabricating a harmonious nature in fiction so as to deny the discordant realities of history; the guilt of bourgeois deception. More specifically, though, Keller might be charged with fabricating a very particular idea of nature, one that supports a particular communal identity founded on particular myths and monuments. The origin story that he translates to his Alpine realm risks serving, even against his wishes, as a support for the nation that Schleiermacher envisioned at the "center and heart of Europe." His rooting of Shakespeare in a universalized Swiss soil could lend itself – superficially, but no less potently – to the monumental aspirations of a kind of Pan-Germanism.[61] And if that is the case, if Keller ends up at that point, then the whole line of figures and moments we've traced so far starts to look like a cycle. His root-structure is adopted as one of many expressions of a particular community's legitimacy, and that legitimacy, believed long enough, zealously defended, and passed down through generations, establishes for the community a monumental order. The sequence returns to its starting point, presumably to repeat itself – legitimacy to be unmasked as illegitimacy, monumentality to be uprooted in translation – in violent succession.

But in another way, and with the right theoretical motive, Keller can be saved from the charge of perpetuating a deceptive or destructive cycle. He can be portrayed, instead, as striving to halt the sequence and break the cycle. One could defend him by saying that he is too intent on exhibiting the processes of rooting to allow his roots to lie unquestioned, that he's too concerned with portraying the artifice of divisions to characterize his soil as belonging to any nation in particular. This, then, would be the Swiss-ness that consolidates in Keller: a mountaintop from which he views the spectacle of humanity, all the while criticizing that very viewpoint; a mythical realm shaped and eroded by mundane life; a natural state revealed as a social construct. The conclusion to *Romeo und Julia auf dem Dorfe* offers a convenient figure for such a reading: the story ends with a fictional newspaper report of its lovers' tragedy, conspicuously similar to the report on which the story was based. This final document could be taken as a disruption of the narrative's objective smoothness by a last note of critical irony – the newspaper's condemnation of what it sees as the lovers' wild and immoral passions. It could be labelled a gesture of disclosure, the story's re-acknowledgment of its origins and motivations. The newspaper, then, would act as a window into the historical character of the legitimacy sought by the text. The effect of that window, a narrow slit of self-conscious transparency piercing the epic setting, would prevent the story's absorption into any monumental order. In pointing to the motivations of its rooting, the story would prevent its monument from assuming a timeless nature. In building a monument, it could also claim to be deconstructing one.

Such, then, are two alternatives for judging the text's stance toward translation and legitimacy: to indict Keller for his epic naiveté and for naturalizing his cultural appropriation, or to save him by noting his critical air and naming it that indefinite but generally unimpeachable device, irony. Ultimately, this seems to be a false dilemma. To choose either alternative would be mostly to follow a theoretical impulse determined by its arbitrary position on its own cycle of attraction or aversion to legitimacy. For literary theory, too, is characterized by such cycles. It is itself an anxious negotiation of the problem of legitimacy, verging always in its outcome on either the "post-" or the "new." In the path from new criticism to structuralism to poststructuralism and beyond – a path from rigid, enclosed orders to free-floating signifiers – one sees a retracing of the monumental, the cosmotheistic, and the rootless. I, rather than adopting a judgment consonant with some moment in that cycle, have preferred to represent figures that straddle multiple moments and, through their ambiguity, contain the cycle within themselves. Such figures acknowledge the strain placed on any literary expression as it emerges from and re-enters the turbulence of reception and translation. But the figures have a quality that reflects the forces of translation they confront. The reflection is not single – it is, rather, prismatic – but so much the more does it reveal. It reveals, not least of all, the substance of the reflective figure, the form of its own translatability.

Shakespearean Performance as a Multilingual Event: Alterity, Authenticity, Liminality

ALEXA HUANG[1]

... why do you dress me
In borrowed robes?
Macbeth 1.3.108–9[2]

The age of global Shakespeare 2.0 has arrived. It is an age in which national and transnational performances become self-conscious of the contact zone they inhabit, where dramatic meanings are co-determined by linguistic cohesion and pluralism. If Jacques Derrida's theory of translation makes all writing inherently multilingual, Shakespeare performances as multilingual events at home and abroad complicate the idea of translation and cultural difference. The business of performing Shakespeare has grown into a multilingual affair since the 1990s, as transnational connections and touring have become not only more desirable but necessary for artistic inspiration and success.

In order to address these issues, two frames of reference are useful here: ethnic American performances in New York and international festivals in London. This essay comprises one case study of each of these: John R. Briggs's *Shogun Macbeth* (1985) and the London Globe's multilingual World Shakespeare Festival, which was timed to coincide with the 2012 Olympics. Each of these frames of reference shows how meanings, both intended and unintended, are generated as a result of the shifting cultural and linguistic tensions that inhabit translated Shakespeare from Asian-American to post-imperial British cosmopolitan identities. This hermeneutic is informed not just by the original play, but also by the adaptor's intent, the improvisation and identities of performers, the economics of touring, and the population shifts apparent in the audience, as well as divergent perceptions of intercultural identities.

Multilingual Shakespeare is a boomerang business, inasmuch as it has been transformed from Britain's export to import industry. As touring and transnational productions become a staple of the entertainment industry, translated, bilingual, and multilingual works take centre stage. To celebrate the London Olympics in 2012 and as part of the Cultural Olympiad, the London Globe launched a multilingual Shakespeare project to stage each of the plays in a different language in a single season (thirty-eight in total). Shakespearean plays in translation and adaptation have also inspired English-language performances. John Briggs's English-language play, *Shogun Macbeth*, drew upon Akira Kurosawa's film *The Throne of Blood*, Japanese *kyôgen* comic tradition, Asian-American sensibility, and Shakespeare's language. Even though Briggs's play is in English, its multilingual roots are clearly marked by its sources (Shakespeare and Kurosawa), its performance style, and Pan Asian Repertory Theatre's engagement with notions of otherness and issues of diaspora. Farther afield, numerous productions were designed with multilingual festival audiences in mind, blurring the distinctions between hometown and foreign performances. Kuwaiti-British playwright and director Sulayman Al-Bassam's *The Al-Hamlet Summit* had both English and Arabic versions for touring purposes and demonstrated a keen awareness of the demands and perils of addressing multiple constituencies in one single work. Other artists have experimented with multiple languages within the same production. Singaporean director Ong Keng Sen's pan-Asian *Lear* was performed in multiple Asian languages and theatrical styles to interrogate the fiction of cultural coherence and the issue of inequality in cultural globalization.

This chapter examines the US and UK assumptions behind the production of Shakespeare in multilingual contexts and the patterns of reception, with an emphasis on how cultural authenticity and alterity are reconstructed in the liminal space between languages – a postnational space constructed by festival venues where national identities are blurred by the presence of such entities as transnational corporate sponsors. The organizing principles of London's Cultural Olympiad suggest that beyond the symbolic value of the global at the Globe Theatre, both the celebrated and contrived visions of otherness in Shakespeare as a multilingual event can increase the production value and help to construct a national identity just as the Olympics do. Subsumed under Shakespeare's purported universality, otherness ceases to function as a marker of cultural difference. The space between nations and between languages compels us to rethink Shakespeare's place in today's world, a world dominated by non-Anglophone nations and cultures.

AGENCY, LANGUAGE, AND CULTURAL AFFILIATION

Multilingual Shakespeares put pressure on some of the theoretical models theatre historians have privileged in their documentation of the Western sources of non-Western performances. Some of these touring theatre works are produced under circumstances that may prove challenging or alienating to even the most cosmopolitan audiences. The alienating experience serves important sociocultural and aesthetic functions, and capturing the experience as it unfolds in its shifting cultural location can help us move from narratives driven by political geographies to histories informed by theatrical localities – the variegated locations embodied by touring performances. There are three recurrent themes in the production, touring, and reception of multilingual Shakespeares.

First, the cultural and political conditions of a venue or a production intervene in reception and undercut the work of artistic intent. This genre of stage works is shaped by forms of agency that are not rooted in intentionality. Second, in Shakespearean performance, language is often granted more agency than the materiality of performance, leading to the tendency to privilege certain modernized and editorialized versions of Shakespearean scripts and their accurate reproduction in foreign-language performances. The humanities over the past century have witnessed the so-called linguistic turn, the semiotic turn, and the cultural turn, all of which operate on assumptions about the substantial and substantializing power of language as opposed to the materiality of cultural representation. As opposed to other forms of embodiment, language as a marker is deeply ingrained in identity politics. Language is a tool of empowerment to create solidarity, but it can also be divisive at international festivals, where audience members who do not have access to the immediacy of the spoken language on stage might feel alienated or excluded. Third, non-Western Shakespeare productions that tour to major venues in the West, particularly in the UK, reflect shifting locational terrains of performative meanings that – unlike nationalist imaginations of Shakespeare – do not always correspond to the performers' and audiences' cultural affiliations. The systemic mutations in the politics of cultural production and compression of time and space engender variegated, layered subject positions. These three issues of politics, language, and performative cultural affiliations inform the reception of Shakespeare in multilingual contexts.

MULTILINGUAL SHAKESPEARES IN NEW YORK

John R. Briggs combines both approaches when he brings the Scottish play, Kurosawa, and Asian America together in his *Shogun Macbeth* (1985), a play in English (interspersed with a great number of Shakespearean lines) set on the island of Honshu in Kamakura Japan (1192–1333). Japanese titles or forms of address replace Shakespeare's originals: the Maruyama [Birnam] Wood moves to Higashiyama [Dunsinane]; Thane of Cawdor becomes Ryoshu of Akita; bottom-lit *bunraku* puppets as ghosts are summoned by the witches; "the best of the *ninja*" are the Murderers; and the Porter scene morphs into a *kyôgen* comic interlude performed by a pair of drunken gatekeepers. The emergence of a work such as *Shogun Macbeth* coincided with Japan's rising economic influence in the U.S. in the 1980s and American theatre's continued interest in select Japanese cultural tokens in the new millennium. Briggs notes with enthusiasm the "world-wide rebirth" of Japanese culture that fed into American fascination with "all things Japanese, especially things samurai."[3] As a "samurai" film, *Throne of Blood* has been so successful that it has been cited as inspiration for new works beyond Asia, including Briggs's play, Alwin Bully's Jamaican adaptation (1998), Arne Zaslove's stage production (1990), and Aleta Chappelle's proposed Caribbean film *Macbett* (2010). In contrast to *The Throne of Blood,* which uses *Macbeth* as a launching pad for cinematic experiments, *Shogun Macbeth*, as an American play, deploys fragmented Japanese performance culture to rescue Shakespeare from what Peter Brook has called "cold, correct, literary, untheatrical" interpretations that make "no emotional impact on the average spectator" in a time when "far too large a proportion of intelligent playgoers know their

Shakespeare too well [to be willing to] suspend disbelief which any naïve spectator can bring."[4]

Regarded as a "Kurosawa-lite adaptation," in both the positive and negative senses of the phrase,[5] *Shogun Macbeth* was first staged at the Shakespeare Festival of Dallas in 1985, then by the Pan Asian Repertory Theatre in New York in 1986 (also directed by Briggs). The play has also been performed by non-Asian groups, including a San Francisco State University production directed by Yukihiro Goto in 1992 and The Woodlands High School production directed by Carlen Gilseth at the Edinburgh Fringe Festival in 2003.[6] It was revived in New York in November, 2008, again by the Pan Asian Repertory (directed by Ernest Abuba, who had played the title role in 1986), with a cast of white and Asian-American performers.

The curtain opened to reveal a minimalist stage set cast in ominous green light. All of the action took place in front of an eight-foot statue of Buddha behind a Torii gate (a traditional gate commonly found at the entry to a Shinto shrine), a statue that seemed to look down at the dramatic events with a sense of aloofness, a transcendental indifference; this Buddhist reference informed the framework of the narrative. Biwa Hoshi (Tom Matsusaka), an itinerant blind priest and narrator, opened the production with a powerful delivery of lines from the *Sutra* that echoed the ideas of fourteenth-century *noh* playwright Zeami (*Atsumori*) and anticipated some of Macbeth's later lines:

> BIWA: Life is a lying dream, he only wakes who casts the world aside. The bell of the Gion Temple tolls into every man's heart to warn him that all is vanity and evanescence.[7]
> MACBETH: Life's but a walking shadow, a poor player
> That struts and frets his hour upon the stage
> And then is heard no more.
> It is a tale told by an idiot; full of sound and fury,
> signifying nothing.[8]
> (see *Macbeth* 5.5.23–8)

Fujin Macbeth (Lady Macbeth; Rosanne Ma) walked the stage in *kimono*, while most characters carried *katanas*. The three white-faced *yojos* (weird sisters) in Day-Glo wigs and *kabuki* makeup played a major role throughout the performance, as they manipulated and channelled events and news. Briggs intended "all horrible events or negativity" to spring from the *yojos*.[9] They manipulated the *shoto* (dagger) that Macbeth reacted to ("Is this a *shoto* I see before me, the handle toward my hand?" [see *Macbeth* 2.1.33–4]). Their appearance marked as androgynously "Japanese" through *kabuki* makeup, movements, and chanting, the three *yojos* were played by both male and female performers (Claro Austria, Shigeko Suga, and Emi F. Jones, who doubled as *isha*, the doctor). The *yojos*' cultivation and channelling of various characters' desires and behaviours were enacted by the kinetic energy of their presence in many scenes – seen or unseen by the characters. They delivered armour and a helmet to an agitated Macbeth (Kaipo Schwab) in the final battle scene, and remained on stage as enchantresses and indifferent observers of the end of his story.

Unseen by Fujin Macbeth in the sleep-walking scene but exerting a felt presence, the *yojos* followed her every step of the way, creating the impression that these creatures were both the cause and result of her nightmarish imaginations. Fujin Macbeth's *suri-ashi* ("slide her feet and shuffle along") gait articulated well with the *yojos*' presence in this dreamscape. The doubling of the enchantress (witch) and the healer (doctor), facilitated by a *noh* mask, exemplifies Briggs's investment in the capacity of Japanese signs to generate new meanings from this famous scene (5.1):

> ISHA / YOJO ONE: When was it last she walked?
> *[The lights come up to reveal Yojo One wearing a* noh *mask.]*
> GENTLE WOMAN: Since Shogun [Macbeth] went into the field …
> ISHA / YOJO ONE: In this slumbery agitation, besides her walking and other actual performances, what, at any time, have you heard her say?
> GENTLE WOMAN: That sir, which I will not report after her.
> ISHA / YOJO ONE: You may to me, and 'tis most right you should.[10]

The otherwise benign diagnostic conversation between the doctor and the gentle woman bears a more malignant undertone as the *yojo* (Shigeko Suga) speaks from behind her mask. The very reference to Hell by Fujin Macbeth brings forth the other two *yojos* as she washes her hands:

> FUJIN MACBETH: Yet here's a spot. Out damned spot! Out, I say! One; two; why, then 'tis time to do't. Hell is murky!

YOJO TWO: Fujin Macbeth!
YOJO THREE: Fujin Macbeth!
FUJIN MACBETH: [She does not see or hear the *yojos*] What, will these hands ne'er be clean?!
YOJO THREE: Fujin Macbeth!
FUJIN MACBETH: No more o' that, my lord, no more o' that!
YOJO TWO: Fujin Macbeth!
FUJIN MACBETH: You mar all this with starting.
ISHA / YOJO ONE: You have known what you should not.
GENTLE WOMAN: She has spoke what she should not, I am sure of that.
...
YOJO TWO AND THREE: Oh! Oh! [echo]
ISHA / YOJO ONE: What a sigh is there! [11]

Even though Fujin Macbeth did not interact directly with the *yojos*, the way her lines coincided with those of the *yojos* created a suggestive layer of intertextuality, as she unconsciously danced to the rhythmic hissing and growling of the *yojos* toward the end of this scene. Briggs envisioned an aesthetic structure and "solipsistic" philosophical framework that allowed violence to "scream its horrors beneath the fragrant cherry blossoms."[12] As both observers and instigators, the witches are given substantially more agency than they have in Shakespeare's play.

The artistic and critical focus of *Shogun Macbeth* has thus far rested upon the production's capacity to test Shakespeare's universality and to liberate *Macbeth* from variously defined traditionalist interpretations; as one critic wrote in 1986, "Though language and character are altered, the soliloquies remain and ... at its bloody heart, the play is still *Macbeth*, albeit an exotic one, with a universality transcending time, place and performance style."[13] And yet as a unique English-language adaptation exploiting Japanese sensibilities, *Shogun Macbeth*, as director Abuba points out, also provides an opportunity for exploring what it means to be Asian-American: "One of the major intents of re-visioning *Shogun Macbeth* is to demonstrate the exceptional talent of the new generation of Asian American actors." This vision is in line with the Pan Asian Repertory Theatre's mission to "bring Asian American Theatre to the general theatre-going public and deepen their appreciation and understanding of the Asian American cultural heritage."

Yet is performing in the style of a culture (*kabuki*, for example) actually embodying the culture itself – "not just visiting or importing [it] but actually doing [it]"?[14] Despite its popularity, *Macbeth* is not typically associated with racial questions for Asian-American theatre, a racially defined theatre that was established in 1965 with the founding of the East West Players. *Shogun Macbeth* negotiates challenging cultural terrains as it deploys various elements of Japanese culture to interpret *Macbeth* and to expand the Pan Asian Repertory's slate of otherwise Asian or Asian-American plays. The founder of the group, Tisa Chang, has been criticized for commercializing "Asian-ness" as foreign and exotic. Plays such as *Shogun Macbeth* address the younger generation of performers' resistance to her request to "keep focusing on their Asian identity," which, they believe, limits the creative possibilities even as it promotes Asian-American solidarity.[15] Chang herself seems to be resisting the same concept: "I was so tired of Westerners using Asian-ness as an exotic characteristic."[16] The identity of *Shogun Macbeth* remains unclear, as the blending of different cultures does not necessarily lead to a hybrid one, though the identity of the lead actor, Kaipo Schwab (Macbeth) embodies this ideal: born in Honolulu, he is of Hawaiian-Chinese-German-Irish ancestry. Critics such as Leonard Pronko consider *Shogun Macbeth* a "non-Shakespearean play," albeit with "many of the famous speeches [from *Macbeth*]," but Briggs maintains that the play is still "a Shakespearean play, in the best traditions of what that means."[17] One may wonder whether *Shogun Macbeth*, despite its repackaged Asian cultures and Asian bodies, might not harbour an investment in the notion of "a self-consciously white expression of minority empowerment."[18]

Briggs sought to produce a work that rediscovers Shakespeare's insights by "displacing the audience, forcing involvement in his language, creating an atmosphere that is new and different and capable of spontaneous surprise."[19] Perhaps his displacement succeeded too well; I attended a Sunday matinee performance in the 2008 revival, where more than half of the seats were empty, and quite a few audience members did not sit through the entire performance. Despite their respectable effort, a number of performers appeared to be lost in both the Japanese *mise-en-scène* and the Shakespearean lines, making for an atmospheric but uneven performance that the *New Yorker* called an "ethnic drag show." Perhaps the playwright's "white" identity and the racially mixed cast distracted audience and critics; the reception history of Asian productions of Shakespeare in North America and Europe suggests that reviewers are often more tolerant of cultural differences and artistic innovations when these works are written and directed by artists from Asia.[20] As much as the company, Abuba, and Briggs wanted to break out of the stereotypical association of Asian-American theatre with a necessarily Asian-American repertory which is defined by plays such as David Henry Hwang's *M. Butterfly*, Shakespeare – however Asian – is always "white." However, *Shogun Macbeth* has successfully constructed a contact zone that remains open for future inscription.

MULTILINGUAL SHAKESPEARES IN LONDON

Organizers of the 2012 London Olympics and the Cultural Olympiad proclaimed Shakespeare, once again, the bearer of universal currency. Much more ambitious than the Royal Shakespeare Company's 2006 Complete Works festival, the 2012 Globe to Globe (part of the World Shakespeare Festival) was an integral part of the Cultural Olympiad to celebrate the Olympics. The festival was presented by the Royal Shakespeare Company, the Edinburgh International Festival, and the Globe to Globe program. Opened on 21 April, it brought theatre companies from many parts of the world to perform Shakespeare in their own languages ("37 plays in 37 languages in [the London] Globe, within the architecture Shakespeare wrote for."[21] In fact, thirty-eight Shakespearean plays were performed in languages ranging from Lithuanian to British Sign Language. This is arguably one of the most important festivals since David Garrick's Shakespeare Jubilee in 1769 that jump-started the Shakespeare industry and tourism in Stratford-upon-Avon. Billed as a "great feast of languages,"[22] the Olympiad season featured *Troilus and Cressida* in Maori, *The Tempest* in Arabic, *The Taming of the Shrew* in Urdu, *Richard III* in Mandarin, a Cantonese *Titus Andronicus*, a Korean *Midsummer Night's Dream*, *All's Well That Ends Well* in Gujarati, and *Coriolanus* in Japanese, among other plays. The Globe to Globe's website suggests that the festival "will be a carnival of stories," including inspirational stories by companies "who work underground and in war zones."[23]

The festival planners made choices about the languages to include in the festival and the companies to invite (usually one company for each language including Welsh, though Ninagawa Yukio's *Cymbeline* was staged at the Barbican and Motoi Miura's *Coriolanus* at the Globe), but they worked with the visiting companies to decide on the Shakespearean plays to perform. The World Shakespeare Festival, unlike the previous RSC Complete Works Festival, included almost exclusively non-English-language performances. The WSF also made an effort to cover Africa, the Americas, Russia, Asia, Europe, and New Zealand. In terms of geographical distribution during the WSF, European companies alone offered fifteen touring productions to the festival including British Sign Language performances. Asian companies offered eight productions (not counting the Maori *Troilus and Cressida*), African companies six, and Middle Eastern companies six. Groups from Argentina, Brazil, Mexico, and the U.S. also brought productions to the WSF. The 2012 Globe to Globe, a core component of the WSF, had a few conditions ("the artists will play the Globe way"),[24] including running time under two-and-a-quarter hours, synopsis surtitles, minimal stage set and technology, and no lighting. Some of these limitations are part of the unique architectural space of the London Globe and the need for quick turnaround time among thirty-seven productions in rapid succession, but other conditions are related to the festival's goal to celebrate Shakespeare and world cultures, such as enforced linguistic authenticity, though there were a few exceptions to the ban on English on stage.

Some productions tapped into geopolitical imaginaries. To the Globe's credit, they had an inclusive policy and issued open calls for proposals. Some companies were interested in geopolitical alignment, as evidenced by the Globe's promotional language for Teatro di Roma's production: "Where else but from Rome for *Julius Caesar*?" Andrea Barraco's *Julius Caesar* touts its cultural bona fides: it is set in "a dreamlike yet contemporary Rome."[25] Some companies approached the Globe with plays already in production. For example, Yohangza Company's (*yohangza* means 'travellers') Korean adaptation of *A Midsummer Night's Dream* has toured internationally to critical acclaim. The Globe also commissioned some productions, such as the National Theatre of China's *Richard III*. In still other instances, the Globe suggested plays for the companies to consider, and the companies' rationales for choosing a specific play ranged from interest in creating escapist fantasies and experimenting artistically to a desire to participate in political activism. The Roy-e-Sabs Company of Kabul roundly rejected *Richard II*. *The Comedy of*

Errors performed in Dari suited them better because they wanted to have a laugh amid the realities of harsh Afghan politics, according to director Corinne Jaber. The themes of exile and the darker aspects of the comedy were not lost on the company and their audiences. The play opens with a merchant from Syracuse telling his life story in Ephesus, where he is about to be executed for violating the travel ban between the two warring cities. Jaber's group had to rehearse in Delhi for the Globe-commissioned production after having narrowly escaped being killed in a Taliban attack on the British Council building in Kabul.[26] Ashtar Theatre of Ramallah gladly took on *Richard II* because, according to Globe to Globe festival director Tom Bird, the "Palestinians were desperate to tell their stories" through the Arabic adaptation.[27]

Beyond international politics, the World Shakespeare Festival is also conceived of as a festival of languages that celebrates and recruits London's diverse ethnic communities, some of which have historically been marginalized. Major world languages, as defined by the number of speakers, were obvious choices, including Spanish, Mandarin, Russian, and Hindi; and languages that are important to London communities, such as Bengali, were also included. For eighty-three percent of the audience members who were members of these communities, it was their first visit to the Globe.[28]

The festival at the Globe concluded in early June, but other foreign touring productions continued to arrive in Stratford-upon-Avon and elsewhere in the United Kingdom throughout the summer. Saturated with foreign-language productions, the festival was both boldly experimental and reassuringly British, anchored by the production that both closed the festival and opened the Globe's own season: Dominic Dromgoole's English *Henry V*, which, according to the Globe's marketing material, "celebrates the power of English, or any other language, to summon into life courts, pubs, ships and battlefields, within the embrace of 'the wooden O.'"[29] The World Shakespeare Festival therefore served multiple purposes. First, it has successfully expanded its clientele by inviting London's ethnic communities to occupy the Globe's space. Second, the multilingual Shakespeare festival was a step toward consolidating the underdefined cosmopolitan British identity that was created at the inception of the original Globe. Third, it celebrates diversity within the United Kingdom (Welsh and British Sign Language were among the languages represented).

Finally, though, the festival was directed at the international audience who are the consumers of the South Bank's culture-driven tourism.[30] The timing of the festival coincided with the 2012 Summer Olympics, and the productions were offered in a model of one play per language in quick succession (each production ran for only two to three days). This provided enough diversity to allow tourists who had come for the Olympics to see several different plays during a short stay. The Globe appealed to these particular tourists by offering packages that were named after sporting events: biathlon for two shows, triathlon for three shows, decathlon for ten shows, and Olympian for all thirty-eight shows.

However, unlike the Olympic Games, which focus attention on individual star athletes even when they participate in team sports, the World Shakespeare Festival at the London Globe seemed to have sidelined individual artistic identities: the festival promoted a Bengali *Tempest* (rather than a *Tempest* directed by Nasir Uddin Yousuff), a Turkish *Antony and Cleopatra* (rather than director Kemal Aydogan's production), and so on. It is not always easy to locate the names of participants and further information in English about the director and cast. The Globe did away with programs altogether and instead provided a bilingual leaflet for each production that provided only scanty information. The same is true of their website. By contrast, much more information is readily available for the Royal Shakespeare Company's or the Globe's productions in English. The Globe's strategy of emphasizing the languages of the productions suggests that the main selling point is national or political Shakespeares rather than the backstories of artists, for which festival audiences may not have patience.

UPSTAGING LINGUISTIC DIFFERENCE

Prominent in the marketing language of the World Shakespeare Festival (of which Globe to Globe was a part) was Viola's aforementioned question in *Twelfth Night*, now made rhetorical: "What country, friends, is this?" appears with an image of a marooned ship on the WSF's website to advertise the RSC's "shipwreck trilogy" (*The Comedy of Errors*, *Twelfth Night*, and *The Tempest*) and to serve as a tongue-in-cheek reaction to the deliciously confusing festival.[31] The idea seems to be that if each country's artists fully embody the essence of their culture, the audience would be able to tell which country it is at first blush. The Q Brothers' ninety-minute hip-hop *Othello: The Remix* was invited to represent the US at the Globe. Set in the modern-day United States, the story about the reigning king of hip-hop was acted and narrated by a cast of four men in jumpsuits, with a DJ up in the balcony. The production was among the first show to be sold out, and attracted a large number of young audiences.

There were moments in several productions when questions about cultural and geopolitical identities ceased to be rhetorical and became pressing in a productive way. When the National Theatre of China's *Richard III* opened at the Globe on 28 April 2012, the container that was carrying their exquisite set and costumes was still languishing on the North Sea. The Globe's support team and the Chinese actors quickly assembled substitute costumes and props from the Globe's storage room and the company pulled off a stellar, stylized performance without their full-face masks. They used simple but effective Western costumes, including Richard's red gloves, according to the conventions of the two primary styles the production employed, *jingju* and *huaju* (spoken drama). This is arguably intercultural theatre at its best, because both the hosts and visiting company turned contingencies into opportunities while on the road. Despite the overwhelming success of the performance in London, which was partly due to the effectiveness of the improvisation, director Wang Xiaoying and his crew were not entirely happy about the missing costumes and props.

While the production seems to hail from China, multiple intercultural elements indicate that it is born in a fluid, heterotopic space created by stage designer Liu Kedong. One of the most visible elements is calligraphy. The title "Richard III" is written with English letters morphed into pseudo-Chinese written characters in the style of square word calligraphy pioneered by the artist Xu Bing. The letter R for example is fused with the Chinese character for human (*ren*) and placed on top of a triangular structure that contains the remaining letters of Richard. This is an instance where Viola's question takes on an interesting dimension. For English speakers who cared to look closely, they would realize they could actually read the writing that seemed foreign at first glance. For Chinese speakers who assumed they could claim insiders' knowledge, they would quickly discover that the pseudo-Chinese characters were inscrutable except for individual radicals and elements (such as *ren*) that made up the square word calligraphy.[32] During the performance in Beijing with full stage set and costumes, names of characters that would be killed by Richard appeared in the same fashion on the backdrop of the stage. Buckets of blood were poured down on the names, gradually devouring them and Richard's kingdom.

One of the contributions of multilingual Shakespeares is that Viola's question will be asked with increasing urgency and will prompt more reflections on cultural identities that have been taken for granted. "Shakespeare" is a canon that is supposedly familiar to educated English speakers, but it is increasingly alien to the younger generation. If the Mandarin *Richard III* estranged Shakespeare in linguistic and artistic terms, the hip-hop *Othello* made Shakespeare more familiar and relevant.[33] Thus, the Globe to Globe seasons and other similarly structured festivals, including the EIF and the Barbican International Theatre Events, pitched Shakespeare as global celebrity against Shakespeare as national poet and created a new brand with contemporary currency and vitality.

THE BUSINESS OF WORKING WITH AND AGAINST THE SURTITLES

During the World Shakespeare Festival in 2012, the Globe devised a strategy to divert attention away from the surtitles to the action onstage and applied it uniformly to all of the productions in different languages. The purpose was to remove language as a distraction, if not an obstacle, in order to allow for a certain degree of improvisation. One obvious limitation is that the architectural space of the Globe is not ideal for line-by-line surtitles because of the pillars and the thrust stage. Only short summaries of the scenes – written by the Globe staff in consultation with the visiting companies – were projected on the two screens next to the stage. According to Tom Bird, the synopsis surtitles were meant to avoid the elitism associated with line-by-line translations of Shakespearean texts.[34] The plot summaries were based on Shakespeare's script most of the time rather than on performative choices or improvisational elements. Obviously no synopsis can be neutral whether it is based on narrative or dramaturgical structure, because it involves interpretive acts. As the actors worked with and against the surtitles, the synopsis surtitles redirected the audience's attention to the tension between the plot and dramaturgical structures, highlighting the "Brechtian narrative tension and elements of mediation," as British scholar and artistic director of the Pantaloons Stephen Purcell observed.[35] In the Mandarin *Richard III*, short English phrases were inserted by actors playing the two murderers for more immediate comic effect. In another production, the actors mocked the surtitles. The audiences were told not to trust what was being projected "up there." In the Hindi production of *Twelfth Night* by Company Theatre, the yellow tights Saurabh Nayyar's Malvolio wore onstage provided an interesting contrast with the cross-gartered yellow stockings the surtitles mentioned. Such moments of textual resistance became more noticeable through the synopsis surtitles.

For certain productions with large expatriate communities in London, such as the Hindi *Twelfth Night*, the Korean *Midsummer Night's Dream*, and the Mandarin *Richard III*, few audience members seemed to miss the surtitles, since a majority of them spoke the language. The strategy of projecting summaries rather than fully translated surtitles was not always successful, as the productions had to be designed to work visually and musically against the crude plot summaries. Some productions worked well for the extremely mixed international audiences, such as audience for the Yohangza Company's *A Midsummer Night's Dream* (which had toured to the Barbican in London a few years before in 2006 with a full set of surtitles – a line-by-line translation of the adaptation from Korean into modern English). Other companies played to the expatriate community and neglected audience members who were not versed in the language, such as the Company Theatre's *Twelfth Night* in Hindi, directed by Atul Kumar. Citing "a Hindi-speaking woman sitting next to [him]," Peter Smith applauded the accessible translation in modern prose but lamented the fact that the English-speaking audience had no access to parts of *Twelfth Night* "that cause the emotions to well up: the delicacy of Viola's 'patience on a monument' (2.4.114) or Olivia's pathetic self-abasement as she offers herself to the ungrateful boy (3.4.212)."[36]

Some touring or intercultural productions were seen as showcases for the exotic beauty of unfamiliar performance traditions for cultural elites. Targeting audiences who are bored by an overworked Shakespeare through the education system, these productions are not for purists. A few strands dominate in the narratives surrounding this type of production, ranging from celebration of other cultures' reverence of Shakespeare (e.g., the "Shakespeare Is German" season at the London Globe in 2010) to suspicion about delightful but bewildering (for the press at least) productions that are fully indigenized. The Globe has played host to numerous such productions, and the RSC often sets English-language performances by British actors in non-British locations.

Directors face a dilemma, as they are caught between pursuing authenticity and "selling out." For example, the RSC's recent English-language productions of two plays, one Chinese and the other Shakespearean, have re-ignited debates about cultural authenticity. The first is Gregory Doran's adaptation of *Orphan of Zhao* with an almost exclusively white cast of seventeen. British actors of East Asian heritage have spoken up against the practice of "non-culturally specific casting," in Doran's words, or colourblind casting.[37] The politics of recognition can be a double-edged sword. On the one hand, intercultural theatre is an important testing ground for ethnic equality and raises questions of equal employment opportunity in the UK. On the other hand, can an all-white cast not do justice to *Orphan of Zhao* just as an all-Chinese cast performed *Richard III* at the London Globe and in Beijing? Why would an English adaptation of a Chinese play have to be performed by authentic-looking East Asian actors?[38] The second is Iqbal Khan's *Much Ado About Nothing* that is set in contemporary Delhi and staged at the Courtyard Theatre in Stratford-upon-Avon in August 2012. In her essay in the program, Jyotsna Singh reminds the audience that "the romantic, sexual and emotional configurations underpinning the centrality of marriage in Shakespeare's romantic comedies" are elements that "richly resonate within the Indian social and cultural milieu."[39] Clare Brennan, writing for the *Guardian*, believes that the transposition of Messina to contemporary Delhi works well, because it "plays to possible audience preconceptions about the communality and hierarchical structuring of life in India that map effectively on to similar structuring in Elizabethan England."[40] Performed by a cast of second-generation British Indian actors to Bollywood-inspired music as part of the WSF, the "post-colonial" production (in Gitanjali Shabani's words)[41] was quickly compared by the press and reviewers to the two more ethnically authentic productions at the Globe from the Indian Subcontinent (Arpana Company's *All's Well That Ends Well* directed by Sunil Shanbag in Gujarati and Company Theatre's *Twelfth Night* directed by Atul Kumar in Hindi). Cultural, linguistic, and ethnic pedigrees are part of the picture.[42] Some critics question the RSC's form of internationalism. Birmingham-born director Khan's treatment of Indian culture is seen as too simplistic. Kate Rumbold wishes the production had not ignored but "ironized the company's inevitable second-generation detachment from India."[43] Taking issue with the production's "pastiche of 'internationalism', with apparently second generation British actors pretending to return to their cultural roots in a decidedly colonial way," Kevin Quarmby states that the production offers "the veneer of Indian culture, served on a bed of Bradford or Birmingham Anglicized rice." He concludes that "as the World Shakespeare Festival and Globe to Globe seasons have shown, 'international' is best understood in the context of the nations who embrace Shakespeare as their own."[44] The more difficult part of these debates concerns commercialized cultural and ethnic identities. Obviously art and commerce are not antithetical activities, but they have become inescapable predicates in the debates about the sociological and expressive values of touring and intercultural Shakespeare performances.

CONCLUSION

While multilingual Shakespeares may celebrate polyglot cosmopolitanism, their reception is governed by the logic of cultural prestige. In the case of the 2011 Edinburgh International Festival, a bridge was built between Europe and Asia, as EIF director Jonathan Mills had hoped, but Asia's economic prowess did not quite translate into cultural prestige or meaningful ways to intervene in Western cultural hegemony. Oh Tae-suk expressed a strong desire to validate the cultural value of Korea through his production in Edinburgh.[45] The Korean press took pride in the British approval of Oh's production by noting how it captured the imaginations of the demanding audiences in Shakespeare's home country, as was reported in the *Donga News*,[46] and the YTN *News* referred to the British media's attention: "Oh Tae-suk's *Tempest* drew critical interest from England's prominent newspapers such as *The Guardian, Telegraph,* and *The Financial Times* and was given four out of five stars."[47] One of South Korea's major newspapers noted, when the production visited Russia, that the "Korean *Hamlet* works well on international stages" because Shakespeare could help condense select aspects of Russian and Korean cultures and facilitate an otherwise challenging cross-cultural encounter.[48] This kind of sentiment enabled high-profile touring productions to receive government support and become part of South Korea's branding effort. Along with corporate sponsors such as HSBC and Shell UK, several Asian government agencies co-sponsored the tours of productions to Edinburgh, as they did again for the 2012 World Shakespeare Festival, in the hope of elevating of the status of their cultural productions. The PRC's Ministry of Culture supported *The Peony Pavilion* and *The Revenge of Prince Zi Dan*, and its rival Republic of China in Taiwan backed *Lear Is Here*. Public unease about these sources of funding led Mills to clarify for the *Scotsman* that "there was no pressure placed on the Festival by either government agencies" and to stress that "it is extremely important to remain connected in China ... but it is not an attempt to be a Chinese festival in any way."[49] During the World Shakespeare Festival 2012, the London Globe did not share box-office income with the guest artists, but it gave each company a fixed fee, local accommodation, and fifteen round-trip tickets to London.[50] Despite the Globe's offer, most companies had to rely on other sources of funding.

Multilingual Shakespeares have a de-territorializing effect, in the anthropological sense, that unmarks the cultural origins of intercultural productions because they work against assumptions about politically defined geographies in theatre historiography – artificial constraints that no longer speak to the realities of theatre-making. Touring productions can also re-territorialize the plays upon arriving in a new location.[51] In a world constantly in motion, representations of certain aspects of culture transcend territorial boundaries. These touring works can be best understood through theatrically defined cultural locations (e.g., a French-Japanese *Richard II* in Paris and on tour, a "culturally neutral" *Richard III* made in Beijing but presented in Berlin) rather than through political boundaries (e.g., when "Shakespeare in India" is used as unproductive shorthand for literary universalism). Simplified notions of the universal can be self-deceptive and even self-effacing, as Marvin Carlson points out in his study of Brook and Mnouchkine, because it "den[ies] the voice of the Other in an attempt to transcend it."[52] Locality criticism, as I have suggested elsewhere, focuses on the multilayered cultural localities within and around a production (and its venue) so as not to impose on the work the nation-state as a critical criterion.[53] Theatre can produce and redefine visible and invisible cultural localities. Recent publications have begun to explore these fronts to show that theatrical cross-fertilization and mobility is the norm, not the exception. As Steve Tillis points out in his study, theatre history is currently driven by polity, by periodization, and by continental divisions, and as a result it inadvertently creates myths of multiple unknowable objects.[54]

Afterword

JAMES LOEHLIN

Early in *The Merchant of Venice*, the maid Nerissa is asking the heiress Portia her opinions of the various suitors, defined mainly by their nationalities, who have come to Belmont to court her.

> NERISSA: What say you then to Falconbridge, the young Baron of England?
> PORTIA: You know I say nothing to him, for he understands not me, nor I him. He hath neither Latin, French, nor Italian, and you will come into the court and swear that I have a poor pennyworth in the English. He is a proper man's picture, but alas, who can converse with a dumb show? How oddly he is suited. I think he bought his doublet in Italy, his round hose in France, his bonnet in Germany, and his behavior everywhere. (1.2.57–64)

This passage is interesting for several reasons relating to the concerns of this collection, *Interlinguicity, Internationality, and Shakespeare*. Falconbridge is one of a range of suitors from nations as far afield as Scotland and Morocco; Portia's Belmont is evidently as cosmopolitan as Antonio's Venice, where "the trade and profit of the city / Consisteth of all nations" (3.3.30–1). In the introduction to this volume, Michael Saenger writes of early modern London in similar terms, as "a mercantile boomtown, thriving in large part because of its inclusion of multiple languages and its corresponding fluency in international trade." Young Falconbridge has apparently been exposed to the dress and behaviour of other Europeans – whether in London or on the grand tour that has brought him to Belmont – and has adopted them as his own. However gracelessly, Falconbridge has defined himself partly through international exchange, even if only as a tourist or borrower of fashion. Yet there is a suggestion of English insularity or xenophobia in his failure to learn any of the languages that distinguish Portia, by contrast, as an educated European, a woman of the world.

In the Elizabethan theatre, this moment from *The Merchant of Venice* gave the predominantly English spectators a chance to laugh at themselves. Perhaps that laughter was self-congratulatory and jingoistic; perhaps it brought with it a brief troubling vision of themselves as other, as foreign, as mute and marginal within a busy polyvocal Europe. In any event, this moment calls attention to something that is true but unacknowledged in the majority of Shakespeare's plays: that the characters are understood, throughout, to be speaking a language other than English. This is a point that Shakespeare usually resists calling attention to, even when the matter of language is foregrounded within a given play. "Where the devil should he learn our language?" Stephano asks about Caliban in *The Tempest*, without making mention of what language (presumably Italian) it is (2.2.63–4). Ferdinand reacts in a similar manner to Miranda's speech: "My language! Heavens!" (1.2.432). For Ferdinand, this language is a reminder of his royal status – "I am the best of them that speak this speech" – whereas for Caliban it is a mark of his subjection and, perhaps, a means of resistance: "You taught me language, and my profit on't / Is I know how to curse" (1.2.433, 366–7). But in neither case is the language linked specifically to national identity, nor is the audience forced to hear it as anything other than English.

This apparent transparency of the vernacular language is the rule throughout the twenty-five of Shakespeare's plays, well over half, to have non-English settings. Some of the early plays do flirt with linguistic specificity. Characters in *The Taming of the Shrew* throw around the occasional "*Basta*" or "*Mi perdonato*," and the "feast of languages" in *Love's Labour's Lost* is one of its defining features (perhaps drawing on its resonances with the tangled history of Navarre, as Elizabeth Pentland's contribution to this volume suggests). But for much of Shakespeare's oeuvre, self-conscious attention to the plays' supposed language is surprisingly rare. It is in the English history plays, accordingly, that language is most fully made an issue, connected, as it so often is, with national identity. The banished Mowbray tells Richard II that "Within my mouth you have enjailed my tongue," complaining that being cast out of England is tantamount to "speechless death" (1.3.160, 166). In *1 Henry VI*, Joan la Pucelle speaks French to talk her way past the sentries guarding Rouen, though elsewhere she and her compatriots speak English (3.2.13). In *Henry VIII*, the Spanish-born Queen Katherine insists that the Cardinals address her cause in English rather than Latin, saying, "I am not such a truant since my coming / As not to know the language I have lived in. / A strange tongue makes my cause more strange suspicious" (3.1.42–4). All of these moments highlight the predominance of English as the language of the text, but promote an awareness of linguistic alternatives within and beyond it.

The history plays that explore most fully the issues of language and nationality are those most extensively considered in this volume, *1 Henry IV* and *Henry V*. In the former, as Philip Schwyzer here suggests, the presence of unscripted Welsh dialogue destabilizes not only the question of British identity within the play, but our notion of the Shakespearean text itself; perhaps it should be considered a multilingual work of which only the English portion survives. *Henry V* calls attention to matters of language most famously through the French dialogue between Princess Catherine and Alice in 3.4 – the only substantial scene in the canon not written in English, and one that provocatively addresses language, nationality, gender, and power. The play also raises questions about identity within the British Isles through the use of dialect markers for Welsh, Scottish, and Irish characters – "What ish my nation?" the Irish MacMorris demands to know, and the play never fully answers his question (3.3.61). Moreover, the substantial presence of French characters in *Henry V* allows for a variety of linguistic effects, including the translingual homophonic puns Patricia Parker describes (as when Pistol hears French "bras" as English "brass"), and the coarse equine jesting of the French tent scene, analyzed by Lauren Coker, which exploits the English pun on "horse/whores" to foster a stereotype of perverse Continental sexuality.

In a play such as *Henry V*, the issues raised around matters of language and nation are unavoidable. But Portia's English suitor reminds us that language should never be taken for granted in Shakespeare. The contributors to this volume reveal the fertile field of linguistic and cultural interaction within which Shakespeare's work was produced, as well as the ongoing problems of speech, authority, and nationhood it continues to raise as it is reproduced in our own global century. Early modern Europe was a place where language, as Gary Waite's essay suggests, could create kinship with religious or cultural others, but could also literally demonize them. The historical development of English, its hybrid history, gave Shakespeare the tools for unparallelled verbal inventiveness, as several of the essays attest. The "twinomials" that Scott Newstok identifies throughout Shakespeare's work undoubtedly enrich its poetic fabric, juxtaposing differing linguistic heritages, rhetorical registers, and sonic textures. These pairings not only allow Shakespeare to make effective use of the contrast between the Latinate and the Germanic elements of Early Modern English; they also, as Robert N. Watson notes, often serve to provide glossaries for the auditor, with more familiar words reinforcing the meaning of those perhaps less often heard.

Patricia Parker and Lauren Coker point out how this linguistic layering gives the active listener multiple options for understanding the spoken text, providing a wealth of possible puns, wordplays, and suggestive mishearings, extending productively beyond the permeable borders of English. Paula Blank's essay offers a nuanced and generative way to hear Shakespeare with the ears of modern English speakers without losing the linguistic range and depth of the text; our evolving language can provide new ways into a corpus of work that is, after all, still being continually reproduced in performance.

The essays in the final section productively examine the ways the cultural currency of Shakespeare may or may not be conditioned by the linguistic authority of the text. Brian Gingrich demonstrates how Gottfried Keller succeeded in transplanting Shakespeare's *Romeo and Juliet* from its linguistic roots into the cultural soil of central Europe, creating a new prose work with its own rival authority in the German-language world. Alexa Huang, by contrast, notes the cultural tensions and anxieties surrounding multilingual productions of Shakespeare in international contexts such as the 2012 London Olympiad. What does it mean to produce Shakespeare in a global context? What kinds of authority do linguistic and cultural translations of Shakespeare invoke or appropriate? Who is speaking through Shakespeare's language?

Some years ago, Sir Peter Hall predicted that in another century or two Shakespeare's language will have become so remote from modern English that it will no longer be performable. My own experience teaching Shakespeare through performance leads me to hope otherwise. In working with the University of Texas Shakespeare at Winedale program, I have found that both students and audiences are more than willing to meet Shakespeare halfway. The very fact that we live in such a diverse and dynamic linguistic moment means that people, especially young people, are continually learning unfamiliar words, coining neologisms, adjusting frames of verbal reference. Moreover, the linguistic text has always been only one of the many languages of the stage, and what may seem archaic and incomprehensible on the page can often be communicated in performance with startling clarity. Finally, the eloquence and power of Shakespeare's language should never be underestimated, even in situations where many of its nuances are lost. English would have to change very drastically indeed before its speakers would lose the force of "I do, I will" or "Never, never, never, never, never." But the essays in this collection impel us not to take Shakespeare's language for granted. As the central element in one of the most influential bodies of work in human history, Shakespeare's language necessarily warrants the array of searching and vigorous scholarship the present collection represents. The questions these essays raise – about language, authority, nationality, and culture – become even more compelling as Shakespeare's canon enters its fifth century of existence, and continues to be reinvented "in states unborn and accents yet unknown" (*Julius Caesar* 3.1.114).

Notes

INTRODUCTION

1 The presence of active foreign-language communities in London, particularly speakers of French, Italian, and Dutch, is most easily visible in the churches that performed services in those languages. On the Stranger Churches, see Douglas Kibbee, *"For To Speke Frenche Trewely": The French Language in England, 1000–1600: Its Status, Description, and Instruction* (Amsterdam: Benjamins, 1991), 106–7, 131.

2 See Kathleen Lambley, *The Teaching and Cultivation of the French Language in England During Tudor and Stuart Times* (Manchester, UK: Manchester University Press, 1920), 144–5.

3 Carla Mazzio, for example, has traced the powerful ways in which gestures to the failure of language, such as mumbling and stammering, point to both deep epistemic conflicts and specifically linguistic anxiety; as she notes, for "many writers of the period, attempts to enrich the language could seriously compromise natural bonds integral to both communal intelligibility and national coherence." *The Inarticulate Renaissance: Language Trouble in an Age of Eloquence* (Philadelphia: University of Pennsylvania Press, 2009), 99.

4 Deanne Williams, in *The French Fetish from Chaucer to Shakespeare* (Cambridge, UK: Cambridge University Press, 2004), has influentially elucidated the continuing tension between French and English, both as languages and as perceived identities, well after the Norman Conquest.

5 For example, Abigail Dings, in *Developing Interactional Competence in a Second Language: A Case Study of a Spanish Language Learner* (Doctoral dissertation; Austin: University of Texas, 2007), suggests that language learners in particular tend to exhibit a variety of quasi-linguistic

and non-linguistic behaviours to align themselves with foreign-language speakers as they transition into foreign fluency.

6 Jean-Christophe Mayer has recently suggested that the fact that the English army in *Henry V* has such trouble communicating stands in pointed contrast to the perfect English of the French camp in that play, thus hinting at a broad and delicate questioning of linguistic integrity; see "The Ironies of Babel in Shakespeare's *Henry V*," in *Representing France and the French in Early Modern English Drama*, ed. Jean-Christophe Mayer (Newark, NJ: University of Delaware Press, 2008), 127–41.

7 Daniel Vitkus, "The New Globalism: Transcultural Commerce, Global Systems Theory, and Spenser's Mammon," in *A Companion to the Global Renaissance: English Literature and Cullture in the Era of Expansion*, ed. Jyotsna Singh (Malden, MA: Wiley-Blackwell, 2009), 31–49.

8 Jacques Derrida, "What Is a 'Relevant' Translation?" in *The Translation Studies Reader*, 2nd ed., edited by Lawrence Venuti (New York and London: Routledge, 1999), 423–46. Derrida focuses on the ways in which ethical judgments and textual valuation almost invariably accompany translation. In a similar way, Mikhail Bakhtin argues for a concept of "heteroglossia," or a condition where a "unitary language" is understood to operate in relation to various other languages; see *The Dialogic Imagination: Four Essays by M.M. Bakhtin*, ed. Michael Holquist, trans. Caryl Emerson and Michael Holquist (Austin: University of Texas Press, 1981), 271. In my view, Bakhtin's concept grants the unitary language a kind of integrity, however much stress it suffers, whereas Derrida's concept opens the door for a more radical view of linguistic slippage.

9 Michael Saenger, "Interlinguicity and the Alchemist," in *Multilingualism in the Drama of Shakespeare and his Contemporaries*, ed. Dirk Delabastita and Ton Hoenselaars; *English Text Construction* 6 (2013): 176–200.

10 Paula Blank, *Broken English: Dialects and the Politics of Language in Renaissance Writings* (London: Routledge, 1996).

11 Russ McDonald, *Shakespeare and the Arts of Language* (Oxford: Oxford University Press, 2001), 23.

12 Philip Sidney, *The Defense of Poetry*, *The Oxford Authors: Sir Philip Sidney*, ed. Katherine Duncan-Jones (New York: Oxford University Press, 1989), 248.

13 Peter Burke, "Cultures of Translation in Early Modern Europe," in *Cultural Translation in Early Modern Europe*, ed. Peter Burke and R. Po-chia Hsia (Cambridge, UK: Cambridge University Press, 2007), 16.

14 On the instruction of languages such as Arabic in early modern London, see Vivian Salmon, "The Study of Foreign Languages in Seventeenth-Century England," *Histoire Epistémologie Langage* 7 (1985): 45–70.

15 See Peter Burke, "Cultures of Translation in Early Modern Europe," 7–38, as well as the influential work of Lawrence Venuti, for example, "Local Contingencies: Translation and National Identities," in *Nation, Language, and the Ethics of Translation*, ed. Sandra Bermann and Michael Wood (Princeton, NJ: Princeton University Press, 2005), 177–202.

16 See, for example, Lisa Hopkins, *Shakespeare on the Edge: Border-crossing in the Tragedies And* The Henriad (Burlington, VT: Ashgate, 2006), as well as Alexander Leggatt, "The Disappearing Wall: *A Midsummer Night's Dream* and *Timon of Athens*," in *Shakespeare and the Mediterranean: The Selected Proceedings of the International Shakespeare Association World Congress, Valencia, 2001*, ed. Tom Clayton, Susan Brock, and Vicente Forés (Newark, NJ: University of Delaware Press, 2004), 194–205. Critics such as Martin Orkin have put particular focus on Shakespeare's treatment of romance, a genre which is founded upon travel, as a locus for theorizing both Shakespeare's own imagination of strange places and also the subsequent appropriation of Shakespeare all over the world. As Orkin puts it, "The characters of *Cymbeline* are … repeatedly situated in changing locations in which the challenges of travel and cultural encounter, with their potentials for epistemological uncertitude, recur." Martin Orkin, *Local Shakespeares: Proximations and Power* (New York: Routledge, 2005), 82.

17 See, for example, Patricia Parker, *Shakespeare from the Margins: Language, Culture, Context* (Chicago: University of Chicago Press, 1996), and more recently, Timothy Billings, "Masculine in Case: Grammar Lessons and Gender Identity in *Hic Mulier* and *The Merry Wives of Windsor*," in *Class, Boundary and Social Discourse in the Renaissance*, ed. Alexa Huang, I-Chun Wang, and Mary Theis (Taiwan: National Sun Yat-sen University, 2007), 63–86.

18 Marianne Montgomery, *Europe's Languages on England's Stages, 1590–1620* (Burlington, VT: Ashgate, 2012), 5.

19 Claire McEachern, *The Poetics of English Nationhood, 1590–1612* (Cambridge, UK: Cambridge University Press, 1996), 160.

20 Alexa Huang, "Shakespearean Localities and the Localities of Shakespeare Studies," *Shakespeare Studies* 35 (2007): 186–204.

21 Sonia Massai, "Defining Local Shakespeares," in *World-wide Shakespeares: Local Appropriations in Film and Performance*, ed. Sonia Massai (New York: Routledge, 2005), 10.

22 Richard Helgerson, *Forms of Nationhood: The Elizabethan Writing of England* (Chicago: University of Chicago Press, 1992), and "Language Lessons: Linguistic Colonialism, Linguistic Postcolonialism, and the Early Modern English Nation," *The Yale Journal of Criticism* 11 (1998): 289–99.

23 Patricia Parker, *Literary Fat Ladies: Rhetoric, Gender, Property* (New York: Methuen, 1987), 37.

24 Lloyd Edward Kermode argues that there were two competing ways of portraying foreigners on the early modern English stage; one was antagonistic, but the other mode, predominating in the latter years of Elizabeth's reign, opened the option of incorporating foreign ethnicities and linguistic traits into Englishness; see *Aliens and Englishness in Elizabethan Drama* (Cambridge, UK: Cambridge University Press, 2009), especially 17.

25 Lien Bich Luu, *Immigrants and the Industries of London, 1500–1700* (Burlington, VT: Ashgate, 2005), 1, 303.

26 See, for example, the central work of Sidney Lee, *The French Renaissance in England: An Account of the Literary Relations of England and France in the Sixteenth Century* (Oxford: Clarendon Press, 1910).

27 Grigori Konzintsev elucidates his demystification of the regicide at the center of *Hamlet* in his book *Shakespeare: Time and Conscience*, trans. Joyce Vining (New York: Hill and Wang, 1966): "The overthrow of government effected by Claudius is an ordinary criminal act; it is not even a seizure of power, but petty larceny," 139.

28 Quotations from Shakespeare in the Introduction are taken from *The Norton Shakespeare*, ed. Stephen Greenblatt et al. (New York and London: Norton, 1997).

29 Marjory Garber, *Shakespeare and Modern Culture* (New York: Pantheon, 2008), xii.

30 Samuel Coleridge, *Coleridge's Criticism of Shakespeare* (Detroit: Wayne State University Press, 1989), 68.

31 Ton Hoenselaars addresses this issue, focusing on the meaning of Dutchness in Shakespeare's contemporaries, in "The Topography of Fear: The Dutch (M/F) in Early Modern Literature," in *Class, Boundary and Social Discourse in the Renaissance*, ed. Alexa Huang, I-Chun Wang, and Mary Theis (Taiwan: National Sun Yat-sen University, 2007), 41–62.

32 Bradin Cormack, *A Power to Do Justice: Jurisdiction, English Literature, and the Rise of Common Law, 1509–1625* (Chicago: University of Chicago Press, 2007), 219.

33 *Twelfth Night* 1.2.1; this quotation was used to promote the World Shakespeare Festival and is discussed by Alexa Huang in her essay in this volume.

SHAKESPEARE, NAVARRE, AND CONTINENTAL HISTORY

1 Gillian Woods, "Catholicism and Conversion in *Love's Labour's Lost*," in *How to Do Things with Shakespeare*, ed. Laurie Maguire (Malden, MA: Blackwell, 2008), 104. See following note.

2 Ibid. As critics have pointed out, Navarre's courtiers and would-be scholars all bear conspicuously French names: Berowne and Longaville have been linked to well-known allies of Henry of Navarre – Charles de Gontaut, the Duke of Biron (1562–1602), and Henry of Orleans, the Duke of Longueville (1568–1595), respectively – while Dumaine is usually identified with Henry's Catholic opponent, Charles of Lorraine, the Duke of Mayenne (1554–1611). Critics have also suggested that Boyet and Moth had their historical counterparts in the Huguenot leader Boyset and the French governor of Gravelines, la Motte (Woods, 104). See also Mary Ellen Lamb, "The Nature of Topicality in *Love's Labour's Lost*," *Shakespeare Survey* 38 (1985): 49n2, 57.

3 Writing in 1918, H.B. Charlton observed: "Since Sir Sidney Lee's article in the *Gentleman's Magazine* (1880), it has been universally conceded that the names of Navarre, Biron, Longaville, and Dumain point to a period of time during which, or immediately following which, these were the protagonists in the French civil wars." See Charlton, "The Date of '*Love's Labour's Lost*,'" *Modern Language Review* 13.3 (July 1918): 258. See also Lee's *The French Renaissance in England* (Oxford: Clarendon Press, 1910).

4 Eric Griffin recently observed, however, in a footnote to his book, *English Renaissance Drama and the Specter of Spain* (Philadelphia: University of Pennsylvania Press, 2009), that "plays like *Love's Labour's Lost*, *Much Ado About Nothing*, *The Winter's Tale*, and *The Tempest* are by implication as much Spanish plays as Kyd's famous tragedy. For Navarre, Sicily, Naples, Milan, and Algiers are in Shakespeare's day either among the Kingdoms of the Spanish monarchy or within the Spanish orbit" (Griffin, 222n58).

5 The story occurs in the same volume where we find the story of *Amleth*, a probable source for Shakespeare's *Hamlet*.

6 Jean Froissart, *Cronycle*, trans. John Bourchier, Lord Berners (London, 1523), fo. C.liiiv.

7 Mariano Carlos Solano y Gálvez, Marqués de Monsalud, "El Palacio Real de Olite," *Boletín de la Real Academia de la Historia* 49 (1906): 440.

8 Ibid., 446.

9 William Shakespeare, *Love's Labor's Lost*, in *The Pelican Shakespeare*, ed. Peter Holland (New York: Penguin, 2000). All citations of the play in this chapter refer to this edition.

10 "one of the wisest and most lettered Princes of his time, having been so nourished by Greek and Latin literature that he translated out of Greek into Spanish the Ethics of Aristotle. He was, moreover, well versed in history and there remains, by him, an epitome and chronology of the Kings of Navarre, his predecessors up to the reign of his father." Pierre de Belloy, *Declaration du droit de legitime succession, sur le royaume de Portugal* (Anvers, 1582), 82v. All translations from Belloy's text are my own.

11 "one of the most ambitious and malicious creatures who ever lived."

12 "the ruin of the legitimate Kings of Navarre." Belloy was also, incidentally, an outspoken supporter of Henry of Navarre's right to inherit the French crown.

13 Patricia Parker, "Preposterous Reversals: *Love's Labor's Lost,*" *Modern Language Quarterly* 54.4 (1993): 435–82.

14 The expression means "to cool (a hot or boiling liquid) by stirring, skimming, or pouring in something cold, in order to prevent it from boiling over" (OED, s.v. "keel").

15 Here, I quote Peter Holland's note at 3.1.202.

16 Prior to her wedding to Charles the Bad of Navarre, Joan of Valois had been betrothed to John of Brabant.

17 Froissart, *Cronycle*, fo. CCxvii.

18 Mary C. Ekman, "'Satisfaite de soy en soy mesme': The Politics of Self-Representation in Jeanne d'Albret's *Ample declaration*," in *The Rule of Women in Early Modern Europe*, ed. Anne J. Cruz and Mihoko Suzuki (Urbana, IL: University of Illinois Press, 2009), 30.

19 See Bethany Aram, "Queen Juana: Legend and History," in *Juana of Castile: History and Myth of the Mad Queen*, ed. Maria A. Gómez, Santiago Juan-Navarro, and Phyllis Zatlin (Lewisburg, PA: Bucknell University Press, 2008), 33–46. Records show that before her death, Isabella "indicated that her husband, Ferdinand (and pointedly not Philip), should govern Castile until the majority of Juana's eldest son, Charles" (Aram, 34).

20 Gabriel Richardson, *The State of Europe* (Oxford, 1627), Aa3v. Pierre de Belloy also refers to Blanche as "fille de Sanxi 7" (82v).

21 Belloy, 97v–98.

22 Ferdinand II's first wife, Isabella of Castile, died in 1504.

23 William Warner, *Albion's England* (London, 1597), P8v.

24 *so-eare*: soever.
25 *Sampson*: Sancho III ("the Great") of Navarre (ca. 992–1035) is credited with having unified, temporarily, all of Christian Iberia during his lifetime.
26 *stauld*: installed or enthroned.
27 *quits*: requites.
28 Ferdinand II ruled Castile after the death of his wife, Isabella I, in 1504. He invaded Navarre in 1512.
29 *hether*: hither. The Spanish Armada set sail from Lisbon in 1588.
30 Francesco Guicciardini, *The Historie of Guicciardin: Containing the Warres of Italie and Other Partes*, trans. Geffray Fenton (London, 1599), 517. Guicciardini's account was widely cited by Elizabethan writers. Thomas Bilson, for example, quotes the Italian historiographer on "the ancient desire of the kings of *Spaine* to be Lords of *Nauarre*" in his *True Difference between Christian Subjection and Unchristian Rebellion* (Oxford, 1585), 482.
31 Richard Sergier, *The Present State of Spain. Translated out of French* (London, 1594), A4v.
32 "It was necessary, at all costs, to join the Kingdom of Navarre to the rest of Spain, and, at the first available opportunity, to chase out the Counts of Foix, who were French at heart and in nation, and had come to plant themselves there and hold a district of it" (Belloy, 94).
33 Elizabeth I and Henry of Navarre both faced bulls of excommunication, in 1570 and 1586 respectively.
34 André Thevet, *Cosmographie Universelle*, Tome 2 (Paris, 1575), 503. My translation.
35 See also François Hotman, *The Brutish Thunderbolt* (London, 1586), 304–5. This tract was Hotman's polemical response to the excommunications of Henry of Navarre and the Prince of Condé by Sixtus V.
36 "Guien" (or "Guyenne") was another name for "Aquitaine."
37 Henry Wotton, *The State of Christendom* (London, 1657), 58. Wotton, writing in 1594, was of the opinion that the king of Navarre had little choice in the matter:

> As it is most certain that the Kings of *Naples* and of *Scotland* hold their kingdomes the one of the Pope of *Rome*, the other of the Queen of *England* as of their Soveraigns, so it is undoubtedly true, that the Kings of *Navarra* owe homage, faith, fealty, and obedience unto the king of *France*, as unto their Lord and Soveraign, for their kingdom; in regard whereof they are bound to many conditions of services unto him as their Soveraign, and especially to aid and assist him in his just quarrels,

wars, and contentions against any other Prince whatsoever, and never to leave him, upon pain of forfeiture of their States and Dominions holden of him" (58).

Belloy also comments on the legal obligation of Jean d'Albret to side with the French king against his enemy, the Spaniard, in this case (Belloy, 103v).

38 "Returned to the heirs of John of Aragon, father of the heiress of Nauarre, who were not able to claim this succession because they were not in the direct line for this crown. And in this way were united the Provinces of Navarre and Castile under a single Prince three hundred and seventy-eight years after the time of Sancho the Great, when these realms were separated and given to different Princes." François Belleforest, *Les Grandes Annales* Tome 2 (Paris, 1579), 1396v. All translations from Belleforest's text are my own. The "heiress of Navarre" was, after the death of Charles of Viana, his sister Blanche (Blanche II of Navarre, 1424–64); Eleanor, their younger sister, was next in line and reigned briefly in 1479. From Eleanor, the crown passed to Francis Phoebus (r.1479–83), her grandson, and then to his younger sister, Catherine of Foix (Catherine of Navarre).

39 "Owe" is normally glossed as "own," although it might well retain its implication, here, of indebtedness.

40 Joshua 2:2, in William Whittington, *The Bible and Holy Scriptvres Conteyned in the Olde and Newe Testament* (Geneva, 1562). All the biblical citations that follow refer to "The Boke of Iosva" in this edition.

41 A Huguenot tract called *The Masque of the League and the Spanyard discouered* (1592), translated from the French by Anthony Munday, describes in colourful terms how partisans of the Catholic League "scornfully call [the King] a **Bearn-nish man.*" See L.T.A., *The Masque of the League and the Spanyard Discouered*, trans. Anthony Munday (London, 1592), B2r. Elsewhere, Henry Wotton explains, alluding to Pedro Cornejo's *Compendio y breve relation de la lyga y confederation Francesca* (1591), that "the Spaniards (as I have said before) considering that their King enjoyeth a great part of that Kingdom, and layeth claim to the whole, vouchsafeth him not the honour to call him king of *Navarra*, but in all their Writings they call him either the Prince of *Bearn*, or more plainly, the *Bernois*." See Wotton, *State of Christendom*, 51. Gabriel Chappuys confirms this fact, noting that, in letters concerning the siege of Paris, Mendoza and the king of Spain referred to Navarre as "le Prince de Bearn." See Chappuys, *L'Histoire du Royaume de Navarre* (Paris, 1596), 787.

42 Christopher Marlowe, *The Massacre at Paris: With the Death of the Duke of Guise* (London, n.d.), B7r. This play, Marlowe's last, was first staged in January 1593.

43 François Belleforest confirms that this is a reference to François II d'Orléans (1470–1512), who held many titles including Count of Longueville and of Dunois (Belleforest, *Grandes Annales*, 1397).

44 "If it was impossible to do any good, so long as this jealousy grew between them, it also prevented their service of the king and the advancement of the king of Navarre."

45 For more on English perceptions of Santiago or Saint James, the patron saint of Spain, see Griffin, especially chapter 6, "*Othello*'s Spanish Spirits Or, Un-sainting James," 168–206.

46 Chappuys, *L'Histoire*, 627.

47 William Cecil (later Lord Burghley), acquired a copy of this work in 1548; it is now in the British Library.

48 Antonio de Nebrija, *Aelii Antonii Nebrissensis Rervm a Fernando & Elisabe Hispaniarum foelicissisimis Regibus gestar Decades duas. Necnon belli Nauariensis libros duos. Annexa insuper Archiempi Roderici Chronica, aliensque historiens antehac non excussis* (Granada, 1545), fol. LXXVIIr.

49 "All of this took place on the twenty-fourth of July, 1512, which was a Saturday, on which day the Count of Lerin, Constable of Navarre entered the city. And the next day, which was the feast of Saint James, the patron saint of Spain, the Duke of Alba made his entry as Lieutenant of the King of Castile, in whose name he took possession of the Kingdom of Navarre. And this was the first time ever that Pamplona abandoned its natural King to give itself up to the Castilian and Aragonese, even though there had been great and cruel wars in the past between Navarre, Aragon and Castile."

50 Bartolomé de Las Casas, *The Spanish Colonie*, trans. M.M.S. (London, 1583), D4r.

51 Thomas L. Berger and William C. Bradford, Jr., *An Index of Characters in English Printed Drama to the Restoration* (Englewood, CO: Microcard Editions, 1975), 56.

52 [Thomas Kyd], *The Tragedye of Solyman and Perseda* (London, n.d.), A4r–v.

53 "The Spaniard … pursued the war of Navarre with more animosity than he had shown against the Infidel, whom he sent back to his lands, and expelled a Christian from his patrimony." François de Belleforest, Argument, "Harangue du Duc d'Albe aux citoyens de Panpelonne, lors

que par force il leur feit iurer faulte au Roy d'Espaigne," *Harangues Militaires* (Paris, 1572), fol. 129б.

54 William Camden, *Annales, or The History of the Most Renowned and Victorious Princesse Elizabeth, Late Queen of England*, 3rd ed. (London, 1635), 371.

55 L.T.A., *Masque*, B4r–v. The French author of this tract is likely punning on the Latin *mendosus* (faulty, erroneous, incorrect), related to the Latin *mendax* (whence we derive "mendacious" and "mendacity"). The OED also cites the sixteenth-century French medical writer Ambroise Paré for his use of the term "mendeux" in describing something "false" or "spurious" in the anatomical sense (s.v. "mendose, *adj*.,"). An aural pun on "Lyar" (or "liar") and "lyre" (the poet's instrument) would also be particularly apt in this case because poets were regularly accused of lying, because the job of the ambassador was to sing praises and convey messages on behalf of monarchs or other powerful parties, and because the form of Mendoza's "lie" about the Armada was a published song, or poem.

56 "That is also why Ferdinand, judging well for himself that he had violated the principles of justice and the common alliance of Princes, and that beyond the blame that posterity would give him, he might by his bad example, have given occasion to one more powerful than he, to pay him with the same or stronger coin … wished and ordered Antonio de Nebrija, who was still alive then, to research and set down the reasons that might pertain to some defence or other of this incursion, and to publish them, as he did, along with that which occurred in Navarre after the war made by the aforementioned King Jean 3 for the recovery of the Kingdom." "Roy Iean 3" refers to Jean d'Albret, the ousted king who made several attempts to recover his lost territory.

57 "The second reason given by Nebrija is that Jean d'Albret, King of Navarre, had been declared a schismatic by Pope Julius II and his territories put in the hands of their first usurper, the Kingdom's remaining subjects discharged of their oath of fidelity. To this there are excellent replies, firstly that the Kingdom of Navarre did not belong to Jean d'Albret, since it was his wife Catherine who held the right of succession, and since Ferdinand was her uncle he ought to have guarded and protected her against those who might do her wrong. But I believe that the Pope had no intention to excommunicate a poor woman and give away her worldly goods, when she had never caused him any displeasure."

58 "a history-wrecking grammarian"

59 François Hotman, incidentally, refers to Nebrija disparagingly as a "Spanish peasant" (Hotman, *Brutish Thunderbolt*, 304).

60 For an argument that links the play's rhetoric to its gender politics, and to problems of inheritance and succession, see Katherine Eisaman Maus, "Transfer of Title in *Love's Labor's Lost*: Language, Individualism, Gender," in *Shakespeare Left and Right*, ed. Ivo Kamps (New York: Routledge, 1991), 205–23 (especially 212–13).

61 That is, "pumpkin."

62 Gerhard Mercator, *Historia Mundi, or Mercator's Atlas* (London, 1635), 211.

"*THE LADY SPEAKS IN WELSH*"

1 I wish to thank Paul Bryant-Quinn for invaluable assistance in matters of Welsh language, stylistics, and academic history.

2 William Shakespeare, *Hamlet*, 1.1.38; 1.1.48. All references in this chapter to Shakespeare's plays other than *Henry IV, Part 1* are to *The Norton Shakespeare*, ed. Stephen Greenblatt et al. (New York: Norton, 2008).

3 All references are to William Shakespeare, *Henry IV, Part 1*, ed. David Scott Kastan (London: Arden Shakespeare, 2002).

4 Thomas Heywood, *The Second Part of, If You Know Not Me, You Know Nobody* (London, 1606), sig. H1r.

5 On Welsh song in English drama, see J.O. Bartley, *Teague, Shenkin and Sawney* (Cork: Cork University Press, 1954), 66. A similar circumstance occurs in *The Dutch Courtesan,* where the stage direction "*cantat Gallice*" is followed by a song in English rather than French, probably indicating that Franceschina sings in the French style.

6 See J.O. Bartley and Melville Richards, "The Welsh Language in English Plays," *Welsh Review* 6/1 (1947): 39–50; David Salmon, "Welsh in the Old Plays," *Notes and Queries* 150 (1926): 201–3; Philip Schwyzer, "Thirteen Ways of Looking Like a Welshman: Shakespeare and His Contemporaries," in *Shakespeare and Wales: From the Marches to the Assembly*, ed. Willy Maley and Philip Schwyzer (Farnham, UK: Ashgate, 2010), 34n51.

7 Thomas Dekker et al., *Patient Grissil,* in *The Dramatic Works of Thomas Dekker, Volume 1*, ed. Fredson Bowers (Cambridge, UK: Cambridge University Press, 1954), vol. 1, 2.1.167–75. The Welsh dialogue in this passage has been translated into correct Welsh and English as follows: "*Ble 'roeddech chwi, wraig weddw?; mae'n dda gen i, myn Duw, eich gweld chwi yn wir iawn,* Welsh for 'Where were you, widow woman?; I'm glad, by God, to see you indeed,' and *Syr Owen,* gramercy *i chwi: Gwenllian, mae'n dda gen i (genni hi) eich gweld yn llawen yr un modd,*

'Sir Owen, many thanks to you: Gwenllian, I'm glad (she's glad) to see you content in the same way.'" Cyrus Hoy, *Introductions, Notes and Commentaries to Texts in 'The Dramatic Works of Thomas Dekker,'* vol. 1 (Cambridge, UK: Cambridge University Press, 1980), 157–8.

8 Later in the play, Farneze mistakes Sir Owen's threat to beat Gwenthyan "pob nose" (*pob nos*, every night) for a threat to "bob [her] nose" (4.3.147, 150).

9 Geraint Dyfnallt Owen, *Elizabethan Wales: The Social Scene* (Cardiff: University of Wales Press, 1962), 62. For a more sceptical view of the welcome Welsh immigrants received in London, see Huw Griffiths, "'O, I Am Ignorance Itself in This!': Listening to Welsh in Shakespeare and Armin," in *Shakespeare and Wales*, ed. Maley and Schwyzer, 111–26, esp. 111–12.

10 Citing a private communication from Terence Hawkes, Barbara Hodgdon suggests that "these passages would have been as incomprehensible to early modern auditors as they are, in all probability, to most readers (for Americans, perhaps the best analogue would be a Native American language)." William Shakespeare, *The First Part of Henry the Fourth: Texts and Contexts*, ed. Barbara Hodgdon (Boston: Bedford Books, 1997), 272n1.

11 I have considered these questions from a different angle in "Thirteen Ways of Looking Like a Welshman"; see also Megan Lloyd, "Rhymer, Minstrel Lady Mortimer and the Power of Welsh Words," in *Shakespeare and Wales*, ed. Maley and Schwyzer, 59–73.

12 D. Lleufer Thomas, "Welshmen and the First Folio of Shakespeare's Plays (1623)," *Transactions of the Honourable Society of Cymmrodorion*, Session 1940 (1941), 102–3; Lloyd, "Rhymer, Minstrel Lady Mortimer," 72.

13 See Shakespeare, *Henry IV, Part 1*, ed. Kastan, 117–18.

14 John A. Heraud, *Shakspere: His Inner Life as Intimated in his Works* (London: Maxwell, 1865), 201.

15 See Shakespeare, *Henry IV, Part 1*, ed. Kastan, 90.

16 Max Forster, "Die kymrischen Einlagen bei Shakespeare," *Germanisch-Romanische Monatsschrift* 12 (1924): 349–64; the "reconstructed" Welsh dialogue appears on pages 360–3 of the essay.

17 For the full RSC text, see Shakespeare, *First Part of King Henry the Fourth*, ed. Hodgdon, 272–4.

18 Megan Lloyd, *Speak It in Welsh: Wales and the Welsh Language in Shakespeare* (Lanham, MD: Lexington Books, 2007), 159–71.

19 Forster, "Die kymrischen Einlagen bei Shakespeare," 360–1.

20 Although the full text of the promptbook has been transcribed by Hodgdon (see n. 16, above), here I follow the original 1964 promptbook

as reproduced in *Henry IV, Part 1,* ed. Kastan, 124. Just as Hodgdon's transcription appears to contain some errors, so the typed promptbook contains some mistakes in the Welsh (eg, "aroshebddo" for "aros hebddo").

21 Roger D. Gross, "*1H4* Welsh," in *SHAKSPER: The Global Electronic Shakespeare Conference,* 6 April 1995 (http://shaksper.net/archive/1995/106-april/3194-re-sh-on-tact-sh-on-bravo-1h4-welsh).

22 John Drakakis, "Michael Bogdanov in Conversation," in *Shakespeare Survey 60: Theatres for Shakespeare*, ed. Peter Holland (2007): 201.

23 As Jones remarks, "It is fortunate that my first experience in acting I was able to write my own lines in a Shakespeare play!" *Sianed Jones: RSC Histories* (http://sianed.co.uk/the-histories). Jones composed her own Welsh song, *Fy Nghariad* (My Darling) for the production. Other productions have used a range of Welsh folk songs and lullabies of the eighteenth and nineteenth centuries, such as *Dafydd y Garreg Wen* (Roger Gross) or *Suo Gân* (BBC, 1979).

24 Gross, "*1H4* Welsh."

25 See Lloyd, "*Speak It in Welsh,*" 160–1.

26 Craig Barrow, "The Experimental and the Traditional: The 2006 Alabama Shakespeare Festival's *A Midsummer Night's Dream* and the 2006 Stratford Festival's *Henry IV, Part 1,*" *Upstart Crow* 26 (2006/7): 108.

27 Drakakis, "Michael Bogdanov in Conversation," 201.

28 See Shakespeare, *First Part of Henry the Fourth,* ed. Hodgdon, 272n1.

WHERE DID THE DEVIL GO?

1 For confessionalization, see Heinz Schilling, "Confessional Europe," in *Handbook of European History, 1400–1600: Late Middle Ages, Renaissance and Reformation*, ed. Thomas A. Brady Jr., Heiko A. Oberman, and James D. Tracy (Leiden, Netherlands: Brill, 1995), vol. I: 640–81. On Mennonite confessions of faith, see Karl Koop, ed., *Confessions of Faith in the Anabaptist Tradition, 1527–1660* (Kitchener, ON: Pandora Press, 2006).

2 See Mark Konnert, *Early Modern Europe: The Age of Religious War, 1559–1715* (Toronto: University of Toronto Press, 2006).

3 For a brief overview, see William Monter, "Heresy Executions in Reformation Europe, 1520–1565," in *Tolerance and Intolerance in the European Reformation*, ed. Ole Peter Grell and Bob Scribner (Cambridge, UK: Cambridge University Press, 1996), 48–64. On the Habsburg persecution, see Gary K. Waite, *Eradicating the Devil's Minions: Anabaptists and Witches in Reformation Europe* (Toronto: University of Toronto Press,

2007). On France, see E. William Monter, *Judging the French Reformation: Heresy Trials by Sixteenth-Century Parlements* (Cambridge, MA: Harvard University Press, 1999). For England, see, among others, Eamon Duffy, *Fires of Faith: Catholic England under Mary Tudor* (New Haven, CT: Yale University Press, 2010), and Eamon Duffy, *Saints, Sacrilege and Sedition: Religion and Conflict in the Tudor Reformations* (London: Bloomsbury, 2012).

4 Ralf Klötzer, "The Melchiorites and Münster," in *A Companion to Anabaptism and Spiritualism, 1521–1700*, ed. John D. Roth and James M. Stayer (Leiden, Netherlands: Brill, 2007), 217–56.

5 See Sigrun Haude, *In the Shadow of 'Savage Wolves': Anabaptist Münster and the German Reformation during the 1530s* (Leiden, Netherlands: Humanities Press, 2000).

6 James D. Tracy, *Europe's Reformations, 1450–1650* (Lanham, MD: Rowman and Littlefield, 1999), 146–53.

7 See James A. Parente Jr., "Drama," in *The Oxford Encyclopedia of the Reformation*, ed. Hans J. Hillerbrand (Oxford: Oxford University Press, 1996), vol. II: 4–9, and the literature he cites.

8 Peter Blickle has called it instead the "Revolution of the Common Man." Peter Blickle, *The Revolution of 1525: The German Peasants' War from a New Perspective,* trans. Thomas A. Brady, Jr., and H.C. Erik Midelfort (Baltimore: Johns Hopkins University Press, 1981).

9 For the pamphlet: http://zimmer.csufresno.edu/~mariterel/against_the_robbing_and_murderin.htm

10 Blickle comments that the "most noticeable effect" of the crushing of the Peasants' War was "a new concern for religious discipline on the part of the rulers." Blickle, *The Revolution*, 183.

11 See Andrew Cunningham and Ole Peter Grell, *The Four Horsemen of the Apocalypse: Religion, War, Famine and Death in Reformation Europe* (Cambridge, UK: Cambridge University Press, 2000); and Gary K. Waite, *Heresy, Magic, and Witchcraft in Early Modern Europe* (Basingstoke, UK: Palgrave, 2003), 52–86.

12 Waite, *Eradicating*, 34–62.

13 Ria Stambaugh, ed., *Teufelbücher in Auswahl* (Berlin: de Gruyter, 1970–1980).

14 Waite, *Eradicating,* 57–9, and the literature cited there.

15 See Gary K. Waite, "Sixteenth Century Religious Reform and the Witch-Hunts," in *The Oxford Handbook of Witchcraft in Early Modern Europe and Colonial America*, ed. Brian Levack (Oxford: Oxford University Press, 2013), 485–506, and "Irrelevant Interruption or

Precipitating Cause? The Sixteenth-Century Reformation and the Revival of the European Witch Hunts," in *Chasses aux sorciéres et démonologie: Entre discours et pratiques (XIVe–XVIIe siècles)*, ed. Georg Modestin, Martine Ostorero, and Kathrin Utz Tremp (Florence, Italy: SISMEL edizioni del Galluzzo, 2010), 223–42.

16 An excellent survey of the witch hunts is Brian P. Levack, *The Witch-Hunt in Early Modern Europe* (Harlow, UK: Pearson Longman, 2006). For the devil and demonizing rhetoric, see Stuart Clark, ed., *Languages of Witchcraft: Narrative, Ideology and Meaning in Early Modern Culture* (Basingstoke, UK: Macmillan, 2001), and, of course, his magnum opus, *Thinking with Demons: The Idea of Witchcraft in Early Modern Europe* (Oxford: Oxford University Press, 1997).

17 Dutch artists did turn to the subject: see Claudia Swan, *Art, Science and Witchcraft in Early Modern Holland: Jacques de Gheyn II (1565–1629)* (Cambridge, UK: Cambridge University Press, 2005). On witch hunting in Holland, see Hans de Waardt, *Toverij en samenleving. Holland 1500–1800* (The Hague: Stichting Hollandse Historische Reeks, 1991); he notes that the diabolical Sabbath played no significant role here (217). De Waardt found only three German witch trial accounts were printed in the Netherlands.

18 De Waardt, *Toverij*, English summary 335–9.

19 Waite, *Eradicating*, 37–62.

20 This label was applied especially to the spiritualizers who actually depreciated belief in the corporeal existence of the devil. Ibid., 38–9.

21 Jaap Geraerts, "The Prosecution of Anabaptists in Holland, 1530–1566," *The Mennonite Quarterly Review* 86 (2012): 5–47; also James D. Tracy, *Holland under Habsburg Rule: The Formation of a Body Politic* (Berkeley, CA: University of California Press, 1990).

22 See Emmet McLaughlin, "Spiritualism: Schwenckfeld and Franck and their Early Modern Resonances," and Geoffrey Dipple, "The Spiritualist Anabaptists," both in Roth and Stayer, *A Companion*, 119–162 and 257–97.

23 Perez Zagorin, *Ways of Lying: Dissimulation, Persecution, and Conformity in Early Modern Europe* (Cambridge, MA: Harvard University Press, 1990).

24 Waite, *David Joris and Dutch Anabaptism, 1524–1543* (Waterloo, ON: Wilfrid Laurier University Press, 1990).

25 Alistair Hamilton, *The Family of Love* (Cambridge, UK: James Clark and Company, 1987); Christopher W. Marsh, *The Family of Love in English Society, 1550–1630* (Cambridge, UK: Cambridge University Press, 1994).

26 Daniel Swetchinski, "From the Middle Ages to the Golden Age, 1516–1621," in *The History of the Jews in the Netherlands*, ed. J.C.H. Blom, R.G. Fuks-Mansfeld, and I. Schoffer (Oxford: Litman Library of Jewish Civilization, 2002), 44–84, here 61.

27 Gary K. Waite, "Rhetoricians and Religious Compromise during the Early Reformation (c.1520–1555)," in *Urban Theatre in the Low Countries, 1400–1625*, ed. Peter Happé and Elsa Strietman (Turnhout, Belgium: Brepols, 2006), 79–102. Ben Parsons and Bas Jongenelen note that the chambers were "not merely concerned with their own salvation, but with the spiritual welfare of their communities at large." Ben Parsons and Bas Jongenelen, eds. and trans., *Comic Drama in the Low Countries, c.1450–1560: A Critical Anthology* (Suffolk, UK: Brewer, 2012), 7. See also Gary K. Waite, *Reformers on Stage: Popular Drama and Religious Propaganda in the Low Countries of Charles V, 1515–1556* (Toronto: University of Toronto Press, 2000); and Samuel Mareel, "Urban Literary Patronage in the Early Modern Low Countries: Public Festive Culture and Individual Authorship," *Renaissance Quarterly* 64 (2011): 1–49.

28 Arjan van Dixhoorn, *Lustige geesten: Rederijkers in de Noordelijke Nederlanden (1480–1650)* (Amsterdam: Amsterdam University Press, 2009).

29 On the devil in *rederijker* drama, see Marcel Ficheroux, "Van helse intrigant tot toneelfiguur: De duivel op het toneel in de late Middeleeuwen (1400–1600)," *Trajecta* 8 (1999): 3–30; Gary K. Waite, "Drama, Dutch," in *Encyclopedia of Witchcraft: The Western Tradition*, ed. Richard Golden (Santa Barbara, CA: ABC-CLIO, 2006), vol. I: 291–4.

30 Gary K. Waite, "'Man is a Devil to Himself': David Joris and the Rise of a Sceptical Tradition towards the Devil in the Early Modern Netherlands, 1540–1600," *Nederlands Archief voor Kerkgeschiedenis / Dutch Review of Church History* 75 (1995): 1–30; see also Samme Zijlstra, *Om de ware gemeente en de oude gronden: Geschiedenis van de dopersen in de Nederlanden 1531–1675* (Hilversum, Netherlands: Fryske Akademy, 2000), 148–69.

31 Walter S. Gibson, "Artists and Rederijkers in the Age of Bruegel," *The Art Bulletin* 63 (Sept. 1981): 426–46. Joris also used *rederijker* style in some of his publications, including his proto-nationalistic praise of the Dutch language; see Gary K. Waite, "The Holy Spirit Speaks Dutch: David Joris and the Promotion of the Dutch Language, 1539–1545," *Church History* 61 (1992): 47–59.

32 *Den brullenden Leeuw overwonnen: Ofte Veld-slagh Tusschen eenen Christen ende den Duyvel …* (Amsterdam, 1611). See Gary K. Waite,

"From David Joris to Balthasar Bekker?: The Radical Reformation and Scepticism towards the Devil in the Early Modern Netherlands (1540–1700)," *Fides et Historia* 28 (1996): 5–26, here 17.

33 Stuart B. Schwartz, *All Can Be Saved: Religious Tolerance and Salvation in the Iberian Atlantic World* (New Haven, CT: Yale University Press, 2008), 34. See also Carlo Ginzburg, *The Cheese and the Worms: The Cosmos of a Sixteenth-Century Miller,* trans. John and Anne Tedeschi (Baltimore: Johns Hopkins University Press, 1980).

34 Willem Frijhoff, "Religious Toleration in the United Provinces: From 'Case' to 'Model,'" in *Calvinism and Religious Toleration in the Dutch Golden Age*, ed. R. Po-Chia Hsia and Henk van Nierop (Cambridge, UK: Cambridge University Press 2002), 27–52; see also Benjamin J. Kaplan, *Calvinists and Libertines: Confession and Community in Utrecht, 1578–1620* (Oxford: Oxford University Press, 1995); and on resistance to Calvinist preachers, see Phyllis Mack Crew, *Calvinist Preaching and Iconoclasm in the Netherlands, 1544–1569* (Cambridge, UK: Cambridge University Press, 1973/2008).

35 Benjamin J. Kaplan, "Fictions of Privacy: House Chapels and the Spatial Accommodation of Religious Dissent in Early Modern Europe," *American Historical Review* 107 (2002): 1031–64; Kaplan, *Divided by Faith: Religious Conflict and the Practice of Toleration in Early Modern Europe* (Cambridge, MA: Harvard University Press, 2007), 172–97.

36 Benjamin J. Kaplan, "Remnants of the Papal Yoke: Apathy and Opposition in the Dutch Reformation," *Sixteenth Century Journal* 25 (1994): 653–69; and Kaplan, *Divided by Faith*.

37 Gerrit Voogt, *Constraint on Trial: Dirck Volckertsz Coornhert and Religious Freedom* (Kirksville, MO: Truman State University Press, 2000); Mirjam G.K. van Veen, "*Verschooninghe van de roomsche afgoderye*"*: De polemiek van Calvijn met nicodemieten, in het bijzonder met Coornhert* (Utrecht, Netherlands: HES and De Graaf, 2001); Mirjam G.K. van Veen, "Spiritualism in the Netherlands: From David Joris to Dirck Volckertsz Coornhert," *Sixteenth Century Journal* 33 (2002): 129–50; and Marianne Roobol, *Disputation by Decree: The Public Disputations between Reformed Ministers and Dirck Volckertszoon Coornhert as Instruments of Religious Policy during the Dutch Revolt (1577–1583)* (Leiden, Netherlands: Brill, 2010).

38 Hans de Waardt, "Witchcraft, Spiritualism and Medicine: the Religious Convictions of Johan Wier," *Sixteenth Century Journal* 42 (2011): 369–91; Gary K. Waite, "Radical Religion and the Medical Profession: The Spiritualist David Joris and the Brothers Weyer (Wier)," in *Radikalität und*

Dissent im 16. Jahrhundert / Radicalism and Dissent in the Sixteenth Century, ed. Hans-Jürgen Goertz and James M. Stayer (Berlin: Duncker and Humblot, 2002), 167–85; see also Hans De Waardt, "Religie, duivelspact en toverij," *Tijdschrift voor geschiedenis* 118 (2005): 400–15.

39 Cornelis Kramer, *Emmery de Lyere et Marnix de Sainte Aldegonde: Un admirateur de Sébastien Franck et de Montaigne aux prises avec le champion des calvinistes néerlandais* (The Hague: Nijhoff, 1971).

40 W.P.C. Knuttel, *Catalogus van de pamflettenverzameling berustende in de Koninklijke Bibliotheek*, 9 vols. (The Hague: Algemeene Landsdrukkerij, 1889–1920). Some of these Dutch examples retailed news of supernatural wonders from outside the Republic, rather than Dutch stories. See, for examples, Knuttel numbers 2034, 2088, and 2032. In 1611 an Amsterdam publisher printed a Dutch translation of the English Puritan William Perkins's *A Discourse of the Damned Art of Witchcraft* (1608) as *Tractaet van de ongodlijcke toover-const* (Amsterdam, 1611). The demonic possession of Utrecht resident David Wardavoir caused a stir in 1595: *Cort ende warachtich verhael van de wonderlicke aenvechtinge ende verlossinge van David Wardavoir, trijpwercker, geschiet binnen Utrecht* (Utrecht, Netherlands, 1595), Knuttel, 945; see also Benjamin J. Kaplan, "Possessed by the Devil? A Very Public Dispute in Utrecht," *Renaissance Quarterly* 49 (1996): 738–59.

41 See Margaret R. Greer, Walter D. Mignolo, and Maureen Quilligan, eds., *Rereading the Black Legend: The Discourses of Religious and Racial Difference in the Renaissance Empires* (Chicago: University of Chicago Press, 2007).

42 Its system of fines, however, clearly disadvantaged the minority group. Albert F. Mellink and Samme Zijlstra, eds., *Documenta Anabaptistica Neerlandica*, vol. VII: *Friesland (1551–1601) and Groningen (1538–1601)* (Leiden, Netherlands: Brill, 1995), 232–4. On the earlier demonizing rhetoric, see Waite, *Eradicating*, 34–62.

43 Such as *Tsamenspreeckinghe van drie persoonen/ over het regireus Placcaet van Groninghen* ... (n.p., 1601), Knuttel, 1172.

44 Abraham Costerus, *Historie der Joden, Die t'sedert de verstooringe Jerusalems in alle landen verstroyt zijn: in dry deelen beschreven* ... 2nd ed. (Amsterdam, 1650), 36. See also Swetschinski, "From the Middle Ages to the Golden Age." Contemporaneous with Costerus's book was, however, a translation of a French pamphlet about the birth of the Antichrist which depicted the Jews as celebrating the birth of the Antichrist as their deliverer. *Een wonderlijcke nieuwe Tijdinghe van Het Leuen vanden seer onrechtveerdigen ende Boosen Antechrist* ... (Rotterdam, Netherlands, 1608), Knuttel, 1559.

45 Antonio Feros, *Kingship and Favoritism in the Spain of Philip III, 1598–1621* (Cambridge, UK: Cambridge University Press, 2000), 202–4.

46 Gary K. Waite, "Empathy for the Persecuted or Polemical Posturing? The 1609 Spanish Expulsion of the Moriscos as Seen in Netherlandic Pamphlets," *Journal of Early Modern History* 17 (2013): 95–123.

47 Gary K. Waite, "Menno and Muhammad: Anabaptists and Mennonites Reconsider Islam, 1525–1650," *The Sixteenth Century Journal* 41 (2010): 995–1016; on Moriscos, see Gerard Wiegers, "Managing Disaster: Networks of the Moriscos during the Process of the Expulsion from the Iberian Peninsula around 1609," *Journal of Medieval Religious Cultures* 36 (2010): 141–68, here 157; Benjamin J. Kaplan, *Muslims in the Dutch Golden Age: Representations and Realities of Religious Toleration* (Amsterdam: Universiteit van Amsterdam, 2007), 20.

48 Pieter Iansz Twisck, *Na beter. Religions vryheyt. Een korte Cronijcsche beschryvinghe van de Vryheyt der Religien/ tegen die dwang der Conscientien/ … van Christus tijt af/ tot den Jare 1609* (n.p., 1609).

49 Ibid., 13ff.

50 Ibid., 71–5.

51 Ibid., 46, 70–1, 82.

52 Ibid., 82.

53 Ibid., 231.

54 Dutch pamphleteers did, however, remind readers of the political and military danger offered by Catholicism, which they very clearly linked with Spanish machinations and Jesuit treason. See, for example, *Nieuwe tijdinghe/ ende Handelinghe/ vanden Duyvel/ ende den Paus/ hoe sy met den anderen spraeck hebben ghehouden/ zeer lustigh ende tijdkortich om leesen* (Nieumegen, Netherlands, 1610); Knuttel, 1813 and 1814. A response to this dialogue appeared in 1611, printed likely in Antwerp (Hadopoli), which concludes that only in the Catholic faith can salvation be found. *Nievwe Tiidinge Van den Dvyvel: Ende dry Notabele Persoonen. Hoe sy met malcanderen spraecke ghehouden hebben. Seer lustich ende tijdt-cortich om lesen* (Hadopoli, Netherlands, 1611), Knuttel, 1923.

55 *Helschen Raedt ofte Grouwelicke Practtijcken, die de Jesuvvijten ghebruycken, in 't beraetslaghen van te doen vermoorden eenen Coninck* (Delft, 1610), Knuttel, 1800. These include the rhymed *Het Pater Noster der Ieswiten. Ghegheven aen Philippvs III. Coninck van Spaignien, al seen gheschenck in dit tegenwoordich nieuwe Iaer* (The Hague, 1611), Knuttel, 1917, which characterizes the Society of Jesus as "the Devil's order." See also Knuttel, 1916 and 1918.

56 Tracy, *Europe's Reformations*, 186–96.

57 Good examples are: *Een Tsamen Sprekinghe/ oft Disputatie/ tusschen twee Ghereformeerde Broederen. Vande 1. Predestinatie. 2. Onwederstandelijc ghenaden. 3. Van Perseverantie* (Rotterdam, Netherlands, 1611), Knuttel, 1889; and *Een Corte ende eenvoudige antwoorde op vier poincten. By Doctor Iacob Arminius in syn leven tegen ghesproken/ also te syn ontschrift-matich ende niet noodich om te gelooven : Aengaende de Predestinatie Godts* (Schiedam, Netherlands, 1611), Knuttel, 1890.

58 Such was the concern of Idzardus Nicolai, Reformed minister at Franeker: *Leere der Waerheyt/ Van eenighe Leerstvcken Die door de Drijvers der nieuwicheden berispt endt ghelastert worden* (Franeker, Netherlands, 1611).

59 For the former, see *Grondelijck Bericht Caspari Grevinchovii, vande Dolingen der Nieuwe Luterschen, voornaemlijc opghekomen nat de doot … D. Martini Lutheri …* (Rotterdam, Netherlands, 1611); for the latter, see Augustin de Backer and Aloïse de Backer, *Bibliothéque des écrivains de la Compagnie de Jésus, ou Notices Bibliographiques* (Liège, Belgium: Grandmont-Donders, 1853), 222. See also the strong language used in disciplinary meetings of the South Holland Synod, the records of which were of course not intended for public consumption. W.P.C. Knuttel, ed., *Acta der particuliere Synoden van Zuid-Holland, 1621–1700* (The Hague: Nijhoff, 1908).

60 Casparum Grevinchovium, *Vande vryheydt der Secten/ Hoe schadelijck deselve zij. Tot naedeel der algemeyne warachtige kercke ofte Gemeynte Godes/ … ende tot bescherminghe der kercke Godes van alsulcken lasteringhen/ daermede sy vanden Secten beswaert wert/ …* (Dordrecht, Netherlands, 1611), Air, Knuttel, 1906.

61 Ibid., 11–12.

62 Ibid., 30–2.

63 Ibid., 53. Interestingly, Grevinchoven occasionally cites the Qu'ran, as on p. 61.

64 Ibid., 58.

65 Ibid., 66.

66 *Amsterdamsche Nouvellos, dat is/ Nieuwe Tydinghen/ Van 'tghene datter onlancx is ghepasseert in Bohemen/ Hongarien/ Weenen/ Polen/ Slesien/ Meeren/ Ceulen … Enghelandt/ Brabrandt/ Vrieslandt/ ende Hollandt … tot troost der Calvinisten* (Herderswyck, 1620). Knuttel, 3086.

67 *Een waerachtige beschrijvinghe vant ghene datter geschiet is into lant van Barbarien/ tot den teghenwoordighen Jare 1614 …* (Rotterdam, 1614), Knuttel, 2107a. On the Pallaches, see M. García-Arenal and G.A. Wiegers, *A Man of Three Worlds: Samuel Pallache, A Moroccan Jew in Protestant and Catholic Europe* (Baltimore: Johns Hopkins University Press, 2003).

68 *Antwoorde Op de voor-reden en na-reden: Ghestelt Voor en achter dit gepretendeerde Boeck Sebastiani Kastellij: in welke wort aen-gewezen dat den Auteur van de zelve drijft het Christen-doden ende niet het Ketter-doden* (n.p., 1614).

69 An English translation is Roland H. Bainton, ed., *Concerning Heretics, Whether They Are to Be Persecuted and How They Are to Be Treated, a Collection of the Opinions of Learned Men Both Ancient and Modern* (New York: Columbia University Press, 1935), from the Latin original, *De Haereticis, an Sint Persequendi.*

70 Voogt, *Constraint on Trial*, 62.

71 *Antwoorde Op de voor-reden en na-reden*, 36–7.

72 [I. Verhaghen], *Spieghel der Broeders van de roose Kruysse. In dicht beschreven door een liefhebber der waerheyt* (Amsterdam, 1625), Di r. For the Socinians, see *Socinianisme in de Nederlanden*, special volume of the *Doopsgezinde Bijdragen*, 30 (2004).

73 See, for example, *Het Lof vanden Oorloghe boven den Spaenschen Peys* (The Hague, 1621), Knuttel, 3216; *Wat wonders, wat Nieuws Van den Paus van Alle Sotten. Van Sek'ren Droom ende Gesicht van den Paus van Roomen, Ende van den Engel ende de Duyvel* ... (Utrecht, Netherlands,1624), Knuttel, 3565; Pieter Willemsz, *Den onbedriechlicken Troost Voor alle vervolchde benaude gelovige, die door den Antechrist, ende den Spaenschen Coninck, vervolcht zijn* (Leiden, Netherlands, 1621), Knuttel, 3210; and *Basuyne des heyligen Oorloogs der Openbaringghe S. Johannis Tegen den groten Antichrist den Romschen Paus* (n.p., 1622), Knuttel, 3302.

74 *Nootwendighe ende vrypostighe Vermaninghe van eenighe oprechte Ghereformeerde Patriotten, aen alle Vrome Lief hebbers der Vaderlantsche Vryheyt* (n.p., 1621), Knuttel, 3217; see also *Aen-merckinge Op de Propositie vanden Ambassadeur Peckius. Inhoudende een kort verhael vande wreedtheyd ende bedrijgerije vanden Spaenschen Koning ende zynen Raed aen dese Landen bewesen/ ende de rechtvaerdigheydt van onsen Oorlogh daer tegen* (Amsterdam, 1621), 53, Knuttel, 3196.

75 See Knuttel, 3153–86.

76 [Ewout Teelinck], *Boheemsch Gelvyt ofte Christelyck Gespreck, Over het teghenwoordich Boheemsche wesen, ende de Oorloge daer ontrent ontstaen* ... (Amsterdam, 1620); Knuttel, 3302, *Basuyne des heyligen Oorloogs Der Openbaringghe S. Johannis Tegen den groten Antichrist den Romschen Paus* ... (n.p., 1622), Knuttel, 3038.

77 *Basuyne des heyligen Oorloogs Der Openbaringghe S. Johannis*, foreword, sig. 2v.

78 Ibid., 101.

79 George Gifford, *Sermons vpon the Whole Booke of the Revelation* (London, 1596), 47 (on Libertines), 56 (on Jews as synagogues of Satan), 80 (on Anabaptists), and so on. See Waite, *Heresy, Magic, and Witchcraft*, 176. Gifford's publications on witches are more restrained; see his *A Discourse of the Subtill Practises of Devilles by Witches and Sorcerers* (London, 1587) and *A Dialogue Concerning Witches and Witchcraftes* (London, 1593).

80 Pieter Jansz Twisck, *Chronijck vanden onderganc der tijrannen ofte Jaerlycklche Geschiedenissen in Werltlycke ende Kercklijke saecken … Van Christi geboorte af tot desen tyt toe* (Hoorn, Netherlands, 1620).

81 See *Nievwe-Jaers Dank-Offer Van wegen de groote … Overwinningen, ende Segeningen, die God Almagtig sijne waerde Kerke, ende ons lieve Vaderland, op den Roomschen Antichrist, ende Koning van Spanjen, met hunnen bloedigen aenhang …* (Haarlem, Netherlands, 1630), Knuttel, 3986, which celebrates the victory of the "true Church and our dear Fatherland" over the "Roman Antichrist and King of Spain" at the 1629 siege of Hertogenbosch.

82 See, for example, Ireneum Philaletium *Svlamith, Ofte Baniere des Vredes/ Opgeworpen Om Japhet te locken/ dat hy weder kome wonen inde Hutten Sems. Dat is: Om d'afgewekene Remonstranten weder te brengen tot de gemeenschap vande Gereformeerde Kercke/ daer in zy geboren zyn* (Amsterdam, 1621).

83 My review of the pamphlets in these years is not in any way complete, and there are possibly some pamphlets that make references to Satan that provide no hints of this in their titles; I have merely examined works that, by their titles, would be most likely to have done so.

84 *Vertooninge des Leugenachtigen Miraeckel-Geest, Ofte Wonderlijcke Teeckenen die gebeurt soude zijn binnen de Stadt van s'Hertoghen-bos …* (Granada, Spain, 1632), sig. A2r–v, Knuttel, 4284. This is comparable to the anti-Anabaptist miracle stories that I have described elsewhere: Waite, *Eradicating*, 39–51. See also *Wonderlijcke/ schrickelicke ende noyt ghehoode Predicatie/ van een Jesuijt op den Lantdach tot Warssau in Polen/ teghen de Luthersche/ Calvinische end Mennoniten/ … Item D'artijckelen/ die de Jesuijten in alle plaetsen soecken in te voeren/ om alle Catholijcken onder haer subjectie te brengen* (n.p., 1615), Knuttel, 2215, which says that Calvinists should be burned, but the Mennonites and Anabaptists are a diabolical sect of creeping serpents promoting great ungodliness and devilish evil under the mantel of simplicity and holiness.

85 *Vertooninge des Leugenachtigen Miraeckel-Geest*, sig. A2v–A3r.

86 Waite, *Heresy*, 177–9; Brian P. Levack, *Witch-Hunting in Scotland: Law, Politics and Religion* (New York: Routledge, 2008), 7–14; and Darren

Oldridge, *The Devil in Early Modern England* (Thrupp, UK: Sutton, 2000).

87 Daniel Vitkus, "'The Common Market of All the World': English Theater, the Global System, and the Ottoman Empire in the Early Modern Period," in *Global Traffic: Discourses and Practices of Trade in English Literature and Culture from 1550 to 1700,* ed. Barbara Sebek and Stephen Deng (Basingstoke, UK: Palgrave Macmillan, 2008), 19–38.

88 The essential argument of Gary K. Waite, "Conversos and Spiritualists in Spain and the Netherlands: The Experience of Inner Exile, c.1540–1620," in *Exile and Religious Identities, 1500–1800*, ed. Gary K. Waite and Jesse Spohnholz (London: Chatto and Pickering, 2014), 157–70.

89 De Waardt, "Religie, duivelspact en toverij." For parallel developments in England, see David Wootton, "Reginald Scot / Abraham Fleming / The Family of Love," in *Languages of Witchcraft: Narrative, Ideology and Meaning in Early Modern Culture*, ed. Stuart Clark (Houndmills, UK: Macmillan, 2001), 119–38.

LOVING AND CHERISHING 'TRUE ENGLISH'

1 I thank Gordon Bigelow, Lori Garner, Judith Haas, Lindsay Kaplan, Michael Leslie, Michael Saenger, Marc Shell, and the American Philosophical Society for their support of this project.

2 Citations from Shakespeare in this chapter are taken from *The Norton Shakespeare*, ed. Stephen Greenblatt (New York: Norton, 1997).

3 George Watson, "Shakespeare and the Norman Conquest: English in the Elizabethan Theatre," *The Virginia Quarterly Review* 66.4 (1990): 617.

4 David Mellinkoff, *The Language of the Law* (Eugene, OR: Resource Publications, 2004), 346, 121–2, 363.

5 Tom McArthur, "Bisociation," in *The Oxford Companion to the English Language*, ed. Tom McArthur (Oxford: Oxford University Press, 1992), 131.

6 As recent literary scholars have begun to demonstrate – particularly Patricia Parker in *Literary Fat Ladies* and Jeffrey Masten in his forthcoming *Queer Philology*, and Kenneth Burke before them – a return to 'old' philological inquiries and methods can yield strikingly novel and theoretically sophisticated results, often revealing subtly gendered and nationalistic inflections to the development and study of the English language.

7 Textual scholar Anne Hudson expressed severe reservations about Mueller's book, concluding that "because of its persistent inaccuracy of detail, it could hardly be recommended to students, whether undergraduate or graduate." Review of Janel M. Mueller, *The Native Tongue and the*

Word: Developments in English Prose Style 1380–1580, in *Medium Ævum* 56 (1987): 132. I am grateful to Mueller's chapter for consolidating much of what I had haphazardly gathered over some decade before discovering her study; yet I find frustrating her reluctance to make speculations about how synonymous word pairs were used in the service of *poesis*, and ultimately feel that she unnecessarily discounts the potential linguistic self-awareness of a writer such as Shakespeare to invoke them with deliberation. Even with regard to Caxton, she seems to overlook the fact that his task of translation might reinforce a tendency to exploit twinomials; for instance, even the mere title of Caxton's version of Lefevre's account of Troy contains *four times* as many words as the French original, with a redundant insistence on both Latinate and Germanic words for a number of terms:

composed – drawen out
venerable persone – worshipfull man
gloryous – myghty
translated – drawen out
vertuouse – myghty
translacion – werke

It is as if Caxton wants to point at once to both the original work and to his (interwoven, as it were) translation. I only speculate in passing that Caxton complicatedly reverts to what he must have recognized (through his work with Chaucer) as a deeply and profoundly medieval lexical practice – precisely at the moment his printing press was helping bridge English culture into the Tudor and early modern period.

8 See Yitzhak Avishur, *Stylistic Studies of Word-Pairs in Biblical and Ancient Semitic Literatures* (Kevelaer, Germany: Butzon und Bercker, 1984), 1–52.

9 Indeed, claims to the authenticity of putatively 'ancient' texts, such as the Book of Mormon, sometimes rely on tabulating comparable word pairs as evidence. See James T. Duke, "Word Pairs and Distinctive Combinations in the Book of Mormon," *Journal of Book of Mormon Studies* 12.2 (2003): 32–41.

10 Watson notes that Schäfer's study of *Shakespeares Stil: Germanisches und romanisches Vokabular* (1973) "attracted the criticism that he had exaggerated the extent to which a Tudor poet or audience could have retained any immediate sense of the double derivation of English. These doubts may be put to rest. The truth is that the British to this day retain an immediate and popular sense of the distinction between Germanic and Romance vocabulary, and not only linguists among them"; "Shakespeare and the Norman Conquest," 619.

11 Jürgen Schäfer, "Shakespeare's Synonymy Re-Examined," in *Elizabethan and Modern Studies Presented to Professor Willem Schrickx on the Occasion of His Retirement*, ed. J.P. Vander Motten (Ghent, Belgium: Seminarie voor Engelse en Amerikaanse Literatuur, 1985), 206.

12 I am particularly reluctant to reinforce what I find to be a too easy assertion about Romance-rooted words conveying urbanity, or twinomials as somehow addressing a dual audience, e.g., in "drama and sermon, whose audience might include both the educated and the unlatined, this kind of register-switching and self-paraphrase is particularly common": Sylvia Adamson, "Literary Language," in *The Cambridge History of the English Language,* vol. 3, ed. Roger Lass (Cambridge, UK: Cambridge University Press, 1999), 574.

13 Sir Thomas Elyot, *The book named the governor, 1531*, facs. (Menston, UK: Scolar Press, 1531/1970), 5.

14 Richard Mulcaster, *The first part of the elementary, 1582*, facs. (Menston, UK: Scolar Press, 1582/1970). The frequent sixteenth-century recourse (by Daniel and Camden as well as Mulcaster, among others) to the category "denizen" – that is, a person whose legal status uncertainly straddles between that of a foreign alien and that of a fully naturalized citizen – to describe 'imported' words further attests to the profound ambivalence of English writers to non-'native' elements within their language; Emma Smith catalogues some of these (along with the concurrent metaphor of "usurpation") in "'Signes of a Stranger': The English Language and the English Nation in the Late Sixteenth Century," in *Archipelagic Identities: Literature and Identity in the Atlantic Archipelago 1550–1800*, ed. Philip Schwyzer and Simon Mealor (Hampshire, UK: Ashgate, 2004), 169–79, as does Cathy Shrank in "Rhetorical Constructions of a National Community: The Role of the King's English in Mid-Tudor Writing," in *Communities in Early Modern England: Networks, Place, Rhetoric*, ed. Alexandra Shepard and Phil Withington (Manchester, UK: Manchester University Press, 2000), 180–198; see also speculative work on dramaturgical figurations of the "denizen" by Alan Stewart, "'Euery soyle to mee is naturall': Figuring Denization in William Haughton's *English-men for My Money*," *Renaissance Drama* 35 (2006): 55–81, and Jeffrey Masten, "*More* or Less: Editing the Collaborative," *Shakespeare Studies* 29 (2001): 109–31, as well as more historical studies by Lien Luu, "Natural-Born versus Stranger-Born Subjects: Aliens and their Status in Elizabethan London," in *Immigrants in Tudor and Early Stuart England*, ed. Nigel Goose and Lien Luu (Brighton, UK, and Portland, OR: Sussex Academic Press, 2005), 57–75, and Laura Hunt Yungblut, *Strangers Settled Here*

Amongst Us: Policies, Perceptions, and the Presence of Aliens in Elizabethan England (New York: Routledge, 1996). It is worth noting that many London denizens in Shakespeare's 1590s were French Huguenots, and that the Edict of Nantes preceded *Henry V* by just one year.

15 Richard Rowlands (also known as Richard Verstegan), *A Restitution of Decayed Intelligence: In Antiquities: Concerning the Most Noble, and Renowned English Nation* (London, 1634), 203.

16 See Thomas Fuller, *The Church History of Britain From the Birth of Jesus Christ Until The Year MDCXLVIII*, 3rd ed. (London: Oxford University Press, 1842), 108–9.

17 Sir John Cheke, quoted by Michael Best in "Forswearing Thin Potations: The Creation of Rich Texts Online," in *Mind Technologies: Humanities Computing and the Canadian Academic Community*, ed. Raymond Siemens and David Moorman (Calgary, AB: University of Calgary Press, 2006), 2. "A letter of Syr. J. Cheke to his loving frind Mayster Thomas Hoby," 1557, in Castiglione, *Book of the Courtier*, trans. Sir Thomas Hoby, ed. W.H.D. Rouse (London: Dent, 1561/1966). Such language echoes the terms used in attacks against marrying foreigners: "According to the *Pedlar's Prophecy*, miscegenation is an issue of national security because through interracial marriage foreigners become permanent residents in England where they breed a 'mischieviously mixed' race of children. In addition, much like the projection of disease onto others, describing interracial children as 'mongrels' is a way to differentiate Englishmen and foreigners from one another." Diane Cady, "Linguistic Dis-ease: Foreign Language as Sexual Disease in Early Modern England," in *Sins of the Flesh: Responding to Sexual Disease in Early Modern Europe*, ed. Kevin Patrick Siena (Toronto: Center for Reformation and Renaissance Studies, 2005), 165.

18 In the words of Thomas Watson over a century later, "There is in God not only a sufficiency, but a redundancy"; *A Body of Practical Divinity*, reprint (Aberdeen, UK: George King, 1692/1838), 303.

19 As a satiric commentary on the naively anti-French sentiment Congress fanned in the build-up to the invasion of Iraq, see the following *Christian Science Monitor* op-ed (14 March 2003):

ENGLISH SANS FRENCH

The Franco-American ~~dispute~~falling out over the best ~~approach~~way to ~~disarming Iraq~~take away Iraq's weapons has resulted in perhaps the highest ~~level of~~anti-French feeling in the United ~~States~~Lands since 1763.

A French-owned ~~hotel~~innkeeping firm, Accor, has taken down the ~~tricolor~~three-hued flag. In the House of ~~Representatives~~Burghers, the

> ~~chairman~~leader of the ~~Committee~~Body on ~~Administration~~Running Things has ~~renamed~~named anew French fries "freedom fries" and French toast "freedom toast" in House ~~restaurants~~eating rooms.
>
> To which the ~~question~~asking arises: Why stop with Evian, Total gasoline, and the Concorde (~~just~~only the Air France flights)? Let's get to the heart of the ~~matter~~thing: A ~~huge~~big percentage of the words in ~~modern~~ today's English are of – gasp! – French ~~origin~~beginnings. What if, as a result of the ~~current diplomatic dispute~~today's falling out between lands, the French ~~demand~~ask for their words back? We could all be linguistic ~~hostages~~captives.
>
> It is time for English-speaking ~~peoples~~folk to throw off this cultural ~~imperialism~~lording-it-over-others and ~~declare~~say our linguistic freedom. It is time to ~~purify~~clean the English ~~language~~tongue. It will take some ~~sacrifices~~hardship on everyone's part to get used to the new ~~parlance~~ speech. But think of the ~~satisfaction~~warm feeling inside on the day we ~~are all able to~~can all stare the Académie Française in the eye and say without fear of ~~reprisal~~injury: "Sumer is icumen in ..."

Though *langue*-in-cheek, this recalls the more serious proposals by Cheke for Saxon-inflected Biblical translation, as well comparable attempts by Tudor logician Ralph Lever and Victorian writer William Barnes. For the complicated superimposition of President Bush as a reformed King Henry V (with a mutable Agincourt), see my essay "'Step Aside, I'll Show Thee A President': George W as Henry V?" in *PopPolitics* (May 2003).

20 William Camden, *Remains Concerning Britain*, ed. R.D. Dunn (Toronto: University of Toronto Press, 1605/1984), 40, 43.

21 As Adamson cleverly notes, copia's "grip on the stylistic imagination of the time can be seen when Bacon uses it even in the act of criticising the excesses of copia: 'the whole *inclination and bent* of those times was rather towards copie than weight'"; she goes on to contrast a line from Bacon's 1597 essays to his 1625 revision, which includes synonymous pairs throughout (I've inserted the 1625 additions in italics): "Reade not to Contradict *and Confute*; Nor to Beleeue *and Take for granted*; *Nor to Find Talke and Discourse*; But to weigh and Consider," Adamson, "Literary Language," 559.

22 Swift's satire of the Royal Society's proposed pure language is to be found in the Voyage to Laputa with the visit to the Grand Academy. There, after the complete abolishment of words is rejected, another proposal approves of the goal of "expressing themselves by *Things*": "it would be more convenient for all Men to carry about them, such *Things* as were necessary to express the particular Business they are to discourse on," Jonathan Swift,

The Writings of Jonathan Swift, ed. Robert Greenberg and William Piper (New York: Norton, 1973), 158.

23 See Matti Rissanen, "'Strange and Inkhorne Tearmes'. Loanwords as Style Markers in the Prose of Edward Hall, Thomas Elyot, Thomas More and Roger Ascham," in *Style and Text. Studies Presented to Nils Erik Enkvist* (Stockholm: Skriptor, 1975), 250–62. Repr. in Mats Rydén, Ingrid Tieken-Boon van Ostade, and Merja Kytö, eds., *A Reader in Early Modern English* (Frankfurt, Germany: Peter Lang, 1998).

24 Bradin Cormack, *A Power to Do Justice: Jurisdiction, English Literature, and the Rise of Common Law* (Chicago: University of Chicago Press, 2007), 214.

25 Watson, "Shakespeare and the Norman Conquest," 622. English thus experienced a far more torturous relationship to lexical borrowing from the Continent than did, for instance, Latin from Greek, which was less troublingly emulative. Kenneth Haynes, *English Literature and Ancient Languages* (Oxford: Oxford University Press, 2003), 3. For a more binaristic reading of the antagonism of the English to the French language, see David Steinsaltz, "The Politics of French Language in Shakespeare's History Plays," SEL 42.2 (2002): 317–34. The tensely dialectical relationship between the two polities is better captured by John H. Fisher's observation that the "argument repeatedly used to whip up Parliamentary support for the continuing [14th-century] war with France was that a French victory would annihilate the English language"; yet such charges were recorded by Parliamentary clerks *in French*: "Chancery and the Emergence of Standard Written English in the Fifteenth Century," *Speculum* 52.4 (1977): 879.

26 I am following some of James Simpson's meditations on philology here: "Diachronic History and the Shortcomings of Medieval Studies," in *Reading the Medieval in Early Modern England*, ed. Gordon McMullan and David Matthews (Cambridge, UK: Cambridge University Press, 2007), especially p. 27; see also another finely attuned essay by Bradin Cormack, "Tender Distance: Latinity and Desire in Shakespeare's Sonnets," in *A Companion to Shakespeare's Sonnets*, ed. Michael Schoenfeldt (Oxford: Blackwell, 2006) on Latinity in Shakespeare's sonnets, which I will only commonplace here:

> "Shakespearean etymology is a philology in the sense of being a love of the word … I would call [this] Shakespeare's experimental philology … Shakespearean philology seems especially attracted to discovering a kind of tautological assertion … a philology at the bounds between a

Latin humanist culture and an English vernacular one, at the threshold where language works simultaneously to announce and then overcome historical distance ... Shakespeare's philological thinking, in other words, is etymological when it serves him, but it also looks to whatever acoustic forms are at hand" (243, 245, 246, 251).

27 Richard Rowlands, *A Restitution of Decayed Intelligence*, 203.

28 William Camden, *Remains Concerning Britain*, 32.

29 As Barbara Johnson, "Writing," in *Critical Terms for Literary Study*, ed. Frank Lentricchia and Thomas McLaughlin, 2nd ed. (Chicago: University of Chicago Press, 1995), 45, deconstructs some possible implications of "A AND B":

> A is added to B; A substitutes for B; A is a superfluous addition to B; A makes up for the absence of B; A usurps the place of B; A makes up for B's deficiencies; A corrupts the purity of B; A is necessary so that B can be restored; A is an accident alienating B from itself; A is that without which B would be lost; A is that through which B is lost; A is a danger to B; A is a remedy to B; A's fallacious charm seduces one away from B; A can never satisfy the desire for B; A protects against direct encounter with B.

See also William Empson on "A is B," in *The Structure of Complex Words* (Ann Arbor, MI: University of Michigan Press, 1967), 350–74, with his telling emphasis on "pregnancy," usually of the second term in such a pair.

SHAKESPEARE'S COINING OF WORDS

1 Like the precept that opens *Pride and Prejudice*, this is more assumed than proven. Others such as Thomas Nashe and (as a translator) Philemon Holland were also aggressive minters of words. But (unlike associated claims about the supposedly extraordinary size of Shakespeare's overall vocabulary) it is probably true, even if – because the OED was overly reliant on Shakespeare from its inception – the numbers are inflated by overreliance on the OED; see Jürgen Schäfer, *Documentation in the O.E.D.* (Oxford: Clarendon Press, 1980), and Jonathan Culpeper and Phoebe Clapham, "The Borrowing of Classical and Romance Words into English: A Study Based on the Electronic OED," *International Journal of Corpus Linguistics* 1, no. 2 (1996): 199–218. I will therefore be using several databases – most often, Literature Online (http://lion.chadwyck.com) and EEBO – to determine how new or uncommon certain words or usages probably were among other writers in Shakespeare's lifetime.

2 Vivian Salmon, "Some Functions of Shakespearean Word-Formation," in *A Reader in the Language of Shakespearean Drama*, ed. Vivian Salmon and Edwina Burness (Amsterdam: Benjamins, 1987), 193–206, esp. 198.

3 Paul Yachnin, *Stage-Wrights: Shakespeare, Jonson, Middleton, and the Making of Theatrical Value* (Philadelphia: University of Pennsylvania Press, 1997), ch. 4.

4 Geoffrey Hughes, *A History of English Words* (Oxford: Blackwell, 2000), 149, notes that such conversion becomes "possible only after the loss of grammatical inflections." Much of that loss is already evident in Middle English, but the Elizabethans were well situated to exploit its near completion. See also Dick Leith, *A Social History of English*, 2nd ed. (New York: Routledge, 1997), 99: "the loss of distinctive form for, say, nouns and verbs, could offer enormous syntactic possibilities for a poet and dramatist like Shakespeare."

5 Robert N. Watson, "Coining Words on the Elizabethan and Jacobean Stage," *Philological Quarterly* 88 (2009): 49–75, from which a few parts of this article are drawn, analyzes the purveying of the rapidly evolving English language to a partly illiterate audience at theatres around 1600. The topic united a philological approach with what is commonly supposed its opposite, namely, an emphasis on drama's social functions and material conditions.

6 Christopher Marlowe, *Tamburlaine*, Part I (1587–88), Prologue; because neologisms present special problems (and temptations) for editors, I have tried to work off digital facsimiles of Renaissance editions (silently modernizing the transposed u/v and i/j forms), though with additional information – especially lineation – from standard modern editions where available, to facilitate access for modern scholars.

7 Paula Blank, *Broken English: Dialects and the Politics of Language in Renaissance Writings* (London: Routledge, 1996), makes this point at length and convincingly. Jonson, in *Timber, or Discoveries*, calls custom "the most certain Mistresse of Language, as the publicke stamp makes current money"; see Blank, 39.

8 *Christ's Tears Over Jerusalem*, vol. 4 of *The Complete Works of Thomas Nashe*, ed. Alexander Grosart (London and Aylesbury, UK, 1883–4), 6.

9 For the role of monetary metaphors in the inkhorn controversy, see David Crystal, *The Cambridge Encyclopedia of the English Language* (Cambridge, UK: Cambridge University Press, 1995), 60–1.

10 John Kerrigan, *Archipelagic English* (Oxford: Oxford University Press, 2008), 64.

11 Sir John Cheke, "A letter of Syr. J. Cheke to his loving frind Mayster Thomas Hoby," 1557, in Castiglione, *Book of the Courtier*, trans. Sir Thomas Hoby, ed. W.H.D. Rouse (London: Dent, 1561/1966), 7.

12 Fraunce and Wilson, as discussed in Blank, 41; see also Charles Barber, *Early Modern English* (Edinburgh: Edinburgh University Press, 1996), especially the section on "Attitudes"; and James Siemon, *Word Against Word* (Amherst: University of Massachussetts Press, 2002), 46–90.

13 Ben Jonson, *Poetaster* 5.3.553; Herford and Simpson, ed., IV, 314.

14 "Lanthorne and Candlelight," *The Non-dramatic Works of Thomas Dekker*, ed. Alexander B. Grosart (London and Aylesbury, UK, 1885), vol. 3: 188.

15 George Pettie, *The Civile Conversation of M. Steeven Guazzo* (1581), Preface: quoted in R.F. Jones, *The Triumph of the English Language* (Stanford, CA: Stanford University Press, 1953), 205.

16 Francis Meres, *Poetrie; Poets; and a comparative discourse of our English Poets, with the Greek, Latine, and Italian Poets*, in *Palladis Tamia. Wits Treasury* (1598), 280.

17 Richard Carew, *Remaines Concerning Britaine*, 1595–96); cf. John Davies, "The Holy Roode," 1609, line 507: "O! that there were some new words lawf'lly coyn'd."

18 Thomas Heywood, *Apology for Actors* (1612), 37.

19 Quoted in R.F. Jones, *The Triumph of the English Language*, 198.

20 Alexander Gill, as discussed by Blank, 24–5. Kerrigan, 66, points out the ironic fact that Gill made this suggestion in Latin. The same is true of Richard Sherry's dedication to his *Treatise of the Figures of Grammer and Rhetorike* (1555).

21 Claire McEachern, *The Poetics of English Nationhood, 1590–1612* (New York: Cambridge University Press, 1996), 83–137, is especially helpful on this topic.

22 Thomas Dekker, *English villanies eight severall times prest to death by the printers, but (still reviving againe) are now the ninth time (as at first) discovered by Lanthorne and candle-light* (1609; rpt. 1648), sig. L3v.

23 Thomas Deckar (Dekker), *The Guls Horne-booke* (London, 1609), 27–8, 32 (misprinted as "30").

24 Anonymous, *The returne from Pernassus, or, The scourge of simony* (London, 1606), sig. B2v.

25 As if in ironic fulfillment of this point, the 2008 Scripps National Spelling Bee prize was won by spelling "guerdon." Shakespeare seems aware that Costard is doing what the audience would also be doing: recognizing the

words as presumptively nouns by their endings (the obvious "-ation" and the less obvious "-on"; Donka Minkova, private communication, 2009, reports that all English words ending in "-on" are nouns, except "common" and "wanton"). Costard again speaks truer than he realizes with "contempts" at 1.1.190. These and all further citations from Shakespeare are based on *The Riverside Shakespeare*, ed. G.B. Evans et al., 2nd ed. (Boston: Houghton Mifflin, 1997).

26 With a noteworthy persistence, the coining of words was associated with the coining of money in this period. Jonson, in *Timber, or Discoveries*, calls custom "the most certaine Mistresse of Language, as the publicke stampe makes the current money" in *Ben Jonson*, edited by C.H. Herford, Percy Simpson, and Evelyn Simpson (Oxford: Clarendon, 1947), VIII, 622. For a more extensive discussion of this point, see David Crystal's entry in *The Cambridge Encyclopedia of the English Language*, 60–1.

27 Terttu Nevalainen, "Shakespeare's New Words," in *Reading Shakespeare's Dramatic Language: A Guide*, ed. Sylvia Adamson et al. (London: Arden Shakespeare, 2001), esp. 238. Debates about imported words regularly took on the shape and even the vocabulary of mercantilist economic controversies; cf. Watson, 53.

28 Blank, 51.

29 *Oxford English Dictionary*, definitions verb1.II.5.a and verb1.I.1a (e.g., *Romeo*, 5.1.67); this pun recurs at 4.4.184 of *The Winter's Tale*; both link back to the sense of "coin, issue currency," verb1.I.2a.

30 Thomas Tomkis, *Albumizar* (1614), 2.1.

31 Edmund Gayton, *Pleasant notes upon Don Quixot* (1654), 271.

32 Ralph Alan Cohen, *ShakesFear and How to Cure It!* (Clayton, DE: Prestwick House, 2007), 109.

33 T.W. Baldwin, *William Shakespere's Small Latine and Less Greeke* (Urbana, IL: University of Illinois Press, 1944) and Stuart Gillespie's *Shakespeare's Books* (New Brunswick, NJ: Athlone, 2001) have helped clarify that these diminutives are misleading by modern standards. Jonson was always ready to take a more-classicist-than-thou stance, but Shakespeare received and demonstrated a good classical education.

34 On Shakespeare's high tolerance for such combinations, see Bryan A. Garner, "Latin-Saxon Hybrids in Shakespeare and the Bible," in *A Reader*, 229–34.

35 Garner; also Garner, "Shakespeare's Latinate Neologisms," in *A Reader*, 207–28; Jürgen Schäfer, *Shakespeares Stil: Germanisches und romanisches*

Vokabular (Frankfurt, Germany: Athenäum, 1973); and the more recent and accessible David Crystal, *'Think on my Words': Exploring Shakespeare's Language* (Cambridge, UK: Cambridge University Press, 2008). A perfect list may be impossible, since we certainly cannot recover and date the full spoken lexicon of the period, and what to count as a new and distinct word is open to many different interpretations. Jeffrey McQuain and Stanley Malless, *Coined by Shakespeare* (Springfield, MA: Merriam-Webster, 1998), is written for a non-academic audience and deals with a limited set of words (many of which were not quite as new as it supposes), but is still helpful.

36 Garner, "Shakespeare's Latinate Neologisms," in Salmon and Burness, 214.

37 Simon Palfrey, *Doing Shakespeare* (London, 2005), 51.

38 David Crystal, *The Cambridge Encyclopedia of the English Language* (Cambridge, UK: Cambridge University Press, 1995), 166–7.

39 E.g., "this dwarfish war, this pigmy arms" (*King John* 5.2.133–5); "a giant's robe / Upon a dwarfish thief" (*Macbeth* 5.2.20–2). Even with the simpler form, Shakespeare offers guidance: Berowne calls Cupid "This senior-junior, giant-dwarf" (*Love's Labour's Lost* 3.1.180).

40 2.1.150; see Hilda M. Hulme, *Explorations in Shakespeare's Language: Some Problems of Lexical Meaning in the Dramatic Text* (London: Longmans, 1962), 279–80.

41 "Pious," which the Literature Online database suggests was almost never used in the sixteenth century, became a decade-long project for Shakespeare. Duke Vincentio's speech to Friar Thomas goes from "My holy sir" to "Now, pious sir" (*Measure* 1.3.7–16). Belarius in *Cymbeline* speaks of "pious debts to heaven" (3.3.72). Norfolk's sarcasm about Cardinal Wolsey builds (with references to souls and angels and submissive blessings) toward the then-unusual word: "How holily he works in all his business! / And with what zeal! ... is not this course pious?" (*Henry VIII* 2.2.23–36). Two scenes later Queen Katherine is praised as "saint-like ... and pious" (2.4.139–41). See similarly *Macbeth* 3.6.27, *Cymbeline* 3.3.72; and *Timon* 4.3.136–41.

42 William Empson, *Seven Types of Ambiguity*, 3rd ed. (London: Chatto and Windus, 1956), 88–101; George T. Wright, "Hendiadys and *Hamlet*," PMLA 96 (1981): 168–93; Frank Kermode, *Shakespeare's Language* (New York: Farrar, Straus and Giroux, 2000), 100–2, 167–9; Patrick Cheney, *Shakespeare's Literary Authorship* (Cambridge, UK: Cambridge University Press, 2008), 142–5, 204–6.

43 Schäfer, *Shakespeares Stil.*

44 Inna Koskenniemi, *Repetitive Word Pairs in Old and Early Middle English Prose* (Turku, Finland: Turun Yliopisto, 1968), 109, similarly assumes that two symbols expressing a single meaning must be – if not "pathologic" – intended "to convey a message more accurately and more effectfully than one word would." She does acknowledge cases pairing "a loan-word and a native synonym," but supposes these are usually the result of "the authors' wish to display a knowledge of two languages, or to various stylistic motives" such as "a search for alliterative synonyms" (116), rather than anything pedagogical. M. Görlach, *Introduction to Early Modern English* (Cambridge, UK: Cambridge University Press, 1991), 195, assumes that the main use of synonymy is "to avoid repetition."

45 The First Folio and First Quarto read "league," which Alexander Pope plausibly emended to "leagued." Iago's use of "affin'd" at 1.1.39 is an exception.

46 Sylvia Adamson, "Synonymia, or in Other Words," in *Renaissance Figures of Speech*, ed. S. Adamson, G. Alexander, and K. Ettenhuber (Cambridge, UK: Cambridge University Press, 2007); this excellent study of *synonymia* recognizes it as an outgrowth of Erasmus's Latin pedagogy, but (even when citing Shakespeare) does not recognize it as a tool for teaching within English.

47 Preface; Jones, 83.

48 Hughes, 156.

49 "Shakespeare's New Words," in *Shakespeare Survey* 56 (2012): 358–77; 368–73 explore this aspect of *Othello* in the context of a broader argument about neologisms.

50 Jonathan Bate, *Soul of the Age: A Biography of the Mind of William Shakespeare* (New York: Random House, 2009), 46.

51 One possible deduction from Russ McDonald's excellent study of *Shakespeare's Late Style* (New York: Cambridge University Press, 2006) is that those final works show an author more determined to please his own rhetorical intelligence with difficult innovations than to offer socially viable forms of speech to his audience.

52 Jones, 272n1: "The Elizabethans borrowed from necessity, vanity, or sheer exuberance. One senses a different spirit, something akin to the metaphysical, a seeking for the strange and out of the way, perhaps a striving for certain imaginative or sound effects, in the borrowing of men like Burton, Donne, Taylor, and Browne."

53 Ben Jonson, *The Case Is Altered*, 1.4.16; in *Ben Jonson*, ed. Herford, Simpson, and Simpson, III.

54 Graham Bradshaw, *Misrepresentations: Shakespeare and the Materialists* (Ithaca, NY: Cornell University Press, 1993); John D. Cox, *Seeming Knowledge: Shakespeare and Skeptical Faith* (Waco, TX: Baylor University Press, 2007); Hugh Grady, *Shakespeare, Machiavelli, and Montaigne: Power and Subjectivity from Richard II to Hamlet* (New York: Oxford University Press, 2003); Anita Gilman Sherman, *Skepticism and Memory in Shakespeare and Donne*, (New York: Palgrave Macmillan, 2007); Ellen Spolsky, *Satisfying Skepticism* (Burlington, VT: Ashgate, 2001).

55 Catherine Belsey, *The Subject of Tragedy* (London: Methuen, 1985); Joel Fineman, *Shakespeare's Perjured Eye: The Invention of Poetic Subjectivity in the Sonnets* (Berkeley, CA: University of California Press, 1986); Harold Bloom, *Shakespeare and the Invention of the Human* (New York: Riverhead Books, 1998); John Lee, *Shakespeare's Hamlet and the Controversies of Self* (New York: Oxford University Press, 2000); Francis Barker, *The Tremulous Private Body: Essays on Subjection* (New York: Methuen, 1984).

56 The First Folio reads "Louely," probably an accidental inversion of the "n" in the reading or typesetting process; the fact that Hanmer could tell this emendation was needed shows how clearly Shakespeare has signalled the idea of "lonely." "Lonely" appears fairly often in the EEBO database, but several instances are actually "alonely," and others are typesetting errors for "lovely." Its only real advocate seems to have been Sir Philip Sidney, who uses "lonely" at least seven times in *The Countess of Pembroke's Arcadia* (1593).

57 Notice that "castigation," then quite rare, receives a gloss here as "exercise devout," in a context emphasizing chastity. At 1.3.345, Iago uses "sequestration," but seems to mean "sequel."

58 Parsons also surrounds the neologism with related ideas to a degree that not even Shakespeare normally attempts: "to beare it in mynde, to ponder in harte, to studdie & meditate upon it both day and night … to make it our cogitation, our discourse, our talke, our exercise & our rumination"; Robert Parsons, *A Christian directorie* (1585), 9.

59 E.g., *Troilus* 3.3.103–11; *Macbeth* 3.4.94–5; *Lear* 3.1.24–5; *Othello* 1.3.270, 3.3.360.

60 Although the Literature Online database finds only 27 entries for "audacious" in sixteenth-century prose, poetry, and drama, the fact that "audaciousness" was in use by 1599 suggests that the root word was well enough established for the compound to be viable.

61 *1 Henry IV* 4.3.39–45; *1 Henry VI* 3.1.8–15, 25–6; 4.1.124–7; *Love's Labour's Lost* 5.1.4–5, 5.2.104.

62 *1 Henry VI* 3.4.3–12; *Love's Labour's Lost* 4.1.88–91; *Taming*, Prologue, 52–4.

63 Russ McDonald, *Shakespeare and the Arts of Language* (New York: Oxford University Press, 2001), 36, drawing on the scholarship of Jane Donawerth and Judith Anderson, observes that "sixteenth-century educators and commentators wrote much more extensively about words than about grammar and syntax."

64 Quoted by Blank, 34.

65 Garner, "Shakespeare's Latinate Neologisms," in Salmon and Burness, 209.

66 Norbert Elias's *The Civilizing Process* (1939) has become very influential, over the past forty years, in studies of the functions of the early modern *habitus*.

67 Cathy Shrank, *Writing the Nation in Reformation England, 1530–1580* (Oxford: Oxford University Press, 2004), 190.

68 Shrank, 190. Adamson, "With Double Tongue," 209, perceives a shift from early dictionaries which are fundamentally remedial and focused on written language, to those of the later eighteenth century, which provided "the social aspirant" with "instruction in prestige forms of speech." I believe that the theatrical instances I have been describing bridge the gaps between those two types.

69 Charles Whitney, *Early Responses to Renaissance Drama* (Cambridge, UK: Cambridge University Press, 2006), 118.

70 Thomas Harman, *A Caveat or Warening for Commen Cursetors* (1567; reprint, London: n.p., 1573), sig. G3v.

71 Robert Copland, *The hye way to the spyttell hous* (London, 1535–6?), sig. C1r.

72 3.1.200–32; in John Dryden, *Marriage à la Mode*, ed. Mark S. Auburn, Regents Restoration Drama Series (Lincoln: University of Nebraska Press, 1981). Kerrigan, 68, notes in Restoration England a "hostility to the fashionable borrowing of words from the national enemy, France."

73 Mikhail Bakhtin, in *Rabelais and His World* (1940), trans. Helene Iswolsky (Bloomington, IN: Indiana University Press, 1984), sees the marketplace as a theatre; Jean-Christophe Agnew, in *Worlds Apart: The Market and the Theater in Anglo-American Thought, 1550–1750* (Cambridge, UK: Cambridge University Press, 1986), sees the anxieties of the early modern marketplace reinforced by theatrical practice.

74 Mikhail Bakhtin, *The Dialogic Imagination* [1930s], trans. Caryl Emerson and Michael Holquist (Austin: University of Texas Press, 1981), 17.

SHAKESPEARE'S SOUND GOVERNMENT

1 The edition used for all quotations from Shakespeare is *The Riverside Shakespeare*, ed. G.B. Evans et al. (Boston: Houghton Mifflin, 1974). Through Line Numbers, where used, are cited throughout as TLN.

2 See also Wes Folkerth, *The Sound of Shakespeare* (London: Routledge, 2002), passim and 25. I am very grateful to Neil Rhodes for comments that prompted the revision of this paper and to Lorna Hutson, who both shaped and delivered it to the original conference held at St. Andrews in 2006.

3 For this contemporary sense of sound, see also *A Mad World, My Masters* (4.2.12: "Recovered, well, and sound again") in Thomas Middleton, *A Mad World, My Masters, and Other Plays*, ed. Michael Taylor (Oxford: Oxford University Press, 1995), 312.

4 See OED s.v. "sound," noun 4. In *Henry VI Part 2*, the stage direction in the Folio for the swooning of the king reads "*King sounds*" (TLN 1729). See Alan Dessen and Leslie Thomson, *A Dictionary of Stage Directions in English Drama, 1580–1642* (Cambridge, UK: Cambridge University Press, 1999), 223.

5 William Shakespeare, *Titus Andronicus*, ed. Jonathan Bate (London: Arden Shakespeare, 1995), 220.

6 Desiderius Erasmus, *De Copia*, in *Collected Works of Erasmus*, vol. 24, ed. Craig R. Thompson (Toronto: University of Toronto Press, 1978), 577.

7 I am indebted here as elsewhere to Folkerth, 91–8.

8 Alan Dessen, *Rescripting Shakespeare: The Text, the Director, and Modern Productions* (Cambridge, UK: Cambridge University Press, 2002), 75.

9 Patricia Parker, *Shakespeare from the Margins: Language, Culture, Context* (Chicago: University of Chicago Press, 1996), 255.

10 Q1, F3r; Alan Dessen, *Recovering Shakespeare's Theatrical Vocabulary* (Cambridge, UK: Cambridge University Press, 1995), 21.

11 Jonathan Gil Harris, "All Swell That End Swell: Dropsy, Phantom Pregnancy, and the Sound of Deconception in *All's Well That Ends Well*," *Renaissance Drama* 35 (2006): 169–89.

12 Patricia Parker, *Shakespeare from the Margins*, 48.

13 Barnabe Riche, *Faultes faults, and nothing else but faultes* (London, 1606), sig. 10v.

14 1.1.110, 2.2.29; Middleton, *A Mad World, My Masters*, 301, 305.

15 John Day, *The Isle of Guls: A Critical Edition*, ed. Raymond S. Burns (New York: Garland, 1980), Induction, 65–71.

16 Folio *TLN* 2122; Alan Dessen, *Rescripting Shakespeare*, 21.

17 Though there is not room here to cite all of the treatments of this pervasive homophonic network, its importance within and beyond the sonnets is treated by Joel Fineman, in *Shakespeare's Perjured Eye,* while its relation to ears as well as eyes is foregrounded in Jonathan Baldo, *The Unmasking of Drama: Contested Representation in Shakespeare's Tragedies* (Detroit: Wayne State University Press, 1996), espec. chs. 5 and 6.

18 See the more detailed reading in Patricia Parker, "Spelling Backwards," in *Rhetoric, Women and Politics in Early Modern England*, ed. Jennifer Richards and Alison Thorne (London: Routledge, 2007), 46, with the 1623 Folio text quoted here from *TLN* 1139–43 of the Norton Facsimile of *The First Folio of Shakespeare*, ed. Charlton Hinman (New York, 1623/1968), 282.

19 François Rabelais, *Oeuvres complètes*, ed. Mireille Huchon and François Moreau (Paris: Gallimard, 1994), 501.

20 Patricia Parker, "Cutting Both Ways: Bloodletting, Castration/ Circumcision, and the 'Lancelet' of *The Merchant of Venice*," in *Alternative Shakespeares 3*, ed. Diana E. Henderson (London: Routledge, 2007), 95–118.

21 Thomas Nashe, *Strange Newes* (London, 1592), sig. B4r.

22 Patricia Parker, "Barbers and Barbary: Early Modern Cultural Semantics," *Renaissance Drama* 33 (2004): 233.

23 *The Geneva Bible: A Facsimile of the 1560 Edition* (Madison, Milwaukee, and London: University of Wisconsin Press, 1969), Isaiah 3.20.

24 John Minsheu, *Hegemon eis tas glossas. id est, Ductor in linguas, The guide into tongues bound with Vocabvlarivm Hispanicolatinvm et Anglicum ... A Most Copiovs Spanish Dictionarie* (London, 1617); Patricia Parker, "Barbers and Barbary," 244.

25 Patricia Parker, "The Novelty of Different Tongues: Polyglot Punning in Shakespeare (and Others)," in *Esthétiques de la Nouveauté à la Renaissance*, ed. François Laroque and Franck Lessay (Paris: Presses de la Sorbonne Nouvelle, 2001), 43.

26 Linda Woodbridge, *Vagrancy, Homelessness, and English Renaissance Literature* (Urbana, IL: University of Illinois Press, 2001), 141.

27 Gordon Williams, *A Dictionary of Sexual Language and Imagery in Shakespearean and Stuart Literature* (London: Athlone, 1994), vol. 3, 1439.

28 Patricia Parker, "The Novelty of Different Tongues," 51.

29 Patricia Parker, "Uncertain Unions: Welsh Leeks in *Henry V*," in *British Identities and English Renaissance Literature*, ed. David Baker and Willy Maley (New York: Cambridge University Press, 2002), 81–100.
30 Frankie Rubinstein, *A Dictionary of Shakespeare's Sexual Puns and Their Significance*, 2nd ed. (New York: St. Martin's Press, 1995), 145.
31 William Shakespeare, *Othello, the Moor of Venice*, ed. Michael Neill (Oxford: Oxford University Press, 2006), "Introduction," 22.
32 Deanne Williams, *The French Fetish from Chaucer to Shakespeare* (Cambridge, UK: Cambridge University Press, 2004), 218–19.
33 Paul Bertram and Bernice Kliman, eds., *The Three-Text Hamlet: Parallel Texts of the First and Second Quartos and First Folio* (New York: AMS Press, 1991), 24.
34 For a more extended reading of these connections, see Patricia Parker, "The Novelty of Different Tongues," 45–6; with Mario DiGangi, *The Homoerotics of Early Modern Drama* (Cambridge, UK: Cambridge University Press, 1997), 55; and Patricia Parker, "Spelling Backwards," in *Rhetoric, Women and Politics in Early Modern England*, ed. Jennifer Richards and Alison Thorne (London: Routledge, 2007), 46–7.
35 For detailed citation and discussion of the texts and contexts here and in the next paragraph, see Patricia Parker, "Barbers and Barbary."
36 *The Fair Maid of the West Parts I and II*, ed. Robert K. Turner, Jr. (Lincoln: University of Nebraska Press, 1967), Part 2, 1.1.49–53.
37 Richard Hakluyt, *The Principal Navigations Voyages Traffiques & Discoveries of the English Nation*, 12 vols. (New York: A.M. Kelley, 1904), vol. 5, 301.
38 All citations here are to page references in Bertram and Kliman, eds., *The Three-Text Hamlet*.
39 Patricia Parker, "Black *Hamlet*: Battening on the Moor," *Shakespeare Studies* 31 (2003): 140–1.
40 Patricia Parker, "What's In a Name: And More," in SEDERI, *Revista de la Sociedad Española de Estudios Renacentistas Ingleses*, ed. Pilar Cuder Dominguez, 11 (2002): 101–50.
41 Daniel Vitkus, *Turning Turk: English Theater and the Multicultural Mediterranean, 1570–1630* (London: Palgrave Macmillan, 2003), 86.
42 Kim F. Hall, *Things of Darkness: Economies of Race and Gender in Early Modern England* (Ithaca, NY: Cornell University Press, 1995), 218–21.
43 See Thomas Middleton, *The Works of Thomas Middleton*, ed. A.H. Bullen, 8 vols. (Boston: Houghton Mifflin, 1985), vol. 6, 184 for *The Spanish*

Gypsy (4.1.22–3); with Patricia Parker, "Barbers and Barbary," 226 (on the *mula* or "mule" and *Muley* also sounded in *Don Quijote*).

44 *The Fair Maid of the West*, Part 1, 5.2.80–1, 87.

CONTINENTAL SEXUALITY AND THE AUDITORY CONSTRUCTION OF EARLY MODERN ENGLISHNESS

1 John Webster, *The Duchess of Malfi*, in *English Renaissance Drama: A Norton Anthology*, ed. David Bevington (New York and London: Norton, 2002). All subsequent citations refer to this edition.

2 I argue that early modern English constructions of Continental sexuality through puns on "horse" and "horsemanship" generally refer to an exaggerated sexual appetite or to socially taboo sexual practices. However, I also explore the treatment of sexuality in terms of masculinity – as some of the horse puns, particularly in *Henry V*, work to emasculate the rider.

3 In French, the word for horse is *cheval*, in Italian it is *cavallo*, and in Spanish it is *caballo*. The Latin is *equus* and *caballus*. Moreover, while few native Italians or French would be in the audience, it is likely that several attendees would speak or have some knowledge of Italian or French as a second language.

4 Jonathan Culler, ed., *On Puns: The Foundation of Letters* (New York and Oxford: Blackwell, 1988), 3.

5 Karen Raber and Treva Tucker, eds., *The Culture of the Horse: Status, Discipline, and Identity in the Early Modern World* (New York: Palgrave Macmillan, 2005), 26.

6 Walter J. Ong defines oral residue as "habits of thought and expression tracing back to pre-literate situations or practice, or deriving from the dominance of the oral as a medium in a given culture, or indicating a reluctance or inability to dissociate the written medium from the spoken," in "Oral Residue and Tudor Prose Style," PMLA 80 (1965): 146.

7 Ibid., 149.

8 Paula Blank's concept of "intrelinguistic" reading, as she relays it elsewhere in this volume, is also a useful complement to Ong's approach to the aurality of early modern texts. Specifically, the notion that what one actually hears is equally as important to processing language as what one is meant to hear. In other words, the author's intentions are important, but the audience's varied auditory processing of words – including *double entendres* – also bears weight.

9 I refer to the texts' various taboo sexualizations of horse and horseman as "taboo" because, in the context of early modern social constructs, they

were considered sexually deviant. For a more thorough examination of *how* and *why* actions such as incest and promiscuity were considered taboo, see, for example, Frank Whigham's "Sexual and Social Mobility in *The Duchess of Malfi*," PMLA 100 (1985). Whigham describes "the taboo and its infringements" as "social products ... determined by the pressures and limits of particular social formations," 168.

10 Walter J. Ong, *Orality and Literacy: The Technologizing of the Word* (London: Routledge, 1982), 155.

11 Patricia Parker, "Shakespeare's Sound Government: Sound Defects, Polyglot Sounds, and Sounding Out," *Oral Tradition* 24 (2009): 361. In the same article, Parker also calls attention to Shakespeare's use of "Horace" in *Titus Andronicus*, suggesting there is a "familiar 'sound jest' on 'ass' and 'whore,'" 361. Parker thus reinforces the notion that Shakespeare and his contemporaries demonstrate a keen awareness of not only how words look but also of how they sound – including in aural (but not written) constructions of the word "whore."

12 Paul Saenger, *Space Between Words: The Origins of Silent Reading* (Stanford, CA, 1997), 1.

13 Philip Sidney, *An Apology for Poetry (or The Defence of Poesy)*, ed. Robert Maslen (Manchester, UK: Manchester University Press, 2002), 1.

14 The *Oxford English Dictionary*, 2nd ed., s.v. "horseman," 1a.

15 Ibid., s.v. "horsemanship."

16 Mark Breitenberg, "Anxious Masculinity: Sexual Jealousy in Early Modern England," *Feminist Studies* 19 (1993): 390.

17 In *The Duchess of Malfi*, Antonio juxtaposes the French court to the Italian court. He claims that, unlike the Italian court, the French court is void "Of flatt'ring sycophants" (1.1.8). Bosola, as a member of the Italian court, however, asks if he could be "one of ... [the] flatt'ring panderers" (1.1.52). Both Sidney and Webster make an effort to render Italian rhetoric excessive and inflated.

18 Nicholas Russell, *Like Engend'ring Like: Heredity and Animal Breeding in Early Modern England* (Cambridge, UK: Cambridge University Press, 1986), 77.

19 Walter Redfern, *Puns* (New York: Blackwell, 1984), 20.

20 Parker, 365.

21 In Italian, "whore" translates to *puttana*.

22 Paula Blank, *Broken English: Dialects and the Politics of Language in Renaissance Writings* (London: Routledge, 1996), 18.

23 Ibid., 1.

24 Ibid., 165.

25 Ong, *Orality and Literacy*, 73.

26 William Shakespeare, *The Life of Henry the Fifth*, in *The Norton Shakespeare*, ed. Stephen Greenblatt (New York: Norton, 1997). All subsequent citations in this chapter refer to this edition.

27 The *Oxford English Dictionary* characterizes the verbal form of "vast" as "to lay waste, destroy"; 2nd ed., s.v. "vast," 3. Thus, another *double entendre* emerges with the Prologue's description of the French fields, as "vasty" can denote an immense space: OED, s.v. "vasty." The Prologue suggests that the immense French fields have been wasted and destroyed; he also figuratively suggests that, in the drama's ability to depict the space, the fields have been contained, appropriated, and dominated by the "cok-pit" of England.

28 For those who speak or know French, "*le cheval volant*" translates to "the flying horse." There is nothing overtly erotic in this translation. It is therefore probable that Shakespeare appropriates this phrase to link the speaker's identity more overtly with the French (as he likely is an English actor). Moreover, this appropriation fits Paula Blank's claim that "[f]or Shakespeare, Jonson, and their contemporaries, the attainment of another language is not always a matter of borrowing freely from the national linguistic coffers, but of 'filching' words for a profit, at another's expense" (*Broken English*, 34).

29 Arguably, Bourbon's lack of awareness makes his horse-turned-whore boast more comical. His unawareness contrasts with Cleopatra's deliberate aural nod to horses/whores and bestiality in Shakespeare's *Antony and Cleopatra*. Cleopatra fantasizes about Antony's whereabouts, wondering if he rides his horse. She then says "O happy horse, to bear the weight of Antony!" *The Norton Shakespeare*, ed. Stephen Greenblatt (New York: Norton, 1997), 1.5.21.

30 Italics in the original. Bruce Boehrer, "Shakespeare and the Social Devaluation of the Horse," in *The Culture of the Horse: Status, Discipline, and Identity in the Early Modern World*, ed. Karen Raber and Treva Tucker (New York: Palgrave Macmillan, 2005), 93.

31 Lynda Birke and Keri Brandt, "Mutual Corporeality: Gender and Human/Horse Relationships," *Women's Studies International Forum* 32 (2009): 193.

32 Birke and Brandt, 193.

33 Pistol offers a similar commentary on the origin of pox as French. He conflates war wounds in France with the physical effects of venereal disease by his grouping of "Gallia wars," the "malady of France," and skin patches: "To England will I steal, and there I'll steal; / And patches will

I get unto these cudgeled scars, / And swear I got them in the Gallia wars" (5.1.78–80).

34 Michael Drayton, "The Ballad of Agincourt," in *The King's Lyrics*, ed. Fitzroy Carrington (New York: R.H. Russell, 1899), 114.

35 Ibid., 116.

36 Nicholas Morgan, *The Horse-mans honour, or The beautie of horsemanship* (London, 1620), sig. D1r–v.

37 Morgan, sig. C3r.

38 Russell, 77.

39 It is, however, worth noting that although approaches to riding and breeding varied depending on nationality, the physical appearance of a horse only varies slightly – often being most visibly different through colour and grooming. Therefore, the authors' perception of their nation's horses as superior is largely a fantasy.

40 While early modern English dramatists often represent local concerns in other locations in order to deflect any potential for criticism from royalty or the patronage system, the nation-specific labels for various characters in *The Duchess of Malfi* allow for a more overt distancing between off-stage English viewers and Italian characters such as Ferdinand.

41 Blank, *Broken English*, 101.

42 Breitenberg, 390.

43 Birke and Brandt, 193.

44 This wilderness is much like Shakespeare's "vasty fields" of France in *Henry V*.

INTRODUCING "INTRELINGUISTICS"

1 Ton Hoenselaars, "Introduction," in *Shakespeare and the Language of Translation*, ed. Ton Hoenselaars (London: Arden Shakespeare, 2004), 18.

2 Russ McDonald, *Shakespeare and the Arts of Language* (Oxford: Oxford University Press, 2001), 36.

3 David Crystal, "To Modernize or Not to Modernize: There Is No Question," in *Groundlingo* (2002), http://www.davidcrystal.com/?fileid=-4232, accessed 1 March 2014.

4 Roman Jakobson, "On Linguistic Aspects of Translation," in *The Translation Studies Reader*, 2nd ed., ed. Lawrence Venuti (New York and London: Routledge, 2000), 139.

5 David Crystal, *"Think on my Words": Exploring Shakespeare's Language* (Cambridge, UK: Cambridge University Press, 2008), 231, emphasis added.

6 Ibid., 179.
7 Hilde M. Hulme, *Explorations in Shakespeare's Language: Some Problems of Lexical Meaning in the Dramatic Text* (New York: Barnes and Noble, 1962), 7.
8 Gayatri Chakravorty Spivak, "The Politics of Translation," in *The Translation Studies Reader*, 2nd ed., ed. Lawrence Venuti (New York and London: Routledge, 1992), 372.
9 Walter Benjamin, "The Task of the Translator," in *The Translation Studies Reader*, 2nd ed., ed. Lawrence Venuti (New York and London: Routledge, 1923), 77.
10 Ibid.
11 Ibid., 82.
12 Ibid., 77.
13 Ibid., 78.
14 Ibid.
15 George Steiner, *After Babel: Aspects of Language & Translation*, 3rd. ed. (Oxford: Oxford University Press, 1998), 251.
16 Ibid., 252.
17 Ibid., 253.
18 Ibid., 255.
19 Ibid., 256.
20 Ibid., 257.
21 Ibid., 316.
22 Ibid., 312.
23 Ibid., 399.
24 Ibid., 315, 314.
25 Ibid., 381.
26 Ibid., 378.
27 Ibid., 338.
28 Lawrence Venuti, *The Scandals of Translation: Towards an Ethics of Difference* (London and New York: Routledge, 1998), 6.
29 Antoine Berman, cited in Anthony Pym, *Exploring Translation Theories* (London and New York: Routledge, 2010), 104.
30 Jacques Derrida, "What is a 'Relevant' Translation?" in *The Translation Studies Reader*, 2nd ed., ed. Lawrence Venuti (New York and London: Taylor and Francis, 1999), 424.
31 Robert Lado, *Linguistics Across Cultures* (Ann Arbor, MI: University of Michigan Press, 1957), vii.
32 Pit S. Corder, *Error Analysis and Interlanguage* (Oxford: Oxford University Press, 1981), 86.

33 Ibid., 19.
34 Ton Hoenselaars, "Introduction," 20.
35 Lee Strasberg, *A Dream of Passion: The Development of the Method* (New York, 1988), 52.
36 John Barton, *Playing Shakespeare: An Actor's Guide* (New York: New American Library, 1984), 15.
37 Patsy Rodenburg, *Speaking Shakespeare* (New York: Palgrave Macmillan, 2002), 4.
38 Simon Callow, *Being an Actor* (New York: Picador, 2003), 221.
39 Kristin Linklater, *Freeing Shakespeare's Voice: The Actor's Guide to Talking to the Text* (London: Nick Hern Books, 1992), 195–6.
40 Seth Lerer, *Inventing English: A Portable History of the Language* (New York: Columbia University Press, 2007), 129.
41 Jean E. Howard and Marion F. O'Connor, "Introduction," in *Shakespeare Reproduced: The Text in History and Ideology*, ed. Jean E. Howard and Marion F. O'Connor (London: Routledge, 1987), 4.
42 W.B. Worthen, *Shakespeare and the Authority of Performance* (Cambridge, UK: Cambridge University Press, 1997), 99.
43 David Crystal, "*Think on my Words*," ix.
44 John Barton, 17–18.
45 Ibid., 32–3.
46 Ibid., 20.
47 Ibid., 21.
48 Ibid., 245.
49 Ibid., 246.
50 Ibid., 245, 247.
51 Eric Partridge, *Shakespeare's Bawdy*, reprint ed. (London: Routledge, 2007); Gordon Williams, *A Glossary of Shakespeare's Sexual Language* (London: Continuum, 1997).
52 Ibid., 48.
53 Russ McDonald, *Shakespeare and the Arts of Language* (Oxford: Oxford University Press, 2001), 147.
54 Steven Pinker, *The Stuff of Thought: Language as a Window into Human Nature* (New York, 2007), 320.
55 David Crystal, "*Think on my Words*," 12.

MONUMENT, MOUNTAIN, ROOT

1 My idea of translation here is, admittedly, fairly broad; but the broadness is necessary – it suits the metaphorical range with which these texts

themselves treat translation. Beyond the somewhat standard notion of what Roman Jakobson calls "proper translation" – "an interpretation of signs by means of some other language" – I have in mind all varieties of intralingual rewording and intersemiotic transmutation as well as basic acts of physical displacement. (Roman Jakobson, "On Linguistic Aspects of Translation," in *The Translation Studies Reader*, 3rd ed., ed. Lawrence Venuti [New York: Routledge, 2012], 127.) It's worth mentioning that etymologically translation (*trans* + *latus*) is grounded in the simple motion of a carrying-across. (See Sandra Bermann, introduction to *Nation, Language, and the Ethics of Translation*, ed. Sandra Bermann and Michael Wood [Princeton, NJ: Princeton University Press, 2005], 1–10.) The OED's first entry for "translate" is not Johnson's "to change into another language retaining the sense" but rather "to bear, convey, or remove from one person, place or condition to another; to transfer, transport." Among more recent scholars, George Steiner has stood out for his ability to recover such basic features of the term. In doing so, Steiner expands the scope of translation to include "a vast terrain of 'partial transformation'": "This zone of partial transformation, of derivation, of alternate restatement determines much of our sensibility and literacy. It is, quite simply, the matrix of culture." I adopt a similar scope here, and to an extent I practice what Steiner calls a "topological" method, identifying the topoi – the myths, figures, archetypes, or motifs – that remain invariant amidst transformation in order to "arrive at a clearer understanding of the linguistic-semantic motor of culture and of that which keeps different languages and their 'topological fields' distinct from each other." George Steiner, *After Babel: Aspects of Language & Translation*, 3rd ed. (New York: Oxford University Press, 1998), 437, 448–9.

2 Much of *Romeo and Juliet* criticism is dedicated to an argument about whether, in considering the drama, one should focus more on its universal-transhistorical qualities – usually in an effort to defend the play's worth against charges of its inferiority to the later works of the Shakespeare canon – or on its historical-material particularity, as, for example, Dympna Callaghan does in "The Ideology of Romantic Love" (in *Romeo and Juliet: Contemporary Critical Essays*, ed. R.S. White [New York: Palgrave, 2001], 85–115). To me the best answer, supported by the very persistence of the argument, is that Shakespeare's work is both extremely particular and extremely universal – in fact, that its universality becomes present in the very richness of its particularity. My topic, by its nature, must include both of these aspects. As a history of translation, this essay cannot help but consider both the preservation of a work in a

transhistorical and transcultural setting as well as the conditioning of that work by particular historical and cultural forces.

3 Though (sadly) less recognized outside of a German-language context, within that context Keller's "greatness" has been constantly reaffirmed. Walter Benjamin referred to him as one of the three or four greatest prose writers of the German language, and he called *Romeo und Julia auf dem Dorfe* "unvergänglich" [*immortal, unfading*] ("Gottfried Keller: Zu Ehren einer kritischen Gesamtausgabe seiner Werke," in *Gesammalte Schriften*, vol. 2, ed. Rolf Tiedemann and Hermann Schweppenhäuser [Frankfurt a.M.: Suhrkamp, 1980], 283–7). Theodor Adorno listed him alongside Adalbert Stifter and Goethe as one of the three "greatest storytellers of the nineteenth century, at least in Germany" ("On Epic Naiveté," in *Notes to Literature*, vol. 1, trans. Shierry Weber Nicholsen [New York: Columbia University Press, 1991], 26). Georg Lukacs named him as the greatest German realist and the greatest German storyteller since Goethe and Hoffmann (*Gottfried Keller: mit einer Einleitung*, 2nd ed. [Berlin: Aufbau-Verlag, 1946], 9). Max Frisch simply called him "one of the greatest writers of fiction in the German language" ("Foreword," in *Stories: Gottfried Keller*, ed. Frank G. Ryder [New York: Continuum, 1982], vii).

4 William Shakespeare, *Romeo and Juliet*, ed. G. Blakemore Evans, updated ed. (New York: Cambridge University Press, 2003), 5.3.296–304. References are to act, scene, and lines.

5 It would not be difficult to map the so-called monumental order onto Elizabethan stereotypes of Roman Catholicism – an order supposedly dependent on showy rituals and icons, opposed to the (Lutheran, Protestant) activity of vulgar translation. Yet the order I describe is still greater than the sum of anti-Catholic prejudice, and the extent of its dominance in the language of the drama allows it to transcend any reductive status of religious stereotyping, and thus to absorb the English Protestant spectator (however consciously) as well.

6 Harry Levin provides a thorough account of *Romeo and Juliet*'s symmetry in "Form and Formality in *Romeo and Juliet*," *Shakespeare Quarterly* 11, no. 1 (1960): 7–9. See also Callaghan, "The Ideology of Romantic Love," 95.

7 *Romeo and Juliet*, 1.1.80. The volatility of "the word" is foregrounded dramatically throughout the opening: the play's first scene begins with the phrase "on my word" (1.1.1) exclaimed by the belligerent Sampson and echoed soon after by the rival Tybalt's "I hate the word" (1.1.61).

8 *Romeo and Juliet*, 1.2.1.

9 Ibid., 2.2.42–3.

10 Ibid., 3.2.98–9.
11 Ibid., 4.3.39–41.
12 Ibid., 2.2.43–4.
13 Jonathan Goldberg, "*Romeo and Juliet*'s Open R's," in *Romeo and Juliet (New Casebooks)*, ed. R.S. White (New York: Palgrave, 2001), 197–201.
14 Many accounts have focused on the conjunction of love and violence (often expressed through the Elizabethan double-meaning of "death") in *Romeo and Juliet*. The most famous might be Julia Kristeva's "*Romeo and Juliet*: Love-Hatred in the Couple," in *Romeo and Juliet (New Casebooks)*, ed. R.S. White (New York: Palgrave, 2001), 68–84. Still, it might be advisable to temper a commentary like Kristeva's with Stephen Greenblatt's thoughts on "Psychoanalysis and Renaissance culture," in *Literary Theory / Renaissance Texts*, ed. Patricia Parker and David Quint (Baltimore: Johns Hopkins University Press, 1986), 210–24.
15 *Romeo and Juliet* 2.2.163; James L. Calderwood, "*Romeo and Juliet*: A Formal Dwelling," in Romeo and Juliet*: Critical Essays*, ed. John F. Andrews (New York: Routledge, 1993), 92.
16 Jacques Derrida, "Aphorism Countertime," in *Acts of Literature*, ed. Derek Attridge (New York: Routledge, 1992), 426. Derrida's essay, itself structured as a series of aphorisms, seeks to represent a theme of aphoristic separation in language, such as that attempted by proper names. Yet, as I note, it does so in order to reveal the impossibility of such separation: the names *Montague* and *Capulet* cannot separate the feuding families, but neither can Romeo or Juliet be fully separated from their names. At a climactic point Derrida avows, "Romeo would not be what he is, a stranger to his name, without his name" (427).
17 Catherine Belsey, "The Name of the Rose in *Romeo and Juliet*," *The Yearbook of English Studies* 23, special no. (1993): 133.
18 *Romeo and Juliet*, 5.2.30.
19 Ibid., 5.3.179–81.
20 Susan Snyder makes a compelling case for viewing the drama as a generic hybrid that pivots at the point of Mercutio's death in "*Romeo and Juliet*: Comedy into Tragedy," *Essays in Criticism* 20 (1970): 391–402.
21 *Romeo and Juliet* 5.3.305–10.
22 William C. Carroll, "'We were born to die': *Romeo and Juliet*," *Comparative Drama* 15, no. 1 (1981): 67.
23 Johann Peter Eckermann, *Gespräche mit Goethe* (Stuttgart, Germany: Reclam, 1994), 557–8. My translation.
24 Paulin, *Shakespeare in Germany*, 301.
25 Ibid.

26 Trans.: "Shakespeare and his better contemporaries are also German." Paulin, *Shakespeare in Germany*, 149–50, 254; Werner Habicht, "Shakespeare in Nineteenth-Century Germany: The Making of a Myth," in *Nineteenth-Century Germany: A Symposium*, ed. Modris Eksteins and Hildegard Hammerschmidt (Tübingen, Germany: Narr, 1983), 151; Roger Paulin, "Shakespeares allmähliches Bekanntwerden in Deutschland: Aspekte der Institutionalisierung Shakespeares 1840–1875," in *Bildung und Konfession: Politik, Religion und literarische Identitätsbildung 1850–1918*, ed. Martin Huber and Gerhard Laver (Tübingen, Germany: Max Niemeyer, 1996), 13. Paulin describes this activity as exactly opposed to the anxiety of influence that Goethe and Eckermann pondered: "Die Verehrung der Deutschen für Shakespeare beruht auf mehreren Voraussetzungen, die seit Lessing und Herder und erst recht seit der Romantik ihre Gültigkeit haben: die Identification des deutschen Formwillens mit dem Shakespeareschen Genius, die Erneuerung der deutschen Poesie durch eine vitale Transfusion von außen, also gerade das Gegenteil von dem, was der Rezeptionstheoretiker Harold Bloom 'anxiety of influence' nennt" (*Allmähliches Bekanntwerden*, 13).

27 Paulin, *Shakespeare in Germany*, 194. "Shakespearscher Stil" was characterized as "exploiting certain plot devices: prose, frequent scene changes, disarticulated structure, multiple plots, deliberate floutings of Aristotelian properties, set-piece tirades, expressive pitches of passion, 'authenticity' of character, 'nature.'"

28 Ibid., 211, 196.

29 Ibid., 133.

30 Trans.: "had become the full/permanent property of the Germans." Paulin, *Allmähliches Bekanntwerden*, 10.

31 Ibid., 12. On the founding of the *Shakespeare-Gesellschaft*: "Im grunde war er längst eine Institution." Paulin also notes a remarkable instance in which, in 1864, a British cardinal bishop suggested that an artist "aus dem Lande Schillers und Schlegels" be commissioned to work on a British Shakespeare monument (18).

32 Lawrence Venuti, "Local Contingencies: Translation and National Identities," in *Nation, Language, and the Ethics of Translation*, ed. Sandra Bermann and Michael Wood (Princeton, NJ: Princeton Univ. Press, 2005), 177–202.

33 Ibid., 179.

34 Ibid., 189. "Und damit scheint zusammenzutreffen, daß wegen seiner Achtung für das fremde und seiner vermittelnden Natur unser Volk bestimmt sein mag, alle Schäze fremder Wissenschaft und Kunst mit seinen

eignen zugleich in seiner Sprache gleichsam zu einem großen, geschichtlichen Ganzen zu vereinigen, das im Mittelpunkt und Herzen von Europa verwahrt werde, damit nun durch Hülfe unserer Sprache, was die verschiedensten Zeiten schönes gebracht haben, jeder so rein und vollkommen genießen könne, als es dem Fremdling nur möglich ist." Friedrich Schleiermacher, "Ueber die verschiedenen Methoden des Uebersezens," in *Das Problem des Übersetzens*, ed. Hans Joachim Störig (Stuttgart: Goverts, 1963), 38–69.

35 *Lexikon der sprichwörtlichen Redensarten*, 1st ed. (Freiburg i.B.: Herder, 2009), s.v. "Berg."

36 Ibid.

37 See for example Habicht, "Making of a Myth," 147, 152–3.

38 By alluding to a monotheistic character here I have in mind Jan Assmann's *Moses the Egyptian: The Memory of Egypt in Western Monotheism* (Cambridge, MA: Harvard University Press, 1997), which I introduce in the next paragraph. Assmann characterizes Western Monotheism by describing what he calls "The Mosaic Distinction": an act of constructing cultural identity by drawing a distinction that creates a cloven or severed space for a group (1–2). But what I describe is also characteristic of the aphoristic form that Derrida attributes to the proper names and the structure of *Romeo and Juliet*: "As its name indicates, aphorism separates, it terminates, delimits, arrests (*horizō*). It brings to an end by separating, it separates in order to end – and to define [*finir – et définir*]" ("Aphorism Countertime," 416).

39 *Romeo and Juliet* 2.2.113.

40 Assmann, *Moses the Egyptian*, 3.

41 Ibid., 2.

42 Gottfried Keller, *Romeo und Julia auf dem Dorfe*, in *Die Leute von Seldwyla: Erzählungen*, ed. Bernd Neumann (Stuttgart: Reclam, 2004), 65–140. Translation modelled after *A Village Romeo Juliet*, trans. Paul Bernard Thomas and adapted by Frank G. Ryder, in *Gottfried Keller: Stories*, ed. Frank G. Ryder (New York: Continuum, 1982), 52–118, with my own amendments. The original version of this introduction was slightly different, though equally suggestive; it was one of the few parts of the story that Keller edited in later years, which can be taken as a sign of the importance he assigned to it.

43 Regarding the word *Fabel(n)*: one might be tempted to liken the term to the Russian formalist *fabula* and see it in opposition to some kind of *syuzhet*. I feel this would be anachronistic and mistaken. I would prefer to leave *Fabel* fairly open as a term, mainly because Keller would have

preferred the same. One might consider it as a combination of all the following: *myth*, *legend*, *source-material*, *fable* (with its full range of meanings), *story* (but not so consciously constructed or historically determined as a *Geschichte*), *tale* (in my translation of the passage), *plot* (in Ryder's translation, and in much German literary theory). Otherwise, it acquires its definition from its relation to the other terms in Keller's model.

44 Keller, *Romeo und Julia*, 65. My translation, modelled after Ryder's.

45 "Slowly and with a certain natural grace they moved forward step by step, and neither said a word ... So that from a short distance they looked completely alike; for they represented the original type of the region." (Ibid., 65–6.)

46 The first lines of *Romeus and Juliet*:

There is beyond the Alps, a town of ancient fame,
Whose bright renown yet shineth clear: Verona men it name;
Built in a happy time, built on a fertile soil
Maintained by the heavenly fates, and by the townish toil
The fruitful hills above, the pleasant vales below,
The silver stream with channel deep, that thro' the town doth flow ...

The opening to Bandello's novella: "If the affection which deservedly I cherish for my own native country does not deceive me, few cities, I take it, can excel Verona in beauty of position, placed as it is on so noble a river as the Adige, whose limpid waters divide the city, and cause it to abound in such merchandise as Germany sends thither. Fair fruitful hills and pleasant valleys environ it ..." (Matteo Bandello, "Of the sad end of two hapless lovers, one dying of poison, and the other of grief; together with sundry events," in Twelve Stories [London: J.C. Nimmo, 1895], 169.)

47 Derrida, "Aphorism Countertime."

48 Keller, *Romeo und Julia...*, 73.

49 Ibid., 71.

50 Ibid., 77.

51 See, for example, "zwei untergehende Gestirne" (Ibid., 66) and "indem jedes Sternbild" (73); for an extended comparison of the Friar and the fiddler, see Robin Clouser, "*Romeo und Julia auf dem Dorfe*: Keller's Variations on Shakespeare," *The Journal of English and Germanic Philology* 77, no. 2 (1978): 161–82; Keller, *Romeo und Julia*, 94–105.

52 "Und wie sehr diese immer herrlich an ihrem Ziele vorbeischiesst, sehen wir an den Romantikern, welche nur das Wlllkürliche und Witzige an Shakespeare gepackt haben, und andrerseits an Gervinus, welcher nur von seiner tiefen Philosophie und männlichen Weisheit zu sagen weiß. Jene lassen sich nachahmen, diese können auch bei jedem andern

ausgezeichneten Menschen vorhanden sein. Von den spezifisch poetischen Urkräften aber, von der eigensten wunderbaren Erfindung dramatischer Situationen und Verläufe, mit denen Shakespeare, entblößt von jedem Zeitgewande, mit seinen olympischen Brüdern konkurriert, davon hören wir nur wenig sagen." This is from a letter Keller wrote to Hermann Hettner in October 1850, in Emil Ermatinger, *Gottfried Kellers Leben, Briefe und Tagebücher*, vol. 2 (Stuttgart, Germany: Cotta, 1924), 255–6.

53 "hübsch beisamen," "… so daß es zu keinem rechten Trauerspiel und zu keiner guten Komödie kommen kann." Keller, *Pankraz, der Schmoller*, in *Die Leute von Seldwyla: Erzählungen*, ed. Bernd Neumann (Stuttgart, Germany: Reclam, 2004), 42.

54 Peter Villwock et al., *Gottfried Keller: Sämtliche Werke: Historisch-Kritische Ausgabe*, vol. 21 (Basel, Switzerland: NZZ Libro, 2000), 447–8.

55 "Erstens ist ja das, was wir selbst schreiben, auch auf Papier gedruckt und gehört von dieser Seite zur papierenen Welt, und zweitens ist ja Shakespeare, obgleich gedruckt, doch nur das Leben selbst und keine unlebendige Reminiszenz. Hätte ich keine Bemerkung über die wirkliche Vorkommenheit der Anektodte und über die Aehnlichkeit mit dem Shakespearischen Stoffe gemacht, so hätte man mich einer gesuchten und dämlichen Wiederholung beschuldigt, während, jene kurze Notiz voraus gesagt, die Geschichte dadurch eine berechtigte Pointe erhielt; denn diejenigen welche an Romeo und Julie nicht einmal gedacht hätten, und solcher sind viele, da man heut zu Tage ziemlich gedankenlos liest, würden alsdann die Sache für viel zu kraß und abentheuerlich erklärt haben …" Villwock, *Gottfried Keller: Sämtliche Werke*, 448. My translation.

56 "Im Dorfe Altsellerhausen, bei Leipzig, liebten sich ein Jüngling von 19 Jahren und ein Mädchen von 17 Jahren, beide Kinder armer Leute, die aber in einer tödlichen Feindschaft lebten und nicht in eine Vereinigung des Paares willigen wollten. Am 15. August begaben sich die Verliebten in eine Wirtschaft, wo sich arme Leute vergnügten, tanzten daselbst bis nachts 1 Uhr und entfernten sich hierauf. Am Morgen fand man die Leichen beider Liebenden auf dem Felde liegen; sie hatten sich durch den Kopf geschossen." Neumann, *Die Leute von Seldwyla*, 599. My translation.

57 R.S. White, introduction to *Romeo and Juliet: Contemporary Critical Essays*, ed. R.S. White (New York: Palgrave, 2001), 2.

58 Benedict Anderson, *Imagined Communities: Reflections on the Origin and Spread of Nationalism*, revised ed. (New York: Verso, 2006), 35–6.

59 Ibid.
60 Jakob Baechtold, *Gottfried Kellers Leben: Seine Briefe und Tagebücher*, vol. 1 (Berlin: Hertz, 1895), 319.
61 For a discussion of Keller's appropriation through an idea of Pan-Germanism, see Richard R. Ruppel, *Gottfried Keller and His Critics* (Columbia, SC: Camden House, 1998), 86–8.

SHAKESPEAREAN PERFORMANCE AS A MULTILINGUAL EVENT

1 This chapter draws on my previously published materials in "Asian American Theatre Re-imagined: *Shogun Macbeth* in New York." *Weyward Macbeth: Intersections of Race and Performance*, ed. Scott Newstok and Ayanna Thompson (New York: Palgrave Macmillan, 2009), 121–5; and "'What country, friends, is this?': Touring Shakespeares, Agency, and Efficacy in Theatre Historiography," *Theatre Survey* 54.1 (2013): 51–85.
2 References to Shakespeare in this chapter are from *The Riverside Shakespeare*, ed. G.B. Evans et al., 2nd ed. (Boston: Houghton Mifflin, 1997).
3 Briggs interview.
4 Quoted in John R. Briggs, *Shogun Macbeth* (New York: S. French, 1988), 8–9.
5 Mel Gussow, Review of *Shogun Macbeth*, *New York Times*, 21 November 1986.
6 See Sheila Muto, "Shakespeare Turns Japanese," *Asianweek* 13.32 (3 April 1992): 19; Carissa D. Mire, "East Meets … Scotland? Woodlands Thespians Bringing Unique 'Macbeth' to Edinburgh," *Houston Chronicle*, 31 July 2003.
7 John R. Briggs, *Shogun Macbeth*, 11.
8 Ibid., 64.
9 John R. Briggs interview.
10 John R. Briggs, *Shogun Macbeth*, 58; see *Macbeth* 5.1.1–14.
11 Ibid., 59–60; see *Macbeth* 5.1.26–44.
12 Ibid., 8.
13 Gussow.
14 Richard Schechner, *Between Theater and Anthropology* (Philadelphia: University of Pennsylvania Press, 1985), 4.
15 Esther Kim Lee, *A History of Asian American Theatre* (Cambridge, UK: Cambridge University Press, 2006), 91.

16 Quoted in Debra Griboff, "*Shogun Macbeth*," *Encore: The Performing Arts Magazine*, http://encoremag.com/?q=article&id=336, accessed 1 March 2014.
17 Leonard C. Pronko, "Approaching Shakespeare through Kabuki," *Shakespeare East and West*, ed. Minoru Fujita and Leonard Pronko (New York: St. Martin's Press, 1996), 29; John R. Briggs, 9.
18 Hsu, Hua, "The End of White America?" *The Atlantic*, January/February 2009, 5.
19 John R. Briggs, 8.
20 Alexa Huang, "Asian Shakespeares in Europe: From the Unfamiliar to the Defamiliarised," *Shakespearean International Yearbook* 8 (2008): 51–70.
21 Dominic Dromgoole and Tom Bird, "O for a Muse of Fire ..." (statement about the festival), Globe to Globe home page, http://globetoglobe.shakespearesglobe.com/, accessed 29 September 2011; see also the program schedule for the World Shakespeare Festival 2012 (hereafter, WSF Schedule), available at http://globetoglobe.shakespearesglobe.com/schedule, 3, accessed 1 March 2014. According to the BBC, this Globe to Globe season would feature performances in "Afrikaans, Albanian, Argentine Spanish, Armenian, Bangla, Belarusian, Brazilian Portuguese, British Sign Language, Cantonese, Castilian Spanish, Dari Persian, English, French, Georgian, German, Greek, Gujarati, Hebrew, Hindi, Hip-Hop, IsiZulu, IsiXhosa, Italian, Japanese, Juba Arabic, Korean, Lithuanian, Macedonian, Mandarin, Maori, Mexican Spanish, Palestinian Arabic, Polish, Russian, Serbian, Sesotho, Setswana, Shona, Swahili, Turkish, Urdu, and Yoruba." The productions would hail from "Afghanistan, Albania, Argentina, Bangladesh, Belarus, Brazil, China, France, Georgia, Germany, Greece, Hong Kong, India, Israel, Italy, Japan, Kenya, Lithuania, Macedonia, Mexico, New Zealand, Nigeria, Pakistan, Palestine, Poland, Russia, Serbia, South Africa, South Korea, South Sudan, Spain, Turkey, UK, USA and Zimbabwe." Helen Bushby, "Signing and Hip-Hop Shakespeare at 2012 Globe Festival," *BBC*, 27 September 2011, http://www.bbc.co.uk/news/entertainment-arts-15058047.
22 *Love's Labour's Lost* 5.1.32.
23 Dromgoole and Bird, "O for a Muse of Fire," Globe to Globe website, http://globetoglobe.shakespearesglobe.com/, accessed 1 September 2012.
24 Ibid.
25 "*Julius Caesar*: I Termini Company," Globe to Globe, http://globetoglobe.shakespearesglobe.com/plays/julius-caesar/english-33, accessed 29 September 2011. See also WSF Schedule, 8.

26 Amardeep Banerjee, "Shakespeare in Kabul," *The Times of India: The Crest Edition*, 26 May 2012, http://www.timescrest.com/culture/shakespeare-in-kabul-8009.

27 Tom Bird, speaking on "The Globe to Globe Festival" at the International Shakespeare Conference, Stratford-upon-Avon, 9 August 2012 (author's notes).

28 Ibid.

29 "*Henry V*: Shakespeare's Globe," Globe to Globe, http://globetoglobe.shakespearesglobe.com/plays/henry-v/english-16, accessed 30 August 2012. See also WSF Schedule, 25.

30 Figures for summer 2012 are not yet available as of this writing, but the number of visitors to the South Bank and the Bankside Cultural Quarter (where the Tate Modern and the Globe are located) jumped from an annual average in the tens of thousands in the 1990s to 13 million in 2011. Nicholas Serota and Donald Hyslop, "Art and Culture in Regeneration: Tate Modern, Bankside and London," *Journal of Urban Regeneration and Renewal* 4.4 (2011): 328–36; see esp. 332–3. I wish to thank Susan Bennett for drawing my attention to this study and for sharing her draft. Her research has shown why humanities scholars have to pay attention to "new economic profiles of how Shakespeare circulates in the world"; Bennett, "Shakespeare at Work in the Global Leisure Market," at the International Shakespeare Conference, Stratford-upon-Avon, 10 August 2012 (quoted with Bennett's permission). See also Bennett, "Shakespeare on Vacation," *A Companion to Shakespeare and Performance*, ed. Barbara Hodgdon and W.B. Worthen (Oxford: Wiley-Blackwell, 2005), 494–508; Bennett, "Theatre/Tourism," *Theatre Journal* 57.3 (2005): 407–28.

31 "What Country Friends Is This?" World Shakespeare Festival 2012, http://www.worldshakespearefestival.org.uk/themes/what-country-friends-is-this.aspx, accessed 20 September 2012.

32 Shakespearean scholar Andrew Griffin, who attended the performance in Beijing with his Chinese-Canadian partner, was deeply impressed by the intercultural design, but found it ironic that, despite his lack of knowledge of Chinese, he was able to explain the intricate details of the performance to his partner who spoke Chinese. Alexa Huang, interview with Andrew Griffin, Victoria, Canada, 12 October 2012.

33 Erin Sullivan observes that "as opposed to the other 'foreign' offerings in the Globe to Globe Festival," the hip-hop *Othello* had a "noticeably youthful audience" that thoroughly enjoyed the experience, because

the production familiarized Shakespeare through a contemporary genre. Review of *Othello*, in *Year of Shakespeare*, 6 May 2012; http://bloggingshakespeare.com/year-of-shakespeare-othello.

34 Tom Bird, speaking on "The Globe to Globe Festival" (author's notes).

35 Stephen Purcell, presentation at the International Shakespeare Conference, Stratford-upon-Avon, 9 August 2012.

36 Peter Smith, "Year of Shakespeare: Twelfth Night," in *Blogging Shakespeare: Embracing Shakespearean Conversation in a Digital Age*, 1 May 2012, http://bloggingshakespeare.com/year-of-shakespeare-twelfth-night.

37 Matt Trueman, "Royal Shakespeare Company Under Fire for Not Casting Enough Asian Actors," *The Guardian,* 19 October 2012; http://www.guardian.co.uk/stage/2012/oct/19/royal-shakespeare-company-asian-actors?fb=optOut.

38 On the conflicted Asian identities in diaspora, see Alexa Huang, "Asian American Theatre Re-imagined: *Shogun Macbeth* in New York," in *Weyward Macbeth: Intersections of Race and Performance*, ed. Scott Newstok and Ayanna Thompson (New York: Palgrave Macmillan, 2009), 121–5; on colourblind casting in Shakespearean theatre, see *Colorblind Shakespeare: New Perspectives on Race and Performance,* ed. Ayanna Thompson (New York: Routledge, 2006).

39 Jyotsna Singh, "Wooing and Wedding," RSC program, *Much Ado About Nothing*, n.p.

40 Clare Brennan, Review of *Much Ado About Nothing, The Guardian,* 4 August 2012; http://www.guardian.co.uk/stage/2012/aug/05/much-ado-about-nothing-review.

41 Gitanjali Shahani, "Fighting the Merry War," RSC program, *Much Ado About Nothing*, n.p.

42 Kate Rumbold, for example, writes that "the combination of the distinctive space of the Globe, the otherness of its foreign visitors, the absence of English language, and even the Globe's seeming proximity to Shakespeare, has evidently ascribed to participants in the 'Globe to Globe' festival in particular a new degree of 'authenticity.'" Kate Rumbold, Review of *Much Ado About Nothing*, *Year of Shakespeare* blog, 10 August 2012; http://bloggingshakespeare.com/year-of-shakespeare-much-ado-about-nothing-at-the-rsc.

43 Rumbold, Review of *Much Ado About Nothing.*

44 Kevin Quarmby, Review of *Much Ado About Nothing, British Theatre Guide,* http://www.britishtheatreguide.info/reviews/much-ado-about-rsc-courtyard-t-7732, accessed 21 October 2012.

45 Interview with Oh Tae-suk, *Hankooki* [in Korean], 1 August 2011, http://news.hankooki.com/lpage/culture/201108/h2011080102314384310.htm.

46 "*The Tempest*," *Donga News* [in Korean], 15 August 2011, http://news.donga.com/3/all/20110814/39534025/1 .

47 "Favorable Reception of a Korean Production at the Edinburgh Festival," YTN *News* [in Korean], 24 August 2011, http://news.naver.com/main/read.nhn?mode=LSD&mid=sec&sid1=103&oid=001&aid=0005227840 (translation by Dan Kim).

48 "Han'guk-ui [*Hamlet*] segyemudae-sodo t'ong-handa," *Dong-a Ilbo*, 8 October 1996; quoted in the program of Street Theatre Troupe's *Hamlet*, Theater Series 6 (Seoul, 2003), 154.

49 "Edinburgh International Festival 2011: East Meets West in a Festival Aiming to Build Bridges," *The Scotsman*, 23 March 2011, http://www.scotsman.com/news/edinburgh-international-festival-2011-east-meets-west-in-a-festival-aiming-to-build-bridges-1-1544051.

50 Tom Bird, interview by Alexa Huang, Stratford-upon-Avon, 9 August 2012.

51 Deleuze and Guattari developed the concept of deterritorialization to analyze processes that decontextualize sets of fixed relations. Their concept is parallel to that of economic deterritorialization. Gilles Deleuze and Félix Guattari, *Anti-Oedipus: Capitalism and Schizophrenia*, trans. Robert Hurley, Mark Seem, and Helen R. Lane ([*L'anti-Oedipe*, 1972] London: Continuum, 2004); Gilles Deleuze and Félix Guattari, *A Thousand Plateaus: Capitalism and Schizophrenia [2]*, trans. Brian Massumi ([*Mille plateaux, volume 2 of Capitalisme et Schizophrénie*, 1980] Minneapolis: University of Minnesota Press, 1987), 61–3.

52 Marvin Carlson, "Brook and Mnouchkine: Passages to India?" in *The Intercultural Performance Reader*, ed. Patrice Pavis (London: Routledge, 1996), 79–92, at 91.

53 Huang, *Chinese Shakespeares*, 17.

54 Steve Tillis, "Conceptualizing Space: The Geographic Dimension of World Theatre," *Theatre Survey* 52.2 (2011): 301–27.

Index